D1349553

KA 0346439 3

The Pinch

The Pinch

How the baby boomers took their children's future
– and why they should give it back

David Willetts

Atlantic Books

LONDON

UNIVERSITY OF WINCHESTER

305.2
WIL

03464393

First published in hardback in Great Britain in 2010 by Atlantic Books,
an imprint of Grove Atlantic Ltd.

Copyright © David Willetts, 2010

The moral right of David Willetts to be identified as the author of this
work has been asserted by him in accordance with the Copyright,
Designs and Patents Acts of 1988.

All rights reserved. No part of this publication may be reproduced,
stored in a retrieval system, or transmitted in any form or by any
means, electronic, mechanical, photocopying, recording, or otherwise,
without the prior permission of both the copyright owner and the
above publisher of this book.

The author and publisher gratefully acknowledge permission to
quote the following extracts: lines from 'Annus Mirabilis' from
Collected Poems by Philip Larkin © 1988 reproduced by permission
of Faber & Faber for the author; lines from 'Sweeney Agonistes' in
Collected Poems 1909–1962 by T.S. Eliot © 1963 reproduced by
permission of Faber & Faber for the author; extract from 'Tradition
and the Individual Talent' by T. S. Eliot copyright 1919 reproduced by
permission of Faber & Faber for the author.

10 9 8 7 6 5 4 3

A CIP catalogue record for this book is available from the British Library.

ISBN 978 1 84887 231 8

Printed in Great Britain

Atlantic Books
An imprint of Grove Atlantic Ltd
Ormond House
26–27 Boswell Street
London
WC1N 3JZ

www.atlantic-books.co.uk

To Imogen and Matthew

Contents

Contents

List of Tables

Acknowledgements

I have of course learnt much from my constituents in Havant. The problems of the stream of young people coming to my surgery who were trying to do the right thing for their families but were unable to find an affordable place to live particularly set me thinking about the debt we owe them.

I am very grateful to successive researchers who have been of great assistance, particularly Melanie Batley, Henry Cook, Ryan Shorthouse and Laura Fox. Annie Winsbury and Helga Wright provided invaluable support. Gervas Huxley has been an encouraging friend throughout. Nick Hillman has been a great source of wisdom and advice. I have a particular debt to Chris Cook for his wide-ranging research on the book. Georgina Capel, my agent, believed in the project from the beginning. Caroline Knight of Atlantic Books has been a shrewd editor. Responsibility for any errors is of course mine alone.

I have a further debt to the wider academic and research community in Britain and sometimes abroad as well. Rein Jansons of the LSE, Edmund Cannon of Bristol University, Alistair Muriel of the IFS, Bob Pannell of the Council of Mortgage Lenders and Alan Holmans of Cambridge University have provided research on specific issues. But the debt goes wider than that. During my time as a Visiting Fellow at Nuffield College, Oxford, for example, John

Goldthorpe generously gave time to educate me on social mobility, John Mullbauer on housing and Paul Klemperer on game theory. I have greatly benefited from participating in the wide-ranging conferences held at the Ditchley Foundation. Dr Paul Redmond at Liverpool University shares my fascination with the divergent attitudes of successive generations. Social policy experts at the LSE, especially Nick Barr and John Hills, have helped me think about the welfare state and the life cycle. John Ermisch of the Institute for Social and Economic Research and Geoff Dench of the Young Foundation have helped me to understand family change, distinguishing between cohort and life-cycle effects. Paul Gregg and Simon Burgess of the CMPO at Bristol University shared their researches on education and social mobility, as did Jo Blanden; Anna Vignoles of the Institute of Education generously reviewed that whole chapter. Professor Ken Binmore of Bristol and UCL has thought deeply about game theory and its applications to public policy, and his work above all stimulated me to set out some ideas in an earlier lecture at the LSE. Daniel Finkelstein of *The Times* and Matthew Taylor of the Royal Society of Arts share my interest in trying to apply insights from this discipline and evolutionary biology to politics, an approach whose time has come. Matt Ridley has also helped guide me through the literature on this. I have benefited from many discussions on saving and investment with Martin Weale of the National Institute of Economic and Social Research and Andrew Smithers of Smithers and Co. Together with Martin Woolf of the *Financial Times* they persuaded me early on of the importance of national saving rates in explaining what was going wrong with our economy. Dieter Helm of Oxford University links that to the importance of investment, especially in infrastructure. At events at the Royal Society and elsewhere Martin Rees and John Beddington have introduced me to scientists' understanding of the challenges facing us over the next forty years.

Research institutes such as the Institute for Fiscal Studies and the Sutton Trust have been valuable research resources. Policy Exchange hosted the first event, back in 2005, when I attempted to set out some thinking on the shifts in wealth between the generations. Mervyn King of the Bank of England responded encouragingly to my interest in the links between demography and economics, and officials at the Bank have shared some of their data. Philip Booth of the IEA and Nick Bosanquet of Reform have both tackled this issue as well. The National Centre of Social Research and James Lloyd, then of the International Longevity Centre, provided their analyses of the distribution of income and assets which the National Centre generously updated for this book. Kate Barker took me through her work on housing. Adair Turner's reports on pensions provided excellent analytical material. David Coleman of Oxford University has shared his wide understanding of demography. Sitting on the Global Ageing Commission run by the Center for Strategic and International Studies in Washington DC gave me an opportunity to think about demographic change as an international phenomenon. Many other experts, especially from the worlds of education and pensions have patiently shared their knowledge with me. Punter Southall have given me the opportunity to continue to think about pensions after my front bench responsibilities ended.

More than a decade in Opposition could be sterile and frustrating. It is because of the generosity of so many people in universities and research institutes that I have found them intellectually fruitful and I wish to acknowledge my debt and gratitude.

My wife Sarah has shaped the thinking in this book more than she may know. She has always judged every family question by what is best for our two children. This book is dedicated to them.

Introduction

We all know the story. The parents return home from a night away to find a teenage party has got out of hand and the house has been trashed. Every few months a particularly dramatic episode gets into the media – with distraught parents tidying up a mess left by a swarm of young people summoned on Facebook. It plays to a deep-seated fear that younger people will not appreciate and protect what has been achieved by the older generation. This is the eternal anxiety of each generation about what comes after. But what if, when it comes to many of the big things that matter for our futures, it is the other way round? What if it's actually the older generation, the baby boomers, who have been throwing the party and leaving behind a mess for the next generation to sort out?

The boomers, roughly those born between 1945 and 1965, have done and continue to do some great things but now the bills are coming in; and it is the younger generation who will pay them. We have a good idea of what at least some of these future costs are – the cost of climate change, the cost of investing in the infrastructure our economy will need if we are to prosper, the cost of paying pensions when the big boomer cohort retires, on top of the cost of servicing the debt the government has built up. The charge is that the boomers have been guilty of a monumental failure to protect the interests of future generations.

The baby boomers have concentrated wealth in the hands of their own generation. It is far harder for the younger generation to get started on the housing ladder or save for the future in a decent company pension. This leaves them more dependent on their parents for longer. That in turn means new barriers to the spread of opportunity and ownership. Growing to adulthood and starting a family are slower and more difficult. And now young people find themselves by far the biggest victims of the recession – unable to find a job or a mortgage. We are rightly sensitive to the injustices and inequities of life chances within a generation but ignore the injustices between generations, perhaps because they are harder to measure.

I had better declare where I fit in here. I was born in 1956, in the middle of the baby boom and in Birmingham, in the middle of England. It was the year of the Suez crisis and the Soviet invasion of Hungary. My mother remembers being worried about the dreadful, dangerous world into which she had brought me. So far, however, my age group has turned out to be, by and large, a lucky generation. Over the past ten years I have spent a lot of my time involved in education and pensions. I have come to see how they are linked – they are about the obligations of the generation in the middle to the generation coming after and the one which went before. That set me to applying my interest in economic policy to the links between the generations and how some get a better deal than others.

What if instead of being born in 1956 I had been born fifty years earlier in 1906? Then a mother, depending of course on her social class, might have felt things were looking pretty good for her new-born child. Britain was rich and powerful, with social reform on the way as well. She could not have expected that her son's father would die in the trenches of the First World War, that then this young man would not be able to find work in the Great Depression, be conscripted in the Second World War and endure austerity after it. He would finally have retired in 1971 only to find his modest savings then destroyed by the worst ten years of inflation in our nation's history. It was an unlucky generation.

So what of a child born now? These two examples warn us that of course we cannot know. But many boomers are guiltily aware of the heavy burdens being piled on their children and grandchildren. Try asking a group of people who are middle-aged or older whether they have enjoyed greater opportunities and prosperity than their parents. Almost everyone will say they have. But then ask them whether life will similarly be better for their children or grandchildren. They are not so sure. It is what deep-down most parents are most anxious about – the life chances of their children.

How has this happened? It would be easy to slide into generational name calling. That gets us nowhere. It is not that some generations are good and others bad; it is that some are big and others are small. That is why Chapters 2, 3 and 4 track the demographics of boom and bust and what this means for the distribution of wealth and power. Being a great big generation makes you a powerful disruptive force: you pour through society like a flooding river breaking its banks. We can make sense of the economic and social changes around us if we see them as the continuing story of the extraordinary impact of this massive post-War generation. Some economists thought it would be a disadvantage to be in a big generation, with more crowding and competition at every stage: it would be like travelling through life economy class not business class. But, so far at least, being so big has turned out to be a fantastic advantage, enabling that generation to dominate marketplaces and shape politics.

Successive generations at different stages of our lives have

UNIVERSITY OF WINCHESTER LIBRARY

different needs and different things to offer. That is why it makes sense for different generations to co-operate – so we educate the younger generation now and then hope to benefit from what they produce in the future. What you get back need not be a direct exchange but instead an expectation the next generation will do the same for you – so you care for your parents now and hope your children care for you when you are older. These types of exchanges between the generations, explored in Chapters 5 and 6, are how both families and whole societies function. I try to get down to the fundamentals of human co-operation, drawing on the new insights coming from game theory and evolutionary biology. They help us understand how these ties between the generations, the implicit contracts between them, can actually work.

I believe that a lot of our social and economic problems can be seen as the failure to understand and value these contracts between the generations. Much of what we see as social breakdown is the breakdown of relations between the generations, much mistrust is mistrust between generations, much of what has gone wrong with our economy is failure to get the balance right between generations. This is what low savings and big deficits are all about and it is what environmental degradation is about too. Sometimes we do not even appear to understand what we are doing to future generations and how much we owe to previous ones.

The great French thinker Tocqueville put the charge as powerfully as anyone:

Among democratic nations new families are constantly springing up, others are constantly falling away and all that remain change their condition; the woof of time is every instant broken and the track of generations effaced... Those who went before are soon forgotten; of who will come after, no-one has any idea; the interest of man is confined to those in close propinquity

to himself... Thus not only does democracy make very man forget his ances-
try but it hides his descendants and separates his contemporaries from him;
it throws him back forever upon himself alone and threatens in the end to
confine him entirely within the solicitude of his own heart.[1]

There is one obvious explanation why we are failing to protect
the interests of future generations. We can reasonably hope that
successive generations will be more affluent, unless the entire
mechanism of economic growth since the Industrial Revolution is
turned off. In Chapter 7 we look at the argument that economic
growth means we do not have to worry about future generations
as they should be richer than us. I do not believe this does remove
our obligation. We each of us benefit from what we inherit from
previous generations and must do our best to leave something
worthwhile for the next generation. Think of life as a relay race.
We are handed a baton to run our lap and then pass it on to
someone else. We may be able to run faster than the earlier
runners, perhaps because we have better kit and better training,
and we might expect that later runners coming after us will do
better than us. But we still have to try to do the best lap we can. We
cannot escape our obligations to future generations just because
we think they might be richer, any more than previous generations
decided not to educate us or build roads and sewers or leave great
public buildings because we would be rich enough to do all this
for ourselves. Indeed the only reason we can assume that successive generations will be better off is that we invest in the future –
if there is one thing which would turn that process off it would be
a belief that the future did not matter.

Moreover we do actually depend on future generations. Just as
we were provided for in our childhood by the older generation so
in our old age we are provided for by the younger generation. What

we will live on in our old age is not produced now, it will be produced then. The bread we will eat is not baked now and stored in the garden shed; it will be baked by the younger generation and we will hope to get some of it, either by taxing them or owning a stake in what they produce. The challenge is how we can stake a claim now to that future output in a way which ensures that claim is honoured. If the younger generation feel they have had a raw deal they will not protect the boomers in their old age. It is the contract between the generations which binds these two interests together. This is where government fits in too: maintaining the balance between the generations, as we see in Chapter 8. One tribe of American Indians were supposed to have a rule in the tribal council that they should consider the impact of every decision for the next seven generations. Good government values the future; bad government takes from it.

There is nothing more natural in human affairs than the eternal repeating cycle of childhood, adulthood, and old age – or what used to be called the seven ages of man. This cycle gives a deep pattern to our lives which we can all recognize whatever our political and ethical views. The basis for co-operation between the generations is that we can exchange to mutual benefit because we are at different points in the cycle with different needs and capabilities. In the final four chapters I focus on particular stages of our lives to see what they reveal about the relations between the generations. We immediately confront an important paradox here. If anything, relations between parents and their children are better than they used to be: what used to be called the generation gap is disappearing. There is striking evidence of the enormous effort most parents are now putting in to raising their children: parents are closer to their children than a generation ago. Many children are now dependent on their parents for longer than ever – and it is

unwise to row with your banker. The dependence of the generations on each other in the family is more mutual as well, perhaps
because of the speed of technological change – neatly captured in
the cartoon of mother holding gadget like a TV remote and calling
out desperately to her baby: 'How do I get it to work?' But however
close we are to our families we cannot just do our best for the next
generation one by one. We also have to offer a fair share of power
and wealth to the younger generation as a whole. This is where the
gap between the generations is getting wider. It is a different sort
of generation gap from the one we are used to. We may be better
parents than we are citizens.

This is the challenge for the baby boomers. At the moment this
generation dominates just about every important institution in
the country: it has most of the wealth and power. How will this
generation discharge its obligations to younger generation? So far
it has been one of the luckiest generations. Will the boomers be
selfish with their luck, or will they pass it on to the next generation? So far the evidence is not good. The baby boomers, having
enjoyed so far a spectacularly good deal, are dumping too many
problems on the younger generation. It has the great advantage of
being a giant generation but how will it use that power? At the
moment it looks like a selfish giant.

The boomers are a rich and powerful generation. They are now
past the halfway stage but it is not certain their luck will last. Solon,
the great Athenian statesman, visited Croesus, the richest and
most powerful man of his day. Croesus was surprised that Solon
was not more impressed by his good fortune. 'Call no man happy
until he is dead' was Solon's dry response. Subsequently Croesus
lost his wealth, his kingdom and his family and died a captive.[2] So
this is a challenge to the boomers to value not just future generations but also their own futures. It is a matter not just of other

people's futures, but of what, for today's long-lived generations, has been called the 'Long Now'.[3]

Britain is at an unusual point of generational equipoise. Now is a good moment to judge the balance between the generations. If you line up the British population today by order of age, the middle person in Britain would be aged 40. Their life expectancy is 80. So the middle person is likely to be almost exactly halfway through their life. What happens in the next forty years matters to them even if they do not feel any obligation to other generations.

One of our deepest human instincts, somewhere between a desire and an obligation, is to transmit something worthwhile on to the next generation. It is not just wealth but a body of knowledge, a set of values, an understanding of how to lead a good life. We know that each generation is going to move on, and we hope that it will do better than us, but we know its chances of doing better than us are greatest if it is standing on our shoulders. Much of this experience, wisdom, and values is transmitted within the family. This is where the contract between the generations is played out most personally for each one of us. So we will start in Chapter 1 with families and how they shape the deepest features of our society.

Chapter 1

Who We Are

Picture a family gathered around steaming plates of pasta on a massive trestle table under a tree in a Tuscan garden with uncles, aunts, brothers, daughters-in-law, elderly sisters, all engaged in an excited, voluble hubbub. That is a real family, the kind of family in the film *My Big Fat Greek Wedding*. It is easy to assume – I certainly used to – that at some point in the past the English lived like this too. Even if the food was not so good we too surely lived in big, extended peasant families and in those times all the land belonged to a feudal lord as well. Then there came a great transformation – perhaps the rise of Protestantism, or the Civil War, or the Industrial Revolution – which drove the spread of private property and the modern nuclear family. But the truth is that England never was a society of peasants living in extended families, and we never had true serfdom. As far back as 1250, and probably even earlier, it looks as if England had a very different social structure, different even from the rest of the British Isles. Forget everything you think you know about extended families, arranged marriages, serfdom, and seigneurs. As far as we know none of that happened in England – ever. When it comes to families, England was the first nuclear power.

Instead think of England as being like this for at least 750 years. We live in small families. We buy and sell houses. We go out to work for a wage. Our parents expect us to leave home for paid work when we are in our teens. If you are a boy you go off to be an apprentice and if a girl perhaps to be a servant in another house. You try to save up some money from your wages so that you can afford to get married. You are not dependent on inheriting property from your parents so they have a limited hold over you and you can choose your spouse. Indeed, when it comes to choosing your partner what matters is love, actually. It takes a long time to build up some savings from your work and find the right person with whom to settle down, so marriage comes quite late, possibly in your late twenties. If a man gets a girl pregnant before then he might well have to marry her but they tend to avoid full sex, settling instead for elaborate forms of heavy petting.

Because we marry quite late and the two parents then bear a large part of the burden of raising our children, we do not have many of them.[1] If a society has extended families or clans then this spreads the costs of raising children across more adults, who then have more children younger. That means there is a danger of cycles of population boom and bust as surges in the birth rate are followed by famine and collapse. But that is not the English model. Our population grows slowly but steadily after the catastrophe of the Black Death in the fourteenth century, which may have reduced it to 2.5 million. Britain's first great economic statistician, Gregory King, estimated that the population of England in 1688 totalled 5.5 million.[2] His key table includes estimates of average family size. The upper-class 'heads of families' do indeed have many family dependents. But where the wider population is concentrated, categories such as the 750,000 'freeholders of the lesser sort' or the 1,275,000 'labouring people and outservants', estimated family sizes are 5, 4 or 3.5. This first demographic analysis of England offers further evidence that we have long had small nuclear families.

There are a small number of rich families with an enormous

amount of land for whom arranged marriages matter for dynastic settlements and inheritance, but it is a mistake to assume they are typical of everyone else. Most people are, of course, peasants in the sense that they work on the land from generation to generation. But they are not under the exclusive control of a feudal landlord, let alone his property. They can make themselves available for hire at the great seasonal fairs. They are probably paid in cash not in kind. Money matters. There is borrowing and lending and mortgages and, to keep all this going, quite a sophisticated law of contracts. In turn these contracts are enforced by an independent judiciary.

Here is an account of England in the flat language of modern sociology. It is a familiar account of who we are and how we live: 'The majority of ordinary people in England... are rampant individuals, highly mobile both geographically and socially, economically "rational", market-oriented and acquisitive, ego-centred in kinship and social life.'

Some figures for typical English towns and villages confirm that and capture vividly how markets seem to matter more than roots. In Leighton Buzzard, out of 909 transfers of land, 66 per cent are outside the family; only 15 per cent went to the family in the owner's lifetime and another 10 per cent at death. Another study, of a village near Huntingdon, finds on 43 occasions the property is passed on within the family of which 24 are direct blood inheritance. But there are 21 cases of the property being conveyed to someone outside the family and 98 cases of an open market sale. A third study shows 87 per cent of land transactions taking place between people not related to each other through kinship. And a host of studies show lots of buying and selling of property. This is just what we would expect – a nation of cash, contracts, and commerce. The key question is supposed to be whether or not these modern patterns of behaviour are desirable. Has this turbulent individualism eroded our ties of family and community? But there is just one hitch. The statistics for Leighton Buzzard are for the period 1464 to 1508; for the village near Huntingdon the period studied is 1397 to 1457; and the 87 per cent non-family transactions occurred in a manor in about 1400. The quotation is from a description of England back to the thirteenth century by Alan Macfarlane, the historian above all who has revived this understanding of England and whose influence pervades this chapter.[3]

The power of local barons over peasants was limited by an effective national government too. Insofar as medieval England was 'feudal', its feudalism took an unusually centralized form. The Normans successfully increased the power of central government and subordinated local magnates. Peasants could not be called up for military service directly by a local landlord. In the words of Frederic Maitland, the great Victorian historian, the King could directly tax his subjects, 'their lands and their goods, without the intervention of their lords'.[4] There is local administration of the Common Law, that exceptional English creation of the early medieval period. But the Common Law is crucially not local law. You are bound by precedent, a body of case law that is consistent across the country. That is what 'common' means. Royal authority is used to standardize justice, limiting the power of barons to administer the law in their own interests. Indeed, the crown keeps direct control of justice in the regions by sending travelling assize courts around the country. This makes it much harder to do special favours for kith and kin and so helps to ensure protection for the small nuclear family without extended networks of relatives. The standardization is not, however, achieved simply by royal fiat: it is achieved by lawyers meeting at their London Inns to compare notes and establish through these self-governing institutions a shared understanding of the law, built up through precedent – the role of precedent and its limit on discretion being a difference between the English legal system and the more Roman-influenced legal traditions which flourish on the Continent.

An effective national government and a national framework of law bring standardization, which makes geographical and, hence, also social mobility much easier. Internal migration is easier than in the rest of Europe: not least because you are not tied to an extensive network of favours and reciprocal obligations. Indeed, geographical mobility is another exceptional feature of this English model.

This adds up to an extraordinarily balanced political and social system in which an effective national government protects the rights of individuals and families and stops the creation of local clans and concentrations of baronial power. It is not, by and large, possible for local feuds to develop into private wars. Local barons are not able to extract tax at will. And administration of justice remains broadly fair without special favours to networks of relatives. That list is a neat description of the key features of the eighteenth-century English polity when Adam Smith wrote *The Wealth of Nations*, but its roots go back at least 500 years. It might be called merely a nightwatchman state. But this is to underestimate the crucial role of effective national government even then. It is not a libertarian utopia. Maintaining an effective framework of national law and stopping local magnates being too powerful are both crucial national responsibilities, discharged by virtually no other government at the time. This is the paradox of strong but limited government. This strong government protects small families.

These small families are very unusual. Unlike many other cultures we lack specific words for particular types of uncles, grandparents and cousins (how many people could work out what relation a second cousin, twice removed, would be to them?). There is no framework of law setting out obligations between them. Even our earliest law code, King Alfred's, places very weak obligations on families. In the words of one historian of Anglo-Saxon society, 'the duties kinsmen had with respect to [a given family member] were few.'[5] These small families can be extraordinarily strong, held together by powerful attachments between a couple and with marriage increasingly recognized in canon and civil law as a pre-eminent institution. But their unusually small size compared with other types of family also makes them vulnerable to external shocks. An extended family can offer more by way of support and mutual insurance.

This model of law and society is quite different from other models which obtained and still do in many other parts of the world. In parts of Asia for example it is still assumed that if one member of a large extended family gets a good job his responsibility is to distribute the benefits to his relatives and ideally get them a similar job in the same organization. Helping relatives with contracts and jobs is not seen as corruption but as a moral obligation. Big clan-style families are better than nuclear ones at spreading advantage and pooling risks, but for them to be effective people have to stay close to each other, so there is less mobility.[6]

Sometimes we may regret that England does not enjoy the advantages of these clan-style families, and look back to an earlier age when supposedly we did. The earliest recorded example of this sort of nostalgia is a sermon given by Bishop Wulfstan in 1014, in which he expressed regret that vendettas were not what they used to be as family members just would not join in – 'too often a kinsman does not protect a kinsman any more than a stranger.'[7]

These mobile individuals and small families had to look outwards and create alternative networks for support and insurance. So they were very effective at creating local and civic institutions. With small families people need more of these civil networks in order to sustain a given level of social insurance. Medieval guilds are one early example. And early means early – these societies were being created more than a thousand years ago. The rules of the Thegns' Guild in Cambridge in the late tenth century describe the obligations between 'guild-brothers'; for example, 'If any guild-brother dies outside the district, or is taken ill, his guild-brothers are to fetch him and bring him, dead or alive, to where he wishes, on pain of the same fine which has been stated in the event of his dying at home and a guild-brother failing to attend the body.'[8] Instead of families discharging what Bishop Wulfstan thought were their responsibilities, outside groups such as guilds were providing mutual insurance of a sort we can recognize today.

The 'guild-brothers' were not blood brothers. These guilds were not family-based or closed shops. They were usually open to new members: 'if our lord or any of our reeves can suggest to us any addition to our peace guild; [rather] let us accept it joyfully, as becomes us all and is necessary for us.'[9] For the next thousand years the English carried on creating these groups and societies. Thomas Babington Macaulay, the great nineteenth-century politician and historian, looked at them with a hint of amusement: 'This is the age of societies. There is scarcely one Englishman in ten who has not belonged to some association for distributing books, or for prosecuting them; for sending invalids to the hospital or beggars to the treadmill; for giving plate to the rich or blankets to the poor.'[10]

Small families need civil society more. But it was not just voluntary societies which provided mutual support. You need markets and commercial services too. Instead of the mutual exchanges of the extended family, small families must buy services. For example insurance schemes, annuities, and savings help protect you when there is no wider family with any such obligation. This is one reason why England has a long history in financial services.

Small families meant there was a role for government too. Already by Tudor times the national government had stepped in with the Poor Law after the dissolution of those powerful civic welfare institutions, the monasteries.[11] The Elizabethan Poor Law required the provision of welfare, but delivered and financed locally. Despite its harshness and injustices it was a far more ambitious nationally legislated welfare provision than anywhere else in Europe. It set out the entire local parish's obligations to people who could not care for themselves as they were old or infirm or not in work. Unlike in most other countries then or now, it was provided independently of employers or relatives. This left people unencumbered and mobile. When, centuries later, they were trying to reform welfare, Lord Liverpool, the Prime Minister after the Napoleonic Wars, summarized this unique combination very neatly: 'The legislature of no other country has shown so vigilant and constant a solicitude for the welfare of the poorer classes; no other has so generally abstained from the interference with the details and operation of trade.'

This is a very unusual social and political structure indeed. England has had unusually small families, unusually strong national government, unusually weak local magnates, and unusually free peasants. It is not just different from Papua New Guinea or Pakistan; it is also quite different from France and Italy and most of Continental Europe. This difference was recognized by foreigners. After visiting England in 1730 that shrewd French observer of human cultures, Montesquieu, observed: 'I too have been a traveller, and have seen the country in the world which is most worthy of our curiosity – I mean England.'[12]

It is not that England is better or that foreigners are wrong. But England is certainly distinct. How come? One possible explanation, suggested by Alan Macfarlane, is that almost a millennium and a half ago the Anglo-Saxons brought with them the social, legal, and family arrangements of the German tribes. Perhaps because they were frequently on the move they did not have the sense of land held perpetually by some family or group. Instead it was always being exchanged between individuals. The original Germanic model then disappeared on the Continent as Roman law extended its way back across Northern Europe in the Middle Ages. However, it survived in England, to which it had emigrated. This idea was neatly caught by Benjamin Franklin when he wrote that 'Britain was formerly the America of the Germans.'[13] Montesquieu had a similar thought when he wrote that 'In perusing the admirable treatise of Tacitus on the manners of the Germans we find it is from that nation the English have borrowed their idea of political government. This beautiful system was invented first in the woods.'[14] The reference to the woods may be a crucial clue – one suggestion is that the need to cut down trees to create small clearings is why families were small rather than large and clan-based. It is indeed in Central Germany where archaeologists have found the first genetically identifiable nuclear family of a mother, father, son, and daughter buried together and facing each other in graves dating back 4,600 years. The mother was not genetically related to the father and had spent her childhood in a different region, suggesting that the relationship was not based on membership of the same clan.[15]

The range of family structures around the world has been mapped on to political structures by the great contemporary French thinker Emmanuel Todd.[16] The correlation is uncanny and its historical roots deep. The other European countries with the Anglo-Saxon model of the nuclear family are the Netherlands and Denmark. Todd casually notes that these happen to be the areas of Europe once ruled by King Canute, which itself shows the timescale over which we must think about these family structures. Todd shows the fundamental importance not just for social structures but also for shaping political systems of the difference between endogamous societies, where marriages are often arranged and with relatives, looking inwards to reinforce the clan, and exogamous societies, where marriages are to outsiders and partners may be freely chosen. The second key distinction is between societies where inheritance is egalitarian, with all children having an equal claim and societies where it is inegalitarian with no obligation to treat all children alike. Many other European countries have exogamous marriage, but they do not usually have inegalitarian inheritance as well. (When we refer to marriage here its exact legal form and force may change over time, as common-law marriage thrives before the Church gets greater control over the institution but then has to share it once more with a civil authority.)

The Anglo-Saxon model is unusual in being both exogamous and inegalitarian. Instead of all the property belonging to the family as a whole and being automatically divided between many children when the parents died, in England the older son usually inherited. This pushed waves of property-less younger sons out to make their way in the world. At the same time it made it easier to accumulate wealth in the hands of an individual because it was not endlessly being divided amongst many heirs. Hence you get that distinctive English combination of a society that is both mobile and unequal.

So far we have been painting a picture of England as a marketplace, perhaps the world's first and most sophisticated market economy. Inevitably that means we have focused on patterns of behaviour that are rational, calculating, and acquisitive. But that is not the full picture. The market relationships we describe so far are complemented by, and indeed create an intense need for, emotional relationships outside the market economy as well. A small, simple family structure not driven by the need to pass on an inheritance or to sustain ties with brothers and cousins in a clan can be more personal, intense, and emotional – a clue to England's Romantic tradition. Foreign observers have long remarked how the English love their gardens and their countryside. This may be because we were more urban and then more industrial than the rest of Europe. As we were the first country to move from dependence on agriculture, that perhaps explains some of the emotions we now invest in our pets – and the proud claim of the English to be the inventors of pet food. Charles Dickens captures all this brilliantly with his picture in *Great Expectations* of Wemmick retreating over his drawbridge to his little domestic arcadia away from the hurly-burly of market transactions. England displays that strange mixture of calculation and sentiment which marks so many modern societies

There is an obvious romantic appeal in tracing our origins to German tribes from the woods and plains of Central Europe. But is this just nostalgia for a pre-industrial world? Because the account of national identity we have offered goes all the way back to the Middle Ages it is open to the charge that, even if it were once true, now it is out of date. Didn't the Industrial Revolution and class politics change all that? It is easy to assume that Britain had the Industrial Revolution and then became the world's first modern commercial society. The truth is exactly the other way round. We were already the world's first market society and were therefore ripe for the Industrial Revolution. We have rightly been described as enjoying 'capitalism without factories' for many centuries before the Industrial Revolution. That the Industrial Revolution began in England is a crucial piece of evidence in support of the argument that we have a distinctive economic and social structure.

One way of assessing the impact of the Industrial Revolution in Britain is through the historical equivalent of the *Sunday Times* Rich List. One historian, W. D. Rubinstein, has studied the estates left by the richest families before, during, and after the Industrial Revolution.[17] In the early eighteenth century the wealth of the British middle and upper classes came from commerce, finance, professions such as the law, and the global trading networks they serviced. You can then see the impact of the Industrial Revolution as Lancashire and Yorkshire rise from providing 10 per cent of business and professional incomes in 1810 to a peak of 22 per cent in 1860. But after that they begin to decline as a proportion of the richest families. They made their wealth differently from the way anyone had made money in the past – by manufacturing – and they created a proud civic culture in the cities of the Midlands and the North. But by the early twentieth century patterns of income and wealth in Britain had reverted to what they were before the Industrial Revolution. Once again it was trade, finance, commerce, and the great professions.

A similar pattern can be seen in demography. We have seen how traditionally England had an unusually low birth rate and hence a degree of protection from the worst of all possible boom and bust cycles, one in human lives. After the Black Death in the middle of the fourteenth century the population of England appears to have been on a slow upward trajectory for the next 400 years or so, rising perhaps to 8.3 million by the end of the eighteenth century. But the nineteenth century was an exception to this as our population soared to 30 million by the century's end. As we industrialized there was a mass movement of population into the towns and at the same time some of the traditional constraints of the English family system broke down. People had more babies and had them earlier. And of course in the conditions of living then, many of them were sadly to die. Thus England had for a century or so the kind of pattern that many people assume it must always have had. By the end of the nineteenth century mortality in our towns was falling and then the birth rate fell as well. After the Industrial Revolution we therefore went through the two classic phases of the demographic transition which most societies go through as they modernize. It can be summarized very simply – first, we stop dying like flies, and then we stop breeding like rabbits. By the early twentieth century we had resumed a pattern of later marriage and lower birth rate of the sort we can recognize from Alan Macfarlane's account of early medieval England.

Just as aerial photography can reveal the outlines of some long-lost medieval village so, if we know how to look, we can discern deep features of English society that endure to this day. Here is an example. A series of reports have attributed the long-standing weaknesses in the productivity of the British economy to our lack of a *Mittelstand*, the strong medium-sized family businesses of the sort they have in Germany or France.[18] We appear to be very good at starting small businesses and some of our big companies are very strong indeed. It is the high-performance, solid, long-term, high-investment medium-sized companies in the middle that we seem to lack. It is not that we have fewer family-owned firms – about 30 per cent of mid-sized British firms are owned by a family, very similar to France and Germany. But we run them differently. Perhaps England's family structure helps to explain this.

A key difference is that land is not owned by kin groups but by named individuals with unrestricted power over what happens to their property. This is one reason why as soon as you had property you were expected to leave a detailed will. Friedrich Engels recognized that this made England's family law very different: 'In those countries where a legitimate portion of parental wealth is assured to children and where they cannot be disinherited – in Germany, in countries with French law and elsewhere – the children are obliged to obtain their parents' consent to their marriage. In countries with English law... the parents have full liberty to bequeath their wealth to anyone and may disinherit their children at will...'[19] French law reflects a very different view of the family. In France neither land nor a firm is the freehold property of the individual, belonging rather to the family's bloodline with an automatic right of inheritance within the family for all the children – this is how the principle of equal inheritance is delivered in practice. In England it is the absolute property of the individual to do with as they wish. It may be passed on to one child who will have control of the company. In France an asset such as a family firm is not the absolute property of one individual. A father has no right to cut his children out of his will; they (and to almost the same extent, the spouse) are *héritiers réservataires*. If any part of the property or land is willed to other than the children of the deceased, Napoleonic law kicks in and can override any bequest regarding the property.[20]

In England, therefore, family firms are more likely to be run as the personal property of an individual who often manages the business himself or herself. In France and Germany family firms are more likely to be held in common by a whole family and seen as long-term property of a dynasty across several generations. This means the family is more willing to bring in professional managers to run the business on its behalf: 31 per cent of family-owned firms in France are run by an external manager as against only 23 per cent in the UK. (It is 60 per cent in Germany.) Of firms still owned by the founder 44 per cent in France are externally managed whereas it is only 14 per cent in the UK (again it is 60 per cent in Germany).[21] This has a big effect on economic performance – if an inherited family firm brings in an outside manager it raises returns by 6 percentage points, a significant improvement in return on capital.[22] One could even take this further. The role for the family in France as a project for managing property that passes on from generation to generation may be a reason why romantic love may be for a mistress outside marriage. In England romance matters too, but we aspire to find it within marriage.

If you go further afield the differences are far greater, and show up even more starkly the links between the social, the political, and the economic. Why is it so hard to establish liberal democracies and effective governments in large parts of the Middle East? It is not ultimately a matter of religion but of the cultural traditions associated with some versions of Islam. Their family structure may help explain why Western-style democratic government is so hard to establish in parts of the Muslim world. In Pakistan 50 per cent of marriages are to first cousins. In Saudi Arabia this figure is 36 per cent.[23] The political structure of a society of extended families is completely different from that of a society with small families. It means that voting is by clans: it is hard to have neutral contracts enforced by an independent judiciary when family obligations are so wide-ranging and so strong.

It is no accident that there is a Muslim brotherhood – brotherhood really does mean something in parts of the Muslim world. It weakens national governments and makes it hard for the neutral contractual arrangements of a modern market economy to be created. By contrast, as Dr Johnson observed on brotherhood in England: 'Sir, in a country as commercial as ours, when every man can do for himself, there is not much occasion for that attachment. No man is thought the worse of here whose brother was hanged.'[24] The French Revolutionaries ignored the uncomfortable truth that liberty and equality before the law are hard to reconcile with fraternity. That is why it is such a challenge to integrate communities based on fraternity into a host society where the dominant principles are liberty and equality.

England's closest neighbours understood more clearly than the English themselves the components of this distinctive Englishness. A whole stream of French observers were fascinated by this extraordinary English political and social experiment – from Voltaire and Montesquieu in the eighteenth century to Tocqueville and Hippolyte Taine in the nineteenth. But it was above all the Scottish thinkers of the eighteenth century who reflected on this English model. An extraordinary flowering of great thinkers such as David Hume, Adam Smith, and Adam Ferguson put markets, contracts and civil society at the centre of their thinking and in doing so created the political economy of the modern world. As well as political and moral philosophy, David Hume also wrote a history of England. Adam Smith drew heavily on English evidence throughout *The Wealth of Nations* and his *The Theory of Moral Sentiments*. Scottish intellectuals reflecting on England's economy and society created what Gertrude Himmelfarb has boldly called the British Enlightenment.[25]

Britishness is emphatically not the same thing as Englishness. The English model is just one within the British Isles. Scotland has a distinctive history, with a separate legal system and educational arrangements and a different culture. Great Britain provides the political institutions which linked these two nations in an outward-looking endeavour of trade and conquest: it is the British army, the British Empire and the British pound. That connection made both nations different and better than they would have been on their own; and in the early excitement after the Act of Union Scots, such as

David Hume, were willing to describe themselves as living in North Britain. Britishness is a weaker cultural identity than Englishness or Scottishness. That is why H. G. Wells could say that 'The great advantage of being British is that we do not have a national dress.'

That Britishness is essentially an institutional concept makes it very well suited for today when Empire and conquest have long gone. It helps ensure our national identity is not ethnic, giving it a marvellous openness. Instead it is a political identity resting above all in a set of political institutions. Most non-white ethnic groups describe themselves as British rather than English – 78 per cent of Bangladeshis living in the UK for example describe themselves as British and 5 per cent say they are English. But people from the white British group give a very different answer with more describing themselves as English (58 per cent) than British (36 per cent).[26] Our patriotism is not a nationalism of blood and soil. Instead it is a celebration of the institutions that shaped our country and which should be open to everyone. In fact the account in this chapter stresses how successive waves of migration brought distinctive ideas and institutions which between them developed into what we now call Britishness.

Winston Churchill wrote his *A History of the English-Speaking Peoples* in this tradition, including North America and beyond in his celebration of these political institutions. Andrew Roberts has recently carried that tradition forward, adding an extra volume to Churchill's history.[27] Niall Ferguson has also argued for the distinctive identity of what is now called the Anglosphere. These formidable historians show very clearly that in everything from economic structures to cultural attitudes there is a close link between Great Britain, the USA, Canada, and Australia. But they do not fully resolve the question of what makes the Anglosphere distinctive.

UNIVERSITY OF WINCHESTER
LIBRARY

It is easy to think of the English language as what unites this group – after all, the Anglosphere was formerly known as the English-speaking peoples. But this does not tell anything like the whole story. The unusual importance of civil society is crucial. Now, we immediately face a paradox. Alexis de Tocqueville was one of the first people to see that the youthful USA derived much of its dynamism from its extraordinarily rich and self-reliant civil society as a contrast with pre-Revolutionary France: 'When the Revolution started, it would have been impossible to find, in most parts of France, even ten men used to acting in concert and defending their interests without appealing to the central power for aid.'[28] But his most influential book fails recognize that this is what the USA and England share or why. His analysis suffers from one massive disadvantage – he went to America before he visited England. When he wrote his great book *Democracy in America* in the 1830s he was completely unaware of the English origins of the American model. In fact he thought that England was trapped in an aristocratic and feudal past and that the vigour of civil society in America was unique. This is a crucial mistake. It obstructs understanding what links Britain and America, and leaves Brits, metaphorically at least, forever playing aristocrats and butlers in American films.

When he finally visited England Tocqueville was trying to work out when the revolution which America and France had already experienced would also strike England, leading to the overthrow of powerful concentrations of aristocratic wealth. He expected some revolution in favour of agricultural smallholdings belonging to people like the soldier-citizens who were the backbone of Jefferson's America. Free-market English economists had to explain that we had big farms because they were more efficient. He only came to appreciate that what he had seen in America could also be found in England after two visits – the moment of epiphany coming when he visited my home town of Birmingham in the full vigour of the Industrial Revolution and noted in his diary that they are 'generally very intelligent people but intelligent in the American Way'.[29]

Tocqueville thought at first that America was the future for everywhere – and indeed that France having already had its revolution was further on the way than England. But slowly he came to realize that this model was not right. The vigour of civil society in England or the USA is not some universal historic trend. It depends on some very unusual and shared features of our two countries. England and America share a similar civil society because we share the same (rather unusual) family structure. Tocqueville eventually made the connection between this mobility and exceptional family structure, observing that 'England was the only country in which the system of caste had not been changed but effectively destroyed. The nobles and the middle classes in England followed together the same courses of business, entered the same professions, and what is much more significant, inter-married.'[30]

But once more there are frustrating misunderstandings between Britain and America which obscure this crucial point. The leading history of the American family, *Public Vows* by Nancy Cott, talks of the nuclear family as the 'republican family' – showing how it was seen as an example of republican virtue in contrast with the decadence of European model, which was thought to be oppressive both domestically and politically.[31] Meanwhile, one of the best books on the nuclear family, Ferdinand Mount's *The Subversive Family*, treats the nuclear family as essentially a human universal. But the real dividing line is to be drawn differently. American family structure is the same as the English model and very different from much of Continental Europe. This is the explanation of the strength of US and British civil society and the pervasiveness of the market economy in the Anglosphere. The special relationship depends on a special relationship.

Tocqueville appears to have believed that it was political structure which shaped family life. On a visit to Algiers he was shocked by the bare walls of houses turning their backs to the street and attributed it to 'a tyrannous and shadowy government which forces its subjects to hide from the world and tightly encloses all passions in the interior world of the family'.[32] But it could be the other way round because the extended, non-nuclear family behind its walls is self-sufficient and turns its back on civil society. Generally, nuclear families mean a stronger civil society because individuals need support outside the family and turn to a rich network of clubs and friendly societies. A recent study of European families[33] showed that these patterns continue to matter today. People in inegalitarian nuclear family societies, like England, Denmark, and the Netherlands, are the likeliest to join clubs and associations.

We also look out to the market to buy services with contracts instead of the mutual exchanges of the extended family. If we need something we turn to Yellow Pages not to an uncle. This requires respect for contracts, for property and for marketplaces. This too changes the nature of society. It makes it open and market-facing and literally more mobile. Great Britain is one of the few EU countries where more than half of adults have moved house in the past ten years.[34] Even now, when you control for country-level effects, areas of Europe with Anglosphere-style families have a GDP per capita of around €5,000 p.a. higher than regions with say the Southern Italian family form.[35] Indeed, they are higher than all other family forms. Over the past thirty years, they have also outgrown them. These Anglosphere economies are outward-looking and flexible so they are good early adopters of new technologies.

But they may not be so good at steady incremental improvements in performance with a given technology. And sometimes, as we have seen with new financial instruments, their sheer restless innovativeness can do catastrophic damage. Nevertheless, their flexibility can sustain them in the long run – the Anglosphere currently accounts for more than half, 54 per cent, of the economic output of the developed world and one forecast is that by 2050 over two thirds, 68 per cent, of developed world GDP will be generated in English-speaking countries.[36]

It is easy to caricature all this as a picture of sturdy yeoman farmers and heroic offshore islanders. Julian Barnes's novel *England, England* imagines the custodians of Englishness retreating to the Isle of Wight, which becomes a theme park dedicated to a cosy England-land. Some contemporary historians would see this whole account as just one way in which a national 'narrative' is 'constructed', traditions are 'invented', communities are 'imagined', and nations are 'forged'.[37] A modern liberal society is indeed going to see different versions of its own history endlessly contested. Nevertheless, I believe this account of Englishness is empirically rooted and conceptually rigorous. It is right under our noses. It is, quite simply, the main school of English historical writing from its emergence as a serious discipline. David Hume and Sir William Blackstone were key founding figures in the eighteenth century. It includes the leading Victorian historians Sir Henry Maine and F. W. Maitland. Maitland was the mentor of one of the leading founders of the Political Studies Association, Sir Ernest Barker, who wrote of the distinctive strength of our civil society and whose influence carried on to the Second World War. This is not just the dominant strand of English historical understanding; it shapes our political thought too. It is why England saw the first flourishing of classical liberalism. The first great liberal political philosopher, John Locke, celebrated the freedom of the individual, and understood property not as something that belonged to a family or a group but as created by an individual's own efforts. He did not construct such an extraordinary new political theory in a vacuum – it was an abridgement of the political and social arrangements Locke saw around him. The theory followed the practice.

This English political tradition emphasizes the strength and importance of civil society, our country's historic freedoms, a legitimate role for government in providing equitable justice accessible to all, together with a faith in evolutionary social progress. It sustained a political programme – spreading the rights of citizenship widely and generously – which still matters today. That meant widening the franchise and also spreading what Beveridge called social security – mutual insurance against the giant evils of Want, Ignorance, Disease, Squalor, and Idleness. Democracy and the modern welfare state rested on a powerful sense of the birthright of British citizens which did not depend on who your parents were. But that whole tradition got worn smooth and came to seem too complacent. Our weak economic performance after the War showed it just wasn't strenuous enough. And now we fear that, despite the achievements of the welfare state, our society is becoming less cohesive and less mobile.

I believe this great tradition can be revitalized and renewed by enriching it with the insights of the Cambridge school of family history whose leading thinkers such as Peter Laslett and Alan Macfarlane offer a serious and empirically grounded account of our social structure, focusing on our nuclear families. It shows what is distinctive about England: it is our family structure which is the key. It is not that we are right and Continentals are wrong. But we are different, apart from perhaps the Low Countries and Denmark, which do appear to share many features of our social structure and our political tradition.

It also leads us to focus on what we are passing on to our children. Instead of thinking just of the horizontal obligations we have to fellow citizens now, we need to think also about the vertical obligations we have to our children and grandchildren and future generations. We think of haves and have-nots now. But what if the haves are us now and the have-nots are our children and grandchildren in the future? We need to do much better at weighing the claims of the Nows versus the Laters.

If we are failing to pass on full opportunities in life to all our citizens then we may respond by concentrating instead on what we can do for our own children. That is an understandable and indeed admirable instinct. It is not, as we have seen, an instinct that gets automatic protection in the British system. A shrewd nineteenth-century French observer, Hippolyte Taine, was shocked by this feature of the English system: 'they owe nothing but education to their children; the daughters marry without a dowry, the sons shift for themselves.'[38]

You inherit not just a particular set of possessions that belonged to your parents. You also inherit a claim to participate in an extraordinary political, social, and economic system that would give you a chance in life. That is another part of the inheritance that we are obliged to pass on to the next generation – that is the obligation which I fear we are failing to discharge. We discharge our obligation to the next generation not just as parents but as citizens. And to understand our failure to discharge this obligation we need to see how the tumultuous social and economic changes since the war have shifted the balance between the generations.

Chapter 2

Breaking Up

Imagine a society where people live together in quite large nuclear families with traditional roles. The father goes out to work. His wife may work part-time but mostly she is busy running the house and caring for the two kids and her elderly widowed mother who lives with them. She is as much a worker as he is but her work has no direct financial reward. Although it is much smaller than an extended family, nevertheless it is still a kind of mini-welfare state. The man's earnings are transferred to four dependants. It is a transfer from man to woman. It is also a transfer across the generations, from the middle-aged man to children and a pensioner.

Even if he is earning quite a lot, he may not feel very affluent as he has so many commitments. Indeed, the official measures of income and poverty allow for this by counting his income as much less than that of someone with the same earnings who lives on his own ('equivalizing'). The tax system recognizes this too, with special allowances to reduce your income tax if you are married or if you have children, resting on the doctrine that the man we are describing has less 'taxable capacity' than a single person with the same earnings. There is a benefit system too, and its main purpose is to compensate men for loss of earnings – through unemployment, disability, or retirement. He will also get higher benefits such as a higher unemployment benefit or state pension if he is married, so that he can still, in both senses of the word, keep his wife. This further enforces the dependence of women and young people on the male breadwinner, because even state benefits come via the man. There might also be labour market regulations aimed at protecting the jobs this paterfamilias does, even if as a result it is harder for women or young people to get employment.

People may disagree about whether this is what made our community stronger in the past or a monstrous and oppressive paternalism. It was the British model in the earlier part of the twentieth century. Perhaps it is pushing the point to include the elderly relative in the house but these arrangements were quite common for a time after the War because there was such a housing shortage. It is broadly what Japan and Italy are still like today. These are countries with high unemployment benefits and low benefits for single parents, high pensions, and high proportions of pensioners living with their children. (They are also, incidentally, countries with exceptionally low birth rates, suggesting that when women are expected to discharge traditional roles, providing informal care to parents, parents-in-law, and husbands, they refuse to raise children as well. This is why access to birth control poses a particular demographic challenge for these societies with extended families: it gives women the opportunity to escape one of their many obligations.[1])

Then a massive social change fragments millions of families like these – the ultra-individualism unleashed by the post-War baby boomers. The nuclear family always depended on a personal emotional commitment between two adults – in this sense it always was individualistic. But in the past it had been sustained by economic dependence, social pressure, and stern personal morality. From the 1960s onwards all these supports fall away. Instead, each of us focuses on our own personal needs because, in the words of the L'Oréal advert, 'I am worth it.' Or, if instead of L'Oréal you prefer Hegel, whose *Philosophy of Right* is one of the few major works of philosophy to focus on the family, marriage declines into 'reciprocal caprice'. Britain and America are particularly susceptible to this fragmentation because, as we saw, marriage in the Anglosphere relies particularly on its emotional value to each partner.

Let's go back to our opening example. The marriage breaks up in the 1970s or 1980s when the divorce rate surges. The man moves out. His wife becomes a lone parent. The mother-in-law has to go into a flat with some domiciliary care. The lone mother starts to claim benefits. The elderly widow was already getting a basic pension but now she needs a top-up means-tested benefit as well. As they all have their own housing costs to meet with very little income, new benefits have to cover these costs as well. To pay for all these benefits the man finds that his income tax bill goes up. Those special allowances for marriage now seem strangely out of date so they are gradually taken away and the income tax bill goes up even for the couples who have stuck together. Let's take stock of what this new world is like.

Instead of one household there are three. That means we need much more housing, though households are smaller. (Britain's population rose by 8 per cent in the 35 years from 1970 to 2005 but the number of households rose by 30 per cent.[2]) As it is more expensive to run three households than one, people will feel poorer even if there is the same amount of money to go round as before. At the same time these demographic pressures put up house prices much faster than inflation. So people find themselves asset-rich but cash-poor. They stop saving and instead they borrow against the equity in their properties.

Before there was just one working household. Now there are two workless households as well, one of which is headed by a person of working age. Official unemployment doesn't change but workless households are up. People start worrying that children are being brought up without seeing a parent going out to work and that this can damage their own employment prospects in turn.[3] There is pressure to tackle the problem of worklessness by getting tougher on adults such as single parents who aren't working.

Benefits spending has gone up and so has the tax burden. A welfare system that was originally designed to compensate men for loss of earnings is slowly and messily redesigned to compensate women for the loss of men.

The labour market is deregulated so as to get more women and young people into work. The employment rate rises, though there may still be more workless households than before. This reinforces the trend for individuals to be less dependent on each other as more people earn an income for themselves. At the same time there is less deference to tradition and authority and the very idea of the paterfamilias disappears into history.

This model helps us to understand the economic and social changes going on around us. In fact much of our domestic politics is an argument about these changes and their consequences. Why, for example, has Britain become a more unequal society with such pressure on the tax and benefits system to redistribute from rich to poor? Our example provides the clue. The man is counted as richer after the break-up, even though his actual income has not changed. His ex-wife and the children are counted as poorer. The man's equivalized income appears to have risen, as he has fewer family responsibilities. Two new low-income households have been created as well.

In a modern market economy there may well be big gaps in individual earnings (and in Britain and America they are wider than most). We tend to focus on this diversity of individual earnings. But you see things very differently if you measure incomes not by individuals but by whole households. A society where well-paid individuals are sharing their income with other members of the family who are not working can end up quite equal. In Britain, by contrast, we have unusually small households. Our average household size of 2.4 is one of the smallest in the world.[4] Sweden's household size, at 3.1, is much higher, one reason why its level of inequality is much lower.[5] A key difference between more equal and less equal societies is that by and large more equal societies have bigger households.

People talk sometimes as if inequality and poverty, which on some measures have deteriorated over the past twenty-five years, are a result of changes in tax rates and the value of benefits. These have played a role. But at least as important have been changes in the family. One way of measuring this is to take the tax and benefit rates and the employment patterns of Britain today and then impose on them not today's family structure but the family structure of Britain in 1979. Then we get less poverty and inequality than we actually have now. The closest anyone has got to this experiment is researchers who calculated the different factors behind the increase in the proportion of families below 60 per cent of median income from 15 per cent in 1979 to 30 per cent in 1997. Changes in government benefits, other things being equal, actually reduced the poverty rate on this measure by 3 percentage points. But it was more than offset by demographic change which pushed up the poverty rate by 9 percentage points, by far the biggest single factor behind the increase. This demographic change was higher rates of family break-up and more lone parenthood.[6]

There is quite a lot of argument about why these changes occurred. Did the tax and benefits system drive the changes? Did it at least make the changes possible? Or was it just passive, responding to much deeper changes in people's willingness to commit to each other and stick together? Are these changes just an inevitable consequence of living in a society where personal fulfilment matters above all? And are they a good thing? Politicians step in but they find it hard to fit these changes into the conventional political arguments. In a sense people have become more free as taboos are eroded, it becomes easier to leave a relationship that is not fulfilling, and families can take many more different forms. But by becoming more independent of each other we have also become more dependent on the state, which has to take on the financial responsibilities no longer discharged by those traditional male breadwinners. This means there is a growing celebration of personal independence and freedom but it is combined with higher public spending and tax. So it feels as if government is failing to match our individualist values when it is actually picking up the consequences of them. The irony is that it is the hunger for personal fulfilment and happiness which drives these changes but after all this people are no happier than they were before. In fact the research comes in showing that the very arrangements from which we are fleeing seem to offer more happiness for most people.[7] But there are growing gaps between different countries – Denmark has got a lot happier over the past twenty years but Belgium became a bit depressed, and now Italy is rather low[8] – suggesting that we are not just facing the inevitable consequences of modern life. Denmark's high level of equality, high marriage rate and high levels of happiness may all be linked.

There are ambitious attempts to try to measure the wider effects of these changes on the quality of life. President Sarkozy has tried to include them in the French national accounts, believing they will show France does better in quality of life than on some more conventional economic measures. American researchers have even tried to calculate the environmental impact of these changes as smaller households are more energy-intensive per person. They estimate that 'Divorced households in the US could have saved more than 38 million rooms, 73 billion kilowatt-hours of electricity, and 627 billion gallons of water in 2005 alone if their resource-use efficiency had been comparable to married households.'[9]

The old model did work quite well, at least for some, especially for men. Marriage is certainly good for keeping men healthy – when the man in our example moved out to live on his own he started drinking more, smoking more, and going to bed late so his health suffered. His life expectancy falls now he is on his own. Some evidence even suggests that married men are more productive at work.[10] (About half the higher wages of married men can be attributed to a selection effect as women choose men they think will perform better in the jobs market, but the rest appears to arise because the greater commitment in marriage means it is more worthwhile for a spouse to invest in improving their partner's performance at work. When individual American states moved to easier no-fault divorce the marriage premium in wages fell as the commitment device had been weakened.) But the traditional model also involved massive sacrifices of opportunities of jobs and careers by women. It wasn't such a good deal for the woman who sacrificed her career to raise the kids and then found herself on her own without either her husband's earnings or her own. The whole model does depend on very high levels of trust and commitment and it was women and children above all who lost out when the commitment was not kept.

The lesson which the next generation of women take from all this is not to get a man but first to get a qualification and get a career. That is the real pre-nup. Only then can you risk getting married. The feminists would add that it is not just that women cannot trust men to stick to their side of the old marriage contract. Women want to enjoy the same freedom to get a job and make their careers which men have long taken for granted. And before we get too misty-eyed about the intergenerational contract, we should recognize that it was women who did most of the work keeping it going whilst men earned most of the money. So if this contract is to be kept going it will involve a rather different share of responsibilities and burdens between men and women than before.

The political economist who created the first and most coherent account of these massive social changes was Joseph Schumpeter. In *Capitalism, Socialism and Democracy*, published in 1943, he offered a powerful critique of capitalism. Marx had said that capitalism would collapse because people got poorer and poorer and would eventually revolt against the sheer misery of their conditions. But Schumpeter argued capitalism would be destroyed not by its failure but by its success. It would spread material well-being and a consumer culture in which people abandoned projects for the future in favour of living for today. Instead of living by solid bourgeois virtues of prudence and foresight, a counter-culture would mock and then overwhelm them. He predicted the decay of the two most powerful forms of commitment to the future. He argued that saving and investment would decline to catastrophically low levels. Secondly, he believed that the birth rate would decline because children, our ultimate project for the future, get in the way of consuming today. Both his predictions are becoming true across the West, though in very different combinations from country to country. On the Continent they still save but have fewer babies. In the Anglosphere our savings rate fell much lower, but the birth rate is rather higher.

On this model divorce and single parenthood are but transitional stages to a world of full-blown childless singletons: we are on our way to an atomized society of weaker families, transient relationships, and fewer children. We can certainly see this social change in the great world cities of New York, London, or Paris. In London single households are unlike those on say the south coast because many of them comprise a single person, quite possibly a man, under 60. (London has smaller households and more inequality than the rest of Britain. The ratio of income for the 90th to the 10th income percentile is 4.66 across the country, but it is 6.26 for London.[11]) Within London there is one area where almost half of all households comprise one person living on his or her own. It is the greatest concentration of under-60 singletons to be found in Great Britain.[12] It is Kensington and Chelsea. If you want to see the future as a cosmopolitan, mobile, rootless, unattached, affluent network of under-60s living on their own in flats and socializing outside them, then go to Kensington. That is where, as they say, people are thinnest, richest, and singlest.

The contemporary thinker who has done most to provide a theory for all this is the sociologist Professor Anthony Giddens. He astutely identifies a gap in classical liberalism. On the one hand it praises choice and freedom but it rarely asks what the people doing all this choosing are like and how they are created. It just assumes a benign history and culture that shape these robust individuals – and, as we saw earlier, liberalism first flourished in England because of just such a culture. But Professor Giddens argues it was absurd for the economic liberals to think we can restrict choice to holidays and cars: we can choose who we are as well. He argues that our identities are no longer fixed and unchanging but instead are deliberately adopted. And that changes the nature of our relations to others. The pure relationship is one which is chosen and can be 'unchosen'. 'A pure relationship is one in which external criteria have become dissolved: the relationship exists solely for whatever rewards that relationship as such can deliver' instead of ties of 'kinship, social duty, or traditional obligation'.[13] It is not clear where obligations to children or parents fit into this model.

Anthony Giddens's argument is very important for understanding the intellectual currents around us. It is a kind of explanation for the ultra-individualism we described earlier. It reduces all traditions to equally valid costumes in the fancy dress party of life. It sees all unreflective and unquestioned identities as equally anachronistic and equally threatening to the pure untramelled choice which it values above all. Life becomes like channel surfing, with the TV remote in our hands. (Indeed one of the many differences between the generations is that older people tend to watch a single programme, whilst younger people channel surf, holding several different narratives in their head at the same time.[14]) Choice and freedom are everything. We might argue about whether we like it or dislike it but the liberal progressives and the moral pessimists agree on the trend.[15] Then there really is little chance of society meaning much apart from perhaps, if we are lucky, a feeble agreement on how we are going to disagree with each other.

Tocqueville was one of the first people to spot this trend: he traced it back to the breakdown of the contract between the generations, as we saw in the Introduction.

This whole line of thought – from Tocqueville to Schumpeter and Giddens – suggests that as our links with others weaken so posterity ceases to matter for us. This could be the future. But before we settle for the argument that this is what modern life must be like, we are going to investigate what has actually happened and why. In the next two chapters we will look at how changes in the balance between the generations have reshaped Britain and other Western societies since the War. We will look first at the social changes driven by the sheer size of the baby boomers and then the shifts of income and wealth between the generations. It might help us see what the baby boomers really did and why.

Chapter 3

The Baby Boom

The pressures on families were just too much. People were getting married later (aged 26 or more) and having fewer children (down to 670,000 births[1]). One of the popular bestsellers of the day warned of *The Twilight of Parenthood*.[2] How could families afford all these new consumer goods and raise children as well? It was called the dilemma of the pram or the car. Government advisers warned that by the year 2000 the population could fall to 34 million.[3] Pessimism about the future was pervasive. Welcome to Britain in the 1930s.

The greatest minds of the period worried about the long-term effects of this shift towards fewer children and later marriage than in Victorian times. T. S. Eliot feared in 1939 that 'a wave of terror of the consequences of depopulation might lead to legislation having the effect of compulsory breeding.'[4] Aldous Huxley envisaged in *Brave New World* a society where sex was for fun and nothing to do with producing children. In such a future the raising and care of children was taken over by the state, leaving individuals unattached and free to consume.

Keynes's *General Theory of Employment, Interest and Money* was written at the same time as he was wrestling with what he called 'the economic consequences of a declining population' – the title of a lecture he delivered in 1937. He boldly reversed the obvious, but incorrect, conventional wisdom that a growing population is more likely to lead to unemployment because of too many workers

35

– the so-called lump of labour fallacy. Keynes argued the opposite: a population that was shrinking would be at greater risk of unemployment. A youthful and growing population borrowed more, and consumed more, thus stimulating demand and using resources to the full. By contrast, he argued, a shrinking and ageing population diminished demand, leaving resources unemployed. Keynes's lecture on population began with a statement of what then looked obvious:

We know much more securely than we know almost any other social or economic factor relating to the future that, in the place of the steady and indeed steeply rising level of population which we have experienced for a great number of decades, we should be faced in a very short time with a stationary or a declining level.[5]

Those confident words were of course proved wrong by the post-War baby boom, reminding us of the need for some humility in the face of apparently inevitable demographic change. But it was a decade before Keynes's forecast, based on the low interwar birth rate, was to be challenged.

In France and Britain fear of depopulation led to new proposals for supporting families, the origins of family allowances (which later became Child Benefit). But it was the fascist governments of Germany and Italy which worried most about low birth rates and were most successful in reversing the trend – linking pro-natalism with fascism and leaving the issue politically untouchable for half a century. Only in the last few years have the OECD and the EU been willing again to look at the consequences of demographic decline and policies that might raise birth rates.

The Attlee Government and its Conservative successor commissioned earnest reports into the problems of an ageing population and a low birth rate. Indeed one of the Treasury's main fears about the costs of the post-War welfare state was that there would not be enough workers to pay for it. A Royal Commission on Population reported in 1949. A National Advisory Committee on the Employment of Older Men and Women produced a series of reports urging employers not to miss out on the talents of older people. The Phillips Committee warned in 1954 that by 1979 the dependency ratio of pensioners to workers would become unsustainable.[6] Their main proposal was to increase the state pension age for women from 60 to 63 and for men from 65 to 68. More than fifty years after Phillips reported, the slow process of raising the pension age for both sexes is currently planned to start in 2024, after a decade of increasing the female pension age to 65. Eventually a pension age of 68 is supposed to be reached in 2046, almost a hundred years after it was first proposed in a government report – a record even by the standards of Whitehall.

Life was tough in the 1930s. But the actuaries have calculated that 1931 was the best year to have been born to enjoy the greatest improvement in life expectancy Britain has ever experienced. The austerity of those years and the surge in life expectancy may even be linked – our diet was low in calories, sugar, and fat in the 1930s and 1940s and scientists now believe that can prolong life.[7] Another reason that generation has done well is the decline in smoking since the 1970s. Of the 725,000 people born in 1931, 425,000, more than half, have got to the age of 75. But not many people were born in the 1930s. That means, contrary to popular myth, the increase in the numbers of pensioners in Britain over the last two decades has been, if anything, unusually modest.

Then, in the 1940s, contrary to all the official forecasts, the baby boom got underway. The first surge had already started during the War, with births rising from the early 1940s to reach an exceptional peak of more than one million in 1947. Four key factors led to this dramatic rise in fertility rates. First, after the low fertility of the 1930s, women faced the choice of either not having children at all or getting on with it even in the unpropitious circumstances of the War. Think of the decline and surges in birth rates as like someone playing an accordion. Births can be low and spread out as people put off having children, but then births get compressed together in a few years. Second, high wartime employment for women (as well as men) provided financial security that encouraged more children. Third, the Second World War saw a sudden and enormous increase in government-funded local authority nurseries on a scale not to be seen again for at least fifty years. Fourth, there was a direct financial incentive as a soldier's pay was increased if he had children.[8] Britain had a pro-natalist policy, without even realizing it. After the first baby boom there was then a modest decline during the early 1950s before the baby boom reached a second peak in 1964 and 1965, declining steadily over the next decade. These twin peaks are very different from the American post-War baby boom which grew steadily to one sustained high plateau in 1957–61.

With all these babies, the shortage of family homes was a big problem. Churchill wanted to see 'the smoke rising from the chimney of an Englishman's cottage' and won the 1951 Election partly because of the dramatic pledge to build 300,000 houses. Harold Macmillan made his reputation by delivering that pledge. In turn the availability of affordable housing helped to keep the baby boom going. Harold Macmillan went on to become the British Prime Minister and famously said in 1957: 'Most of our people have never had it so good.' Nowadays we may hear a sexual innuendo and, whatever Macmillan's intentions, we are right. The age of first sexual intercourse fell by two years in the fifties, from

21 to 19, more than at any other time in Britain's history.[9] Macmillan's remark could be roughly translated as 'go forth and multiply'. The second phase of the baby boom was underway. Philip Larkin wrote:

> Sexual intercourse began
> In nineteen sixty-three
> (which was rather late for me)
> Between the end of the 'Chatterley' ban
> And the Beatles' first LP.[10]

He got the year exactly right. The following year births across the UK peaked at 1.015 million – the only time they have exceeded a million since 1947.

Delaying gratification is crucial in a society where there is not much to go round. But in the words of one advertisement for a credit card, a modern consumer society takes the waiting out of wanting. There is no more primal example of gratification and our need to manage it than sexual desire. For much of our history and for most people, whatever heavy petting or bundling they might have enjoyed, full sexual activity was delayed. It does indeed look as if by the 1960s we were having more sex and earlier. The conventional explanation is the Pill, but the big change in sexual behaviour was in the ten years from the mid-1950s to the mid-1960s, whereas the Pill only arrived in the late 1960s. A better explanation is that there were more young men in good jobs at an early age than at any other time in the twentieth century. Moreover, marriage as a cultural idea and an economic institution was as powerful as ever: it was still the model for bringing up and providing for a child. If a man got a woman pregnant he was expected to marry her. This meant there was an insurance policy behind the sexual relationship. So there was a host of reliable men with a steady income, and a commitment to marrying a woman if they got her pregnant. It was, in a very different sense from today, safe sex. This was the environment which created the most extraordinary surge in the birth rate modern Britain has seen.

Britons were not just having more sex and getting pregnant. What they were also doing in the Swinging Sixties was getting married. In each year from 1964 to 1971 there were more than 300,000 first marriages in England and Wales – the highest level ever, apart from during the Second World War. And the average age of brides reached a record low of 22 in 1964. One crucial piece of evidence supports our explanation of early marriage as a kind of insurance claim after earlier sex: 22 per cent of brides were pregnant in 1965, a historic peak compared with 15 per cent in 1955 and about 9 per cent today.[11] As well as a baby boom the sixties saw a marriage boom. In particular, the two extraordinary years of 1964 and 1965 saw a record number of marriages, a record number of pregnant brides, and record numbers of babies born. It was a frenzy of mating, like a scene from a David Attenborough nature film – with perhaps a touch of *Romeo and Juliet* as well. After all, one in seven brides in the 1960s was a teenager.

This was a disaster for marriage, brilliantly disguised as a success. It put enormous pressure on marriages. The pressure arose not because people were abandoning marriage but because so many people were piling into it so young. Something that had worked for centuries as a contract that adults chose to commit to in their mid- or late twenties was now being entered into by people who were more youthful, and more pregnant, than ever before. Sadly people who marry young or marry pregnant are most at risk of breaking up. These marriages were fragile. People searched for escape routes, either to avoid getting married in the first place, or to get out from marriage more easily. The first taboo to go was abortion, legalized in 1967. Many of these abortions were to unmarried women: abortion was a way of avoiding the need to marry. But divorce law was still restrictive and again the pressure for liberalization proved irresistible. Divorce law reform was introduced in 1969 followed by an immediate big increase in divorces. Divorces rose from 25,000 in 1960 to 120,000 by 1972. Five times as many 1960s marriages collapsed within ten years as 1950s marriages. Abortion and divorce, key features of the 'permissive society', were a response to this boom in fragile marriages.

The origins of the permissive society lie, paradoxically, in the marriage boom of the 1960s. Instead of deferring marriage, people surged into it earlier. But marriage simply could not bear the pressures that were put on it by so many people trying to join. Then came the bust. This, in turn, was magnified by economic boom and bust as well.

———

Once upon a time, fifty years ago, there were what traditionalists still look back on as real jobs and real families. Men were breadwinners. Women, once they married, became housewives. There were steady jobs in manufacturing which paid enough for a man to keep a family. By and large the old Left looks back nostalgically to the traditional industrial jobs and the old Right looks back nostalgically to the traditional role of women. In reality they were dependent on each other and both were the product of an unusual set of economic circumstances.

This model was itself only perhaps fifty years old. Women had been in paid work for much of the nineteenth century. But as real wages rose it became possible for a man to keep a family on one income and women stopped working when they married. Only one quarter of women were not in paid work in 1851; in 1911 90 per cent of wives were not in paid employment.[12] Responsibility for child care shifted from older siblings (which was then the traditional model) to mothers. The 're-moralization' of late-Victorian society and the surge of voluntary activity may well be linked to these economic forces taking women out of the labour market and making them more available for child care and voluntary work. Large organizations such as the Civil Service even had rules specifically requiring that women cease work when they got married – a rule which was abandoned only in 1946. Marriage was reinforced by economic dependency. If one partner (usually a man) has a paid job and the other does not that makes the marriage less likely to break up, even today.[13] As late as 1964 only 40 per cent of women were in employment.

The economic crisis of the decade following the oil price shock of 1973 destroyed the economic environment on which the twentieth-century model rested. As unemployment rose in Britain in the 1970s and 1980s the big losers were men in traditional industries. The collapse of reliable male industrial employment weakened marriages and families. It is difficult being an unemployed paterfamilias. It is uncomfortable to confront the evidence that the family is affected by its economic environment, as a family rests above all on the intense personal feelings which hold a relationship together. But the evidence is now becoming available which shows how these changes in the jobs market affected families. A man losing his job increased the risk of the marriage breaking up by 70 per cent.[14] One expert estimates that 'the fall in male employment explains between 38 per cent and 59 per cent of the 1.16 m increase in lone parent families over the period 1971–2001.'[15] Men were less able to discharge their traditional breadwinner role so more women gave up on them.

Some other countries tried to protect traditional male jobs. They have higher rates of employment amongst men in traditional jobs: it is women and young people who are unemployed. But in Britain it was older men who lost out from economic change in the 1980s and the young baby boomers who did relatively better. Why was Britain different? A key factor was that we had generous company pension schemes with substantial assets behind them. Employers who made older workers redundant could treat this as early retirement and make the cost a charge on the pension scheme, without the company having to pay anything directly itself. Pension schemes therefore helped finance the social costs of the recessions of the 1970s and 1980s and paid for the restructuring of the British economy but only by targeting unemployment on older workers.[16] It was the traditional breadwinner who lost out. The unusual strength of Britain's funded pensions thus contributed to the unusual weakness of our families.

Young workers may not be so skilled, but they are more flexible, precisely because they have not built up particular know-how tying them to specific industries. They are what you need if you are going through a big change in the structure of your economy – employees who will easily adapt to new technologies. And the peak in the birth rate in the mid-1960s meant there was a surge of young, flexible workers in the mid-1980s. This flow of new workers helped make possible the dramatic structural changes in the British economy as we shifted from traditional manufacturing to services. At the same time there was only a very modest increase in the number of pensioners ahead of them and a fall in the number of children behind them. (The number of pensioners only went up by 400,000 between 1985 and 1995, whilst the number of under-18s fell by 600,000.) So the total number of dependants was falling, making control of public expenditure easier. This combination of a surge in flexible young workers and unusually low public spending pressures was crucial to Thatcherism.

More women went into the jobs market too. One reason was simply the urge for personal fulfilment through education and work. Women have indeed been liberated. But it is not the whole story. There is also the financial pressure of needing a second income to maintain living standards. It is also an insurance policy as more and more marriages break down. And if some women are choosing to work, pushing up their household income and the prices they can afford, everyone else is under pressure to join in as well. As Avner Offer puts it, 'By *choosing* individually to work, women found themselves collectively *compelled to* work.'[17]

The story is taking shape. A couple got married young in the 1960s because they thought it was the only thing to do if you or your partner were pregnant and they were both confident that the husband, the breadwinner, would keep them. But he loses his job. Or maybe he just turns out not to be the husband his wife hoped for when she married him at 18. Then his wife gets a part-time job. But she still has to do the housework as well. He does not bring any money in and does not help her around the house either. More and more women decide the feminists are right, and that a woman needs a husband as much as a fish needs a bicycle, so she divorces him.[18] (Three quarters of all divorces are initiated by women and the rise in divorces since the 1969 reforms matches the increase in female employment.[19]) The tough economic conditions of the 1970s and 1980s did not just have an impact on marriages; they affected the birth rate too. In 1977, the year after Britain had to be bailed out by the IMF, our birth rate reached a historic low. Those who are more interested in the weather than in economics might also observe that the birth rate peaked after the cold winters of

1947 and 1963 and reached a low point after the long hot summer of 1976.

·······

If an economy has not got many young people the temptation is to import them. The Labour Government took a deliberate decision that East Europeans would be an ideal group to encourage to settle here to plug gaps in the labour market. Within a few years several hundred thousand Poles and other East Europeans had come over in one of the biggest deliberately engineered movements of immigrants this country has ever seen. This was, of course, the scheme set up at the end of the Second World War by the British Government to recruit potential workers from the Continent to work in Britain and overcome labour shortages. In the 1940s 350,000 people entered Britain under the European Volunteer Workers' Scheme. There was some controversy immediately after the War about all these Poles arriving. The Attlee Government set up a 'Committee for the Education of Public Opinion on Foreign Workers' and the Ministry of Labour helped produce a leaflet entitled 'What the Poles Have Done for You'.[20]

Demographics drove the policy. The Second World War claimed approximately 400,000 British lives, military and civilian, mostly young adults. It is, however, striking evidence of the power of demographic trends that, even if every British person who died in the Second World War had been aged between 20 and 30, this would have had less of an effect in reducing the size of that age group than the fall in the birth rate in the interwar years. It was this earlier baby bust which meant there was a serious shortage of young people entering the labour market in the 1950s. (It was also one reason why their wages were rising strongly, which in turn created the conditions for the baby boom – so the cycle turns.) The

Royal Commission on Population, which reported in 1949, was quite explicit about the demographic challenge. It calculated that Britain needed to recruit some 140,000 young immigrants and went on, in the language of the day, to say that they should be 'of good human stock and... not prevented by their religion or race from inter-marrying with the host population and becoming merged in it'.[21] These immigrants were assumed to be coming to settle permanently.

The European Volunteer Workers' Scheme was not enough to plug the gap in the jobs market. The first group of immigrants from the West Indies arrived on the *Empire Windrush* in 1948. Unlike the Workers' Scheme this migration had not been deliberately planned by the government, and there was some Cabinet hostility to 'coloured immigration'. However, the migrants were Commonwealth citizens with a legal right to travel to the mother country.[22]

It is easy to assume that there is a steady and constant supply of new workers coming into the labour market, but looking simply at the figures generated by earlier birth rates, the truth is very different. The number of 20- to 30-year-olds fell by 1.5 million in the decade from 1950 to 1960, almost as massive as the fall of 1.8 million between 1995 and 2005.[23] This in turn influenced attitudes to immigration. As the first young people from the wartime baby boom began to enter the jobs market we find more hostility than in the 1950s. The first serious restriction on Commonwealth immigration came in 1962. The National Front was established in 1967 and Enoch Powell's 'Rivers of Blood' speech was delivered in 1968. That year's Immigration Act was also the most dramatic single tightening of immigration controls in the post-War period. That year, twenty years after the first peak in the birth rate, would have seen intense competition for jobs as a very large cohort of young people entered the labour market. From the mid-1960s through to the late 1990s Britain enjoyed the boost from the post-War baby boomers entering the jobs market. In particular 1980 to 1990 saw an unprecedented surge of 1.4 million extra young workers. That was a time when immigration controls were severe and immigration tightly controlled. But the low point of the birth rate in the mid-seventies meant that early in the twenty-first century the experience of immigration immediately after the Second World War repeated itself. The average age of new immigrants in 2005 was 29, neatly matching the low point in the birth rate twenty-nine years earlier.[24] This time, however, immigration has been accompanied by rising unemployment amongst young people in Britain as we have been doing badly at making our own young adults more employable – we will investigate this further in Chapters 10 and 11.

We must not be too deterministic, however. There is not a fixed amount of work to be done. Nevertheless employers may be used to a certain flow of young people on to the jobs market, and rely on taking in a certain number of young people each year. We now face an increase in the number of 20- to 30-year-olds because of the upward trend in the British birth rate through the 1980s and early 1990s. This should mean, other things being equal, that immigration can tail off in coming years. And of course the wider economic scene is crucial – with immigrants returning home in tougher economic times.

Meanwhile, barely remarked upon at first, a new baby boom is underway. The birth rate fell to a historic low in 2001, since when it has grown steadily and strongly. It really has been a significant birth surge – with the number of babies born in England and Wales rising from a historic low point of 595,000 in 2001 to 710,000 in 2008. The birth rate per 1,000 women aged 15–44 shot up from 54.7 to 63.5 between 2001 and 2008. The total fertility rate,[25] the number of children per woman, has risen from a low of 1.63 in 2001 to 1.95 in 2008, its highest rate since 1973, when it was 2.0.[26] (If you want to get a sense of the scale of the original baby boom, however, it hit a peak of 2.95 in 1964.) It looks as if the increase is spread across women of most ages, but especially older women. The birth rate for women aged 35–39 has now, for the first time in our history, overtaken the teenage birth rate. There are two different effects here – one involving women born abroad and another for women born in Britain, but both contributing to the birth surge. The total fertility rate among women born abroad is about 2.5. That rate has remained stable. But the number of women born abroad of child-bearing age has increased from 10 per cent to 15 per cent of all women of childbearing age since 2001. Given their higher birth rate they are now responsible for about 20 per cent of all births in the UK. The number of British-born women of child-bearing age has actually been falling slightly – because of that low birth rate in the 1970s and early 1980s. But their fertility rate per person has risen from 1.7 to 1.8, which has more than offset the slight decline in their numbers and 'since 2004... has been the largest single factor increasing the overall number of births'. It is the women born abroad who push our overall fertility rate up even higher to 1.9.[27]

This increase in the birth rate has taken most of the experts by surprise.[28] High house prices were thought to be a powerful contraceptive, keeping the birth rate down. But it is less surprising if we go back to the four reasons we gave for that first post-War boom. They all apply today. Women who have delayed having children have finally got round to it. Female employment reached a record high with the proportion in jobs rising to a peak of over 70 per cent in early 2008 before they were hit by the rise in unemployment: with flexible working and access to childcare this does actually raise the birth rate. There is more provision for the under-5s. Perhaps most significant is the modern equivalent of the wartime scheme whereby soldiers with children got higher pay. Tax credits mean the financial reward for having children if you are in work is the most powerful it has ever been. We may now be having an extra 45,000 babies a year as a result.[29] We read stories about Continental baby bonuses to boost their flagging birth rates but meanwhile we have a scheme rather like that ourselves whose powerful impact we have largely ignored.

Now our debate about population is the opposite of the one in the 1930s. The new debate in Britain is not about demographic decline but about the pressures of living on a crowded island whose population reached 60 million in, by my reckoning, May 2005,[30] had already in August 2009 exceeded 61 million, and is forecast to be heading to a total of 70 million and beyond. In fact the 2009 projection from the EU is that Britain's population will overtake those of France and Germany to become the largest in the European Union in 2040 and will carry on rising, to reach 77 million in 2060.[31] For the first time in our history Britain will be the most populous nation in Europe. This will excite you if you think big is beautiful. But what matters more for living standards and GDP per head is the composition of this population. Here the news is not so good.

———

We have had an extraordinary demographic bonus over the past twenty-five years. There was a bulge of workers in the middle with no real increase in the number of pensioners and quite a low birth rate. Now that bulge in the middle is turning to a droop and instead the bulges are at the ends of the cycle, among children and pensioners. The baby boomers have been a big generation in the middle of the age range, economically productive and with few dependants either younger or older than them. Between 1985 and 1995 the working-age population increased by 3 million as the baby boomers replaced the older small cohort ahead of them. Earnings peak between the ages of 30 and 45, presumably because people reach a productivity plateau at that age. If that is true, the 1964 birth rate peak had its most positive impact on Britain's economic growth between 1994 and 2009. This matches pretty neatly our successive quarters of economic growth starting in 1992. We had a combination of a modest increase in the number of pensioners because of the low birth rate in the 1930s, a positive impact on the labour market because of the surging population at their peak earnings, and a modest demand for services for children because of another smaller cohort behind. Even without the extraordinary external circumstances of those years, it added up to a very favourable demographic background. The number of pensioners rose by 0.9 million in the twenty years from 1985 to 2005. But because of the ageing of the post-War baby boom it will rise by 1.6 million in the ten years to 2015 (it would have been 2.1 million but for the increase in the women's pension age from 2010). The women born in the first baby boom peak of 1947 became pensioners in 2007, and then the men in 2012.[32]

The demographic environment is now changing – and it will be one of the biggest shocks to our economy since the War. Having had easy sailing with favourable tailwinds, for the next twenty or thirty years we will be battling against demographic headwinds.

We are getting closer to the key question – who is going to be well protected in these tougher times and who is going to find themselves exposed? That is the subject of our next chapter. But there is just one loose end – who exactly are these baby boomers and why should the generation you were born into matter at all?

Nowadays we think of adults as if we are year groups at school, with each successive generation making our way through the system. This is not how people used to understand their world. The first great thinker to set out this way of thinking was Karl Mannheim in his essay 'The Problem of Generations', published in 1928.[33] His argument was that vertical family ties across the generations were weakening. We were all becoming more mobile and he predicted that increasingly our crucial social and cultural links would be horizontal ties to our contemporaries and our friends, not vertical links to our elders and betters, and not even to our parents. It was a challenge to the then conventional wisdom that it was the conflict of classes that would shape the future. And Mannheim was right – apart from within the family, a key feature of our society is the limited contact between the generations. Work, for example, is increasingly segregated by age with more and more of us working exclusively with people of the same age (as we shall see in Chapter 6).

In modern societies our identities are supposed to be shaped by the generation we belong to. Of course, we do not all follow this generational determinism. One traditionalist wanted to claim in a speech that he was a child of the 1960s until an adviser warned him that really he had gone through the 1950s twice and then moved straight to the 1970s. Nevertheless the model is thought to apply to most of us. We think that we can track each distinctive cohort through the system. Each cohort creates its own world. We assume that each generation will carry with them through their lives distinctive patterns of behaviour learnt in their formative years. Social and political change is supposed to be recorded like tree rings, eternally imprinted with the effects of a drought or some ancient volcanic explosion. Part of the appeal of this model is that it looks as if we can understand the present and predict the

UNIVERSITY OF WINCHESTER
LIBRARY

future by seeing where each generation has got to. Sometimes indeed it gets perilously close to astrology as we work out which generational sign you were born under. No one has yet written a history of Britain explicitly in terms of successive generations, but Neil Howe and William Strauss have written a fascinating history of the USA by tracking its thirteen generations:[34] it is only a matter of time before their approach reaches us.

We do not yet have agreed definitions of the different British cohorts. Mannheim argued there are two different ways of doing this. One way of defining cohorts is by hard demographic facts. That would mean we could focus on for example the turning points in the birth rate. Alternatively, you can go for softer cultural measures – intangible shifts in social attitudes as successive generations have different experiences of the world. The most ambitious accounts link hard and soft accounts. One way to do this is through the pattern of cohort size. The cycle of big and small cohorts is not unlike boom and bust in economics and the experience of being in a big cohort may be very different from being in a small one.

One way of categorizing our birth cohorts demographically is to treat them rather like economic cycles. There is a clear pattern with cycles of births around the post-War average annual birth rate of 750,000 for Great Britain (it is a bit higher for the UK as a whole). This figure then defines the low point of some cycles and the high point of others. On this approach the baby boom begins with the mini-dip in 1945 (770,000). Then it runs up to a peak in 1947 (995,000) and down to a dip in 1955 (760,000), with 200,000 fewer births than at the peak. The second phase of the baby boom then runs from 1956 (795,000) up to a peak in 1964 (980,000). The birth rate then falls steadily. It crosses below its post-War average in 1972 to a low in 1977 (630,000) which is 350,000 fewer births than only twelve years earlier. This is Generation X. Unlike the boomers, shaped around high points in the birth rate, this generation is shaped around a post-War low point in the birth rate. We then have a muted echo of the baby boom with Generation Y, reaching a modest peak in 1990 (770,000) and then moving down to a low in 2001 (650,000).

It is tempting to avoid hard chronological definitions because there is no neat and tidy distinction between these generations. There must inevitably be fuzziness around the edges. But then one also avoids being pinned down to real dates and real figures against which one's arguments are tested. So, in the interests of accountability and testability, here is a summary of this rather mechanistic model:

1945–1965	Baby boom
1966–1979	Generation X
1980–2000	Generation Y
2001–	The Millennials

Many people believe that unless you bought the Beatles' first single, were at the Summer of Love and Woodstock, bought your bellbottoms in Carnaby Street and marched against Vietnam and capitalism as a *soixante-huitard* then you can't be a baby boomer. That restricts the baby boomers to the young people who were enjoying the sixties so much that they can't remember them. That surge of people, born in a few years in the second half of the 1940s, produced an exciting teenage movement in the mid-sixties with extraordinary optimism and youthfulness. For many of the people enjoying it, it was brought to an abrupt end with marriage and children, as we saw. But we are not just trying to pin down these narrow and intense cultural moments; we are trying to identify bigger economic and demographic changes. That means focusing on the birth surge which carried on from the 1940s to a second peak in the early 1960s. Looked at as a demographic and economic phenomenon the baby boom covers the twenty years from 1945 to 1965.

The upswing of a boom feels very different from the down-swing. The cutting edge feels very different from trailing edge. These far less optimistic late boomers had punk and the Poll Tax riots. Their emblems were not flower power and psychedelic colours but nose studs and Mohicans – their icon was not Tariq Ali but Johnny Rotten. Indeed many of the big social changes of the permissive era from divorce and lone parenthood to real violent radicalism, which we attribute to the 1960s, actually happened in the seventies – the 1970s were a product of the baby boom too.[35] It may be that Britain's baby boomers do not have as strong a col-lective identity as in America because we have two peaks linked by a more modest surge. This is a contrast to the single high plateau of the American baby boom in the period from 1957 to 1961.

The post-boomers are the product of the low birth rates and the tough times of the 1970s. This is a shorter generation, centring on the historic low in the birth rate in 1976. They are sometimes called the lost generation. Douglas Coupland popularized a better name in his novel *Generation X*.[36] It is a small cohort covering a demo-graphic trough from the mid-sixties to a low point in 1976, through to the arrival of Margaret Thatcher as Prime Minister in 1979, after which we enter a modest demographic recovery. Generation X were born in a recession and hit by successive recessions as they moved to adulthood. The financial pressures they faced are one reason why this is the first generation where women expect to work and have careers like men. As the children of tough times they are seen as tough-minded, even cynical, in contrast to the optimistic baby boomers.

The next group, Generation Y, born between 1980 and 2000, are in many ways an echo of the baby boom, growing up during more sustained economic growth and sharing some of the optimism of the baby boomers. They are also a demographic echo as the surge of boomers to early adulthood produced a second but weaker boom with a modest birth rate peak in 1990, after which the birth rate declines again to a new low at the Millennium. They are digital natives not digital immigrants – they don't print off a document to read it. They may see all knowledge as a matter of opinion and contentious. (Indeed, one suggestion is that some of them may not believe that man landed on the moon; the web is full of accounts of how it was all faked by the authorities and they cannot believe that a previous generation could have achieved anything techno-logical beyond what they have experienced.)

The Millennials take us up from the low in the birth rate in 2001. They are the products of the surprise multicultural baby boom which could eventually push the British population up from 60 million to 70 million and change our country massively in the process. Their impact has already been felt in new pressures on maternity units, childcare centres, and for places at primary school.

We have offered an alternative demographic history of post-War Britain. The conventional approach is to explain a big shift in values in the 1960s and 1970s by claims about affluence or per-missiveness. But these do not really explain much. The patterns of demography and their impact on economics and the family can help to explain this in a much more real way. Why did attitudes to abortion and divorce change so much in 1960s and 1970s – after all there had been assaults on bourgeois values before? The 1960s counter-culture was not unique but what was extraordinary was that it had an effect on wider society in a way that previous Bohemian revolts against the bourgeois did not. The issue is not that there was a Bohemian counter-culture but that it was so successful. Demographics help explain this. The baby boomers were beginning to make themselves felt. But that was only the beginning, as we shall see in the next chapter.

Chapter 4

Spending the Kids' Inheritance

Imagine a primitive family of hunter-gatherers in which every-thing you kill is eaten. Children and elderly people need to be fed out of the surplus food caught or picked by the adult hunters. When they hunt successfully there is more than enough meat for the hunters themselves so it is shared out. This is the simplest form of redistribution across the generations. At any one point of time it might look like one generation, the one that works and does the hunting, paying out to the others. But over their lives everyone would both be a contributor and a beneficiary, so the food you caught and the food you consumed would roughly net out to a balance. Each generation would eventually consume an amount equal to what it produced. Living together in a tribe enables con-sumption to be spread across our lives in this way. This informal contract between the generations is fundamental to the family and society. If we could always just live on what we ourselves killed we would have had little need for society.

Our tribe is stable until there are some mild winters and more babies survive infancy. It has a baby boom on its hands. What happens? The conventional answer has been that it is bad luck to be a big generation because there are more mouths to feed. There are more children fighting for scraps of food from their harassed parents. And then, as the baby boomers become hunters themselves, there are more hunters chasing the same prey. So life is more competitive and times are tougher. Indeed our big generation is so busy fighting for scarce resources that they have fewer children themselves. As a result big generations are followed by smaller ones. This is what Thomas Malthus famously argued in his *Essay on the Principle of Population*. Subsequent thinkers such as Auguste Comte treated this as the fundamental cycle in human affairs. It is why Richard Easterlin, the first great contemporary demographer to think about the impact of the baby boomers, predicted that they would have an unusually hard time.[1] We can recognize some of the patterns these thinkers identified but it is not the whole story.

For a start, we may hope that when there are more hunters they can hunt more mammoths. This is the contemporary response to Malthusian pessimism – that there is no shortage of mammoths, only a shortage of hunters. Human skill and ingenuity is such that we should think of ourselves not just as consumers but as producers and creators.

Moreover, the surge in the number of hunters means that there are more of them relative to the elderly members of the tribe who are not hunters. This is the demographic sweet spot when life seems particularly good. Even though they may hunt just as hunters always did, there is a greater feeling of prosperity as each of them has to distribute less to other members of the tribe. They can spend this gain on higher living standards for working hunters and may even spread the benefits out more widely to other members of the tribe. They can devote more time to cave painting. They can cut back on the frequency of hunting and gather exotic berries and grasses which do not provide much nutrition for hunting but make them feel good at their tribal festivals. It is an age of plenty and of experiment. The young hunters are quite contemptuous of the confined and conventional lives led by their parents. They try to raise their children differently.

There is an even more optimistic version in which our hunter-gatherers can hunt more effectively when there are more of them. They can take on bigger mammoths. The increase in the size of the mammoths the hunters can kill turns out to be more than proportionate to the increase in the number of hunters. Malthus may have worried about the increase in the number of mouths to feed but there is also an increase in the amount of food they can successfully hunt. So big generations enjoy surges of prosperity because of genuine improvements in performance. Our primitive boomers are naturally very susceptible to these arguments about what great hunters they are and how the tribe has increased its hunting performance in their generation. It is only a few tribal elders who worry about the future, but it seems perverse to argue there is a problem when everyone can see there is more meat to go round.

Then this big generation of hunters starts to grow old and want to hand on its spears to the younger generation. Even if they each had just as many children as before, there is no avoiding the fact that there are more old ex-hunters to be maintained. So the next generation of hunters finds that more of what it catches needs to be taken for other members of the tribe. Life seems tougher. Some of the retired hunters argue that younger ones just aren't as good at hunting as they were in the old days.

There is a final twist. The clan is run by a democratic tribal council. That big generation therefore finds it has got the most votes. It uses this power to protect itself, especially as the younger members of the tribe are too busy decorating themselves with woad to turn up for boring tribal meetings. Whilst they were in their prime the baby boom hunters were not very keen on the redistribution of mammoth meat to non-productive members of the clan and were more keen on the rights of hunters to keep as much as possible of what they caught. But as they get older they become more interested in the respect due to senior retired hunters and start voting for more tribute from new young hunters. Younger hunters face a double squeeze – with more retired hunters to support and more expected from each one of them. They have to spend more time hunting. They want to raise their kids in the same generous way their parents raised them but it seems harder to achieve and as a result they don't have so many of them.

Our thought experiment shows a society which worked until a big generation came along which took more of what it produced during its prime and then tried to take more from later generations when it was in need. It was partly just because of its size. Maybe it was also because of how it used the power that came with its size. But, whatever the reason, the principle of fairness across the generations was broken. And it threatened to break that society.

If you could choose, would you rather be part of a big generation like the boomers or a small one? The standard answer from the economists has actually been that it is better to be in a small cohort, travelling through life Club Class not Economy Class. A big group means more competition for jobs, which drives down wages. And public services can be very crowded if you are a big generation – I think of the forty-eight children in my primary school class in the sixties. It may be that, like the rest of life, sometimes you want to be in a crowd and sometimes to be on your own. It might be that in a small generation you have less competition from your contemporaries so your wages may be higher. But in a big generation you have much greater power to shape the political and cultural environment around you.

One of the advantages of being a big, prosperous generation is the power you can exercise as consumers. Your music and your cultural tastes carry on being celebrated through your lives – the baby boomers can still go to Rolling Stones concerts, get Beatles CDs, and drive versions of the Volkswagen Beetle and the Mini. That far smaller group who were teenagers in the 1950s, not the 1960s, are still waiting for a trendy repro version of the Triumph Mayflower. We sent soldiers to Korea and stayed out of Vietnam. But Vietnam happened during the formative years of the baby boomers and so casts a far longer shadow than Korea, which was only a decade earlier, and actually saw British soldiers fighting and dying.

It is hard to measure these cultural effects from changes in the size of generations but here is an attempt. Compare the top 100 albums as selected in a poll of the general public (*Daily Mirror*) and the top 100 albums as selected by music enthusiasts (*Q* magazine).[2] There are only thirty-eight albums in common. Moreover, there is not even any similarity in the rankings of the thirty-eight albums that are common to the two lists. The enthusiasts and the general public deeply disagree. How can such a gap open up? Let us try the following explanation. Most new albums are listened to and bought by young people. Our musical tastes are fixed by those first tracks we bought as teenagers. (I still prefer the real Monkees to the Arctic ones.) So if there were more teenagers around when a pop group was in its prime, it will do better in popular ratings regardless of its quality.

Therefore let us weight the rankings of the albums as voted for by the public so they take into account how many teenagers there were when the album was released; hence, albums in the *Mirror* chart released in years when there were more young consumers are given a handicap, and albums released in years when there were fewer youngsters are given a boost. Once you do that, musicians and the general public start to agree – they agree about which albums are better than others roughly three fifths of the time.[3] This is a first stab at explaining how our culture is weighted towards the baby boomers.[4]

There is a further effect favouring the baby boomers. Albums from the boomers' adolescence do extremely well, even on a demographically adjusted basis. The years when the boomers were youthful consumers are remarkably strong performers, accounting for two thirds of the critics' top 100. This too is a cohort effect, but of a different kind. In the years with lots of teenage music buyers it was easier to sell enough records to break even. You needed a smaller proportion of the total market. So it is easier for more experimental or innovative bands to make a living in a niche market. This means big cohorts enjoy far deeper musical markets with much greater diversity than do their colleagues in other cohorts. As a consequence, a big cohort may actually deliver a genuine improvement in performance that is more than proportionate to its size. So the baby boomers did have something special going for them and this may have magnified their cultural impact. Another survey, on the fortieth anniversary of Woodstock in 2009, shows how the boomers' musical tastes have spread to other generations of Americans. The great bands of the sixties have an extraordinarily wide appeal – the Beatles in particular are in the top four of most popular musical performers for every age group, with the Rolling Stones not far behind.[5]

––––––

We have seen the cultural power of the boomers, but now let's try to measure it economically. Think of a snapshot of Britain today with people from three generations – a 75-year-old, a 50-year-old, and a 25-year-old. These snapshots are of people who are statistical averages (and to make a fair comparison all the figures have been adjusted to 2005 prices). There are of course rich and poor, well-paid and badly paid in each generation. But we have been so preoccupied with the gaps within generations that we have lost sight of the big gaps between them.

The 75-year-olds, born in the 1930s, worked hard and stuck together after they got married. The good news is that many of them are still around. Indeed many more of them are around than anyone forecast – they are called the super-cohort because they have enjoyed the most dramatic surge in life expectancy ever recorded in Britain. If they have got a company pension or they are homeowners then they have probably done well for themselves. The average 75-year-old has been able to build up some of these assets. In 2005 65 per cent of people aged 75 and over were homeowners. And their house was worth then on average about £206,000, which is not bad given they probably bought it for a pittance before the first house price boom of 1965 to 1974, when the first baby boomers entered the market and pushed up prices. And their assets such as their house and savings doubled during the last asset price boom – from £98,000 for a 65-year-old in 1995 to £185,000 when they were aged 75 in 2005.[6]

Membership of company pension schemes peaked as far back as 1967 so, especially for a man who worked in a traditional industry, they may well have built up some pension rights as well. Their pension may well be modest, however, and it won't necessarily have any inflation protection. And our 75-year-old may well be a widow (a third of female pensioners live on their own), in which case they may not have much of a pension because their late husband's pension scheme may not have provided for them.

That is one reason why poverty amongst pensioners is concentrated on older women living on their own.

Our 75-year-old may not feel that well-off as their income has been flat for the past decade or more whilst everyone else's has shot up. This feels worse in a society that celebrates economic growth and assumes that you get better off every year – somehow this did not seem to apply to our old person even in the boom years. Average weekly income for a 65-year-old was £289 in 1995 and £288 when they were 75 in 2005. So over that booming decade the 75-year-old saw a surge in assets but no rise in income.[7] These older people are compensated for their low income, quite rightly, by public spending that focuses on their needs. The two biggest programmes – social security and health – are mainly for them. These transfers are being paid for by the big baby boomer cohort, full of taxpaying workers, coming on behind.

Our classic boomer, born at the mid-point of the boom in 1955, and aged 50 in 2005, was then at his or her peak earnings, with average net weekly household income of £584, the highest of any age group. It had shot up from £433 in 1995 when he was 40.[8] Their assets shot up too, enjoying the biggest increase of any age group in that decade, from £42,000 to £158,000.[9] (More than 80 per cent of our 50-year-olds are homeowners with their house worth in 2005 on average £230,000.[10]) They still had a mortgage but it was down to about £50,000. They are also likely to have been a member of a good occupational pension scheme, at least for a time. Although it may have closed now they have built up some pension rights that are inflation-protected with provision for their widow or widower too. And if anyone still has a company scheme open to them it is likely to be this age group. They are also able to set some money aside, saving almost £200 per month. So this classic boomer did better than the old person as they experienced both an increase in assets and in income. But what about the youngster coming on behind?

The 25-year-olds may well have had to pay for their university education, so they started work with a large amount of student debt. They could well have no assets, once their debts have been deducted, for another decade at least, longer than any previous generation. If they did not get to university they would have found the traditional vocational route to a good job, like apprenticeships, much more rare than a generation earlier. Their jobs are likely to be temporary and with modest pay. Thirty years ago in 1979, when the baby boomers were entering the jobs market, the biggest private sector employer was GEC. That company is now history and the only significant asset which survives is its pension scheme, to pay final salary pensions to its former employees. Instead our biggest private sector employer is Tesco. The biggest employer of young people is McDonald's.

The pay of 20-somethings was growing modestly in the boom years when for most age ranges it was going up. The average weekly income of a 25-year-old was £371 in 2000 and for someone that age in 2005 it was £398. For a 50-year-old it was £534 in 2000 and in 2005 this was up to £584.[11] The biggest gains from higher wages were concentrated on the parts of the age range occupied by the boomers. These new young employees are most unlikely to have any rights to a decent company pension scheme (unless they work for a very big corporation or in the public sector). The proportion of 25- to 34-year-olds contributing to a pension fell from 26 per cent in 1995 to 13 per cent in 2005.[12] In 1995 25- to 34-year-olds were saving £139 monthly, but 25- to 34-year-olds were saving £103 in 2005.[13] Instead their personal debts are higher than ever. The average under 35-year-old now owes more than £9,000 in credit card and student debt. Their repayments average £206 per month, three times as much as they are saving in a pension.[14] We are beginning to see how the distribution of income and wealth is favouring the big boomer generation in the middle. And there is more evidence which confirms this.

We can link these snapshots by measuring the average of when people in Britain do their consuming and the average when we do our producing. Economists take all the consumption going on by adults in one year and work out the average age of the consumer. So imagine that our 25-year-old spends £2,000, our 50-year-old spends £7,000 and our 75-year-old spends £1,000. That adds up to £10,000 of consumption during one year and the average age consumption is 47.5 years.[15] You can do exactly the same calculation for the average age when we do our producing. Two of our leading researchers have done this calculation for contemporary Britain. John Ermisch did so for the mid-1980s and Martin Weale for early this century.[16] They get a broadly similar answer of an average age of production of about 41 years. So half of our national output is being produced by people aged 41 and under. This is stable over the twenty years covered by the two separate calculations. It is incidentally quite young compared with other European countries.

We can also measure the average age of consumption. There is no particular reason why it should be the same as the age of production. A society could have a stable intergenerational contract in which young people did more work and old people did more consuming. Provided that was the deal for all of us in each successive generation we could accept it. The gains from our youthful work might be paid as tribute to the tribal elders but everyone would know that, barring personal misfortune, their turn would come to be on the receiving end. This starts becoming risky, however, if the rules of the game change halfway through. We have evidence that this is what is happening in contemporary Britain. In the mid-1980s the average age of consumption was 46, a bit older than when we were at peak production but so be it. But that age of consumption is now up to 48 and appears still to be rising. So half of all the consuming in our country is now done by people aged 48 and over. It is rising as the baby boomers age. This is a very important piece of evidence. It shows there is indeed a shift of resources towards the baby boomers as they age. But there is no corresponding shift in the balance of who does the producing. Put together with that static figure for the age of production it tells us that, despite all the fuss, we have not yet seen a big enough shift towards later retirement to enable people to keep producing as we live longer, not just consume for longer.

We have now got some hard evidence to back up our intuition that over the past twenty years Britain has seen a shift of power and wealth to the baby boomers. A young person could be forgiven for believing that the way in which economic and social policy is now conducted is little less than a conspiracy by the middle-aged against the young. How has this happened? It is not just that baby boomers have shaped the cultural environment; they have also enjoyed an economic environment that works for them very well. We might have expected a cultural advantage from being a big cohort but why economic as well? In fact, as we saw, the classic Malthusian model proposed that it was worse to be in a big generation. But it has not turned out like that. Why not? Are the baby boomers a lucky generation or a selfish one? And what does this tell us for the prospects of the smaller successor generation coming along behind? We will try to work out what has happened, looking first at wages and then at savings.

Richard Easterlin's path-breaking book *Birth and Fortune* remains one of the few serious attempts to think through the economic impact of successive cohorts of different size. His book, which came out in 1980, argued that you would be better off in a small cohort than a big one. He does not really focus on the value of housing and pension wealth, effects which we can now see matter so much – the book was written just before the great asset price boom which so enriched the baby boomers. Instead he looked at wages and proposed, very plausibly, that if you are in a big cohort you will have so many more people competing for jobs with you that wages will be bid down. By contrast a small cohort of workers are in a much stronger bargaining position and so can bid up wages. That was not a stupid forecast. Indeed, the weight of economic theory was with him. So why haven't things turned out like that? Why were the incomes of the big crowded baby boom generation not lower? And why is the income of the smaller generation after them not higher?

Let us start with the most sympathetic explanation of what has been going on. It enhances the explanation of post-War social change which we offered in the previous chapter. It also concedes some ground to Easterlin's argument. It comes from an American study which compares US data for people aged 25–34 and 35–44 in 1962 and in 1989.[17] The 1962 data measures the incomes and wealth of the boomers' parents and the 1989 data measures the incomes and wealth of boomers themselves. Faced with being an over-crowded cohort the baby boomers adjusted their behaviour so as to maintain their living standards. In particular they postponed marriage and had fewer children, and above all more women went to work. These key social changes are explained as the baby boomers' response to being a crowded generation. Whatever happened to individual wages, household living standards were protected. In particular it reminds us that, even if individual wages had not risen, the massive shift of women into paid work made it possible for total household income to carry on rising. So some of the big social changes with which we associate the baby boomers can be seen as their attempt to maintain family living standards even when they were a big crowded generation.

But we still need to understand why the smaller generation coming along behind the baby boomers have not enjoyed the wage premium they might expect. The explanation is globalization. It happened at just the right moment for the baby boomers. As the baby boomers grew older they needed an infusion of young workers into the jobs market, or else wages would rise behind them and shift resources to the next generation. Bang on cue, hundreds of millions of workers from China and India joined the world trading system. This drives down wages and increases returns to capital, capital which does of course mainly belong to the boomers through their pension schemes. So the younger, smaller generation fail to gain the benefits they might expect from their apparently strong labour market position. This shows up as a widening of the gap between young workers and older ones. One detailed estimate, this time with British data, is that between an earlier cohort born in 1958 and a later cohort born in 1970 there was a 10–12 percentage point decline in the full-time gross weekly earnings of young men aged 21–29 compared to all working men.[18]

Other evidence confirms this clear trend. In 1974 the average 25- to 29-year-old male employee earned more than the average 60- to 64-year-old. He was still significantly ahead in the late 1980s but in 1995 the 60- to 64-year-old caught up and by 2008 on average earned 14 per cent more than the 25- to 29-year-old. In 1974 the average 50- to 59-year-old earned about 4 per cent more than the 25- to 29-year-old – by 2008 it was 35 per cent more.[19]

When the recession came it hit young people particularly hard

– more than 40 per cent of unemployed people are aged 25 or under. One reason is that they were employed in sectors most vulnerable to the recession: 30 per cent of under-25s worked in financial services and 21 per cent of 25- to 29-year-olds but 6 per cent of 45- to 49-year-olds and 5 per cent of 50- to 54-year-olds. By contrast 10 per cent of 45- to 49-year-olds were in manufacturing as against 3 per cent of under-25s.[20] The number of young people not in education, employment or training had risen to over 1 million by late 2009, over 15 per cent of all 16- to 24-year-olds.[21] And young people are particularly vulnerable to long-term damage to their future earnings from periods of unemployment early in their working lives so the latest recession could have blighted the job prospects of an entire generation of young people.

All together British people are worth about £6.7tn or £6,700bn.[22] There are about 60 million of us so that works out at £110,000 for every man woman and child in the country. Most toddlers do not own anything but most 50-year-olds do. So we should expect big disparities in wealth by age, just because most people acquire some property as they go through life. But are there greater gaps than there used to be? Is there a lucky cohort of baby boomers who have ended up unusually wealthy compared with the generation before or after them? And if so, why?

Our financial wealth comes in three main forms: our personal financial assets, our house, and our pension. We will look at each of these in turn.

There is about £1.6tn of wealth which people directly hold as financial assets – in bank and building society deposits and stocks and shares.[23] These assets account for about a quarter of all our wealth. This type of wealth belongs almost entirely to people in their fifties and sixties. The typical 30-something has about £930 in this type of financial wealth. For a 50-year-old that figure is up to an average of £8,300. Half of the population is under 40 but they hold only about 15 per cent of this wealth.[24] We do not really build this wealth up until the children have left home, and then we run it down in the early stages of retirement when we use the money to go diving on the Great Barrier Reef. We do not appear to want to pass it on to our kids. It is the last and most transient form of wealth, like the flowers of an Indian summer.

Before council house sales and the great housing booms of the past thirty years, housing was less than one fifth of total wealth: it used to be worth less than the funds we had got saved up for our pension. By 1997 our housing was worth about the same as our pensions. In fact in 1997, by an extraordinary statistical fluke, the net value of these two crucial assets was identical at £1,301bn each.[25] Then came the pension crisis and the housing boom. Now, even after the house price crash, housing is still worth far more than our pension. Gross housing wealth in 2008 was £3.7tn. Mortgages were £1.2tn. Deducting these gives net housing wealth of £2.5tn. Other physical assets like agricultural land add about £0.8tn. The combined effect of the house price boom and the pension crisis was to shift personal wealth in Britain away from funded pensions and towards housing. The table below gives new estimates of the distribution of housing wealth drawing on work by Dr Alan Holmans of Cambridge University for the Council of Mortgage Lenders. It only covers owner-occupied housing – the exclusion of second homes and buy-to-let property is the reason why it shows net housing wealth rather less than total housing wealth of £2.5tn – that extra wealth is of course very likely to belong to the boomers.

Table 1. Distribution of the UK's housing wealth by age, 2009 (£bn)

	Under 35	35–44	45–54	55–64	65+	Total
Gross	350	690	680	630	810	3,160
Mortgages	280	430	210	70	10	1,000
Net housing wealth	70	260	470	560	800	2,160

The table shows half of all wealth in owner-occupied housing, £1,030bn, belongs to the baby boomers and only about £330bn or 15 per cent to everyone aged under 44. A separate analysis using different data estimates total net housing wealth in 2009 at £2.9tn. Of this only £550bn belonged to the under 50s, and £2,350bn belonged to the over-50s of which £1,300bn belonged to those aged between 50 and pension age. This is stark evidence of the concentration of housing wealth in the hands of the over-50s, particularly the boomers.[26]

Housing is fundamental to shifts in power and wealth between generations. The house price boom of the past fifteen years drove the biggest shift in wealth between the generations since the war. In the cautious words of the Bank of England: 'Changes in house prices redistribute wealth. When house prices rise, those who plan to trade down gain while those who intend to trade up lose... In practice, households planning to trade up tend to be younger households and those planning to trade down are often older homeowners.'[27]

The Bank of England has tried to track changes in the distribution of these assets (financial wealth and housing but excluding pensions) over time using different data. The Bank analysis shows the median net worth in £000s of different age groups.[28]

Table 2. Household net financial wealth plus housing assets by age
(£000s)

	1995	2005
Aged 25–34	3,000	950
Aged 35–44	22,788	54,475
Aged 45–54	44,750	73,500
Aged 55–64	50,000	149,500
Aged 65+	39,500	95,500

It is striking how the wealth of the 55–64 age group has shot up as the early boomers entered it. It is worrying how the wealth of the youngest age group actually fell, showing how much tougher it became for young people to get started.

The baby boomers who were buying their houses and trading up in the 1980s and 1990s did not just see the value of their house rise; they have also got a mortgage that could well have shrunk to a fraction of its former size because of inflation. Inflation redistributes income as powerfully as any tax – it favours the young at the expense of the old. Younger and middle-aged people are borrowers, above all with mortgages, and it is quite helpful for them if inflation wipes out their debts. But it wipes out savings too. Older people are savers and a low inflation world is better for them as it protects their savings as they try to live on a fixed income. Inflation was 4 per cent in the 1950s and 3.5 per cent in the 1960s. Then, when the baby boomers had big mortgages, it shot up to 13 per cent in the 1970s and 7.5 per cent in the 1980s. Now they are looking to retirement when quite possibly their income will be fixed in money terms so they want price stability, and inflation has fallen back to historic lows and even gone negative. Whilst ultra-low interest rates reduce the income received by savers the value of cash they have in the bank rises when inflation is negative. Meanwhile, for the younger generation, trying to borrow to finance a house today, the borrowings they take on are likely to be almost as burdensome in twenty years' time as they are now if inflation remains low. It was all well and good moving to a low-inflation world but it is very convenient for the baby boomers that it was achieved after their debts had effectively been written off.

There have been similar stark shifts in pension wealth. The total value of our savings in company pension schemes and personal pensions is about £1.8tn.[29] Many of the big pension schemes are now maturing, with more and more pensioners and fewer and fewer active contributors. They are closing to new young members. About 30 per cent of men in their fifties are members of such generous schemes but almost no men in their twenties. It is older workers who have this increasingly rare and precious form of pension provision. We can see who gains and who loses when a company announces it is closing its pension scheme to new members, plugging the deficit with an injection of company funds and setting up a new, much less valuable, Defined Contribution pension for new employees. This adds up to a very dramatic redistribution of resources across the generations. The traditional final salary scheme remains for established older employees. Even if it is closed for future accruals the pension rights older employees have already built up are protected. Profits from the company as a whole, earned by employees of all ages, are diverted into plugging the deficit in the scheme which is not available to the younger staff. New employees who are much younger have a much less generous pension to look forward to, or rather not to. It is the young new recruits who are the poor bloody infantry being sacrificed as the generals fight the pensions crisis. The gap between the pension of older employees and younger employees gets even wider.

It is not just that the shift from high to low inflation has helped the baby boomers, via the housing market. Changes in life expectancy have also had a big impact – this time by increasing the value of pension rights. Even the most lurid theory of inter-generational selfishness could not attribute this improvement in life expectancy to a deliberate plot by the baby boomers. Never-theless it does have a big impact on the relative wealth of different generations. For a start it means that people who have already got pension rights are going to enjoy them for much longer, increasing their total lifetime value way beyond what was intended when the pension promise was made. In fact the interaction of high life expectancy and low inflation has been a key to the pensions crisis. Companies are having to pay out more for longer and, as we saw, they respond by cutting the pension entitlements of younger people coming along behind. Because pensions are excluded from many of the calculations of our personal wealth it is easy to ignore the impact of the pension crisis on the younger generation as their prospective wealth is lost.

These two big events of the last fifteen years – lower inflation and greater longevity – have between them delivered a massive shift in the relative wealth of different generations which we have barely begun to understand let alone address. It is their interac-tion which makes them particularly potent, especially in their impact on our pension wealth – if you live longer but inflation is high your pension may lose much of its value. But if you live longer in an age of low inflation your income may keep its value.

When economists try to think through the implications of an increase in the money supply they imagine what would happen if a helicopter dropped £10 notes on the population and attempt to track through the effects both on prices and, temporarily, on output. But imagine instead that the helicopter is dropping pills which increase everyone's life expectancy by ten years. One way it affects us is very similar to the way inflation worked. Inflation redistributed resources because some people (such as elderly savers) had their incomes fixed but the incomes of other people (such as wage-earners) could adjust every year to keep their value. Increased life expectancy redistributes resources when contracts are fixed on specific ages. That redistributes money across the life-cycle as anything you are entitled to from, say, the age of 60 or 65 is worth a lot more. The value of contracts which are fixed by chronological ages goes up. If we index them to life expectancy for the future this means we can offset the effect for future generations, but meanwhile it is older people who gain.

There are no authoritative estimates of the distribution of the £6.7tn of wealth in our country between the different age groups. However, we have seen that there are good reasons to believe that it is particularly concentrated in the hands of the baby boomers, and to some extent the older generation ahead of them, with very little for the younger generations. My personal very rough estimate is that they own about £3.5tn of this wealth, with the older generation owning most of the rest.[30]

Table 3. Rough estimates of distribution of property ownership by age group (£tn)

Age group	Liquid assets	Owner-occupied housing	Other physical assets	Pensions	Total
Under-45s	0.2	0.3	0.1	0.3	0.9
45–65	1.0	1.0	0.75	0.75	3.5
65+	0.4	0.8	0.4	0.75	2.3

This is a massive concentration of property ownership. It would not matter so much if this was just a repeat of the usual pattern with the younger generation always owning less; but the younger generation have much worse prospects of building up their property in the same way. That is the real injustice.

———————

Nothing captures more vividly the theme of this book than the mixed emotions of a baby boomer contemplating the rise in the value of their house in the boom years and more recently watching it crash, wiping out at least some of the gains. When prices were rising we experienced a combination of amazement at our own good fortune, combined with anxiety about how our children were ever going to be able to afford to get on to the housing ladder themselves. We might have hoped that one of the effects of the crash is that now houses will be more affordable for young home-buyers. But even with house prices much lower, access to credit is so difficult that first-time buyers are not being helped – the main beneficiaries so far are well-off boomers with access to credit who can now afford to buy a second home. Already 17 per cent of 50- to 59-year-olds own a second property. One estimate was that by the middle of the decade, when the housing boom was at its peak, the annual yield on property was 22 per cent – so housing became an investment for the boomers, not a place for the young to live.[31] But let us try to work through a bit more carefully what house prices meant on the way up and on the way down.

It felt marvellous as the boomers' houses shot up in value, some years earning more than they did. The boomers increasingly came to think of their house as not just a place to live but their own personal gold mine which could pay for holidays or cars, or be their pension. It was essentially an increase in the price of land – as they say: 'Buy land; they are not making it any more.' It was not produced wealth. It was not that our work was more productive. However, we thought we were richer and acted accordingly. As financial services became more sophisticated we all became alchemists, converting paper increases in the value of our homes into extra money to spend.

Sometimes the conversion of the asset into spending was direct and simple – we borrowed against the house and spent the money. Equally it could be indirect. People felt richer and did not feel they needed to save. It is rather like the holidays from pensions contributions taken by some British companies when the stock market was booming in the 1990s. And saving is net, so even when we carried on putting £5,000 a year into a pension, if at the same time we were remortgaging our house for £5,000 our net saving was zero – it was like paying pension contributions on our credit card.

We did not feel we needed to save so much as we were richer, and when we retired we could eat our house, using it to pay for our retirement. The Treasury were shockingly complacent about this. Indeed, they explained in the following notorious passage why this asset price bubble meant we did not need to save like we used to:

The Government is committed to a policy framework that enables people to choose how and when to save across the full range of asset-building activities. Traditional measures of aggregate saving, such as the saving ratio, often fail both to reflect this variety and to highlight the positive impact asset growth has had on households' balance sheets in recent years. Broader measures, for example including capital growth, indicate that saving behaviour has been more robust in recent years than is often appreciated.[32]

Translated, that means that instead of measuring saving just as a proportion of your income, house price rises really should count as saving too. This was a catastrophic misreading of what was happening to the economy. The Treasury failed to understand the economic cycle – perhaps because their Chancellor claimed to have abolished it. As a result they treated a boom as a structural change in the growth rate and treated an asset price bubble as part of saving. It was a kind of financial levitation in which we appeared to save without actually putting any income aside. It happened above all because of the rise in house prices. It would have been far better to have stuck to the wise words of Adam Smith:

Though a house....may yield a revenue to its proprietor, and thereby serve in the function of a capital to him, it cannot yield any to the public, nor serve in the function of a capital to it, and the revenue of the whole body of the people can never be in the smallest degree increased by it.[33]

People did not gather on street corners, mulling over page 96 of the 2004 Treasury Autumn Statement but the proportion of their incomes that households saved fell to a record low – negative figures which were unprecedented in the recent history of any modern Western economy, as the table below shows.

Table 4. OECD figures for net personal sector savings rate (per cent of household incomes)

	France	Germany	USA	UK
1990	9.4	12.9	7.0	3.9
1995	12.8	11.0	4.6	6.7
2000	11.9	9.2	2.3	0.1
2005	11.7	10.6	0.4	-1.2
2006	11.6	10.5	0.7	-2.8
2007	12.2	10.8	0.6	-4.1
2008	11.9	11.4	1.8	-4.4

These figures show extraordinarily low levels of saving by British households – not just lower than the virtuous French and Germans but also significantly lower than the Americans, with whom we are often compared. The level of saving has increased in the recession. But it tells us that in the boom British households borrowed so much against their increased property value that they basically stopped saving. This incidentally is one reason British mortgage lenders like Northern Rock were so vulnerable in the credit crunch – they did not have a savings base but were still lending: they relied on wholesale lending from abroad rather than retail depositors.

The house price boom led to a fall in the saving ratio and that in turn imposes a heavy burden on our children. Here's why. The swings in house prices can have a big impact on the distribution of wealth between generations – but the effect depends on what we do. Let us start with the case in which we respond to higher house prices with true wisdom and do absolutely nothing. We realize that we have not created any more wealth and have nothing extra to spend or to save. We just leave our house unencumbered for our children to inherit. There are of course tricky questions about equality and social mobility as different houses have different values, but at least we as a generation have not imposed any further burden on our children.

We have not behaved with such wise self-control. Instead we have borrowed against the house or not saved as much as would otherwise have done. That is why the low saving ratio was so important – it is telling us how we responded to the house price boom. We have either borrowed against the house already or we expect to finance our retirement by borrowing against it in future. And where does this money that we thought we had come from? From our children. If we increase our spending because our houses have gone up in value then we were taking from the younger generation. They have to spend more for their house and there is less of an inheritance to pay for it. So they have to pay more for their house out of their lifetime earnings. The flow of resource is from children to parents, not the other way round.

Imagine a country where every couple has two children, and where every house was previously unmortgaged and worth £150,000 and houses were passed on, debt-free, from generation to generation. But each now increases in value to £250,000. We do not see that extra £100,000 as just an increase in the price of land but instead we see it more as a performance bonus, a testament to the extraordinary skills and virtues of our generation. We spend it now or intend to spend it during our retirement. Somehow or other we intend to release that wealth for our use. That means that when we die our children will find that instead of an inheritance of £250,000 to get a house like ours they find there is a mortgage on it and between them they get only £150,000. That means that they have to lower their living standards so they can service a mortgage to enable them to borrow the money to buy a house like their parents or accept lower living standards in the form of smaller and cheaper accommodation than we leave them. It is as if your parents die leaving a treasure chest and when you open it you discover a pile of IOUs which you are obliged to pay. A single generation has had a one-off wealth gain as the price of land shoots up relative to everything else. That one generation is converting this one-off wealth effect into higher consumption. If we thought house prices were going to stay high, our children would need the money to pay for their houses. If we thought they would fall, then it was never there to spend.

Martin Weale has calculated the scale of what we are talking about here.[34] House prices rose between 1987 and 2006 at 1.9 per cent per annum faster than real earnings. That adds up to an extra £1,300bn of housing wealth on top of what would have matched the growth in our incomes. It is approximately 100 per cent of GDP transferred to current houseowners from future houseowners. This is a heavy burden for the next generation – in fact it is as if the government had increased the national debt by that amount and left the younger generation to pay it off with higher taxes.

One might imagine the crash has changed all this, but it has not. Even the precipitous fall in house prices of 2008/9 did not reverse the house price increase of the past two decades – they got back to about the level of the early noughties. This still leaves a big gain for the possessor generation. Even if we went back to the level of 2001, first-time buyers then paid £48,000 more for the average house in real terms than the baby boomers who bought the house in 1975.[35] And it has not helped the younger generation get started in the housing market – as we shall see in Chapter 11.

Let us go back to that opening question – if you had a choice, would you rather be born into a large cohort or a small cohort?

The classic argument is that if you are born into a large cohort you will find that things will be tougher. At every stage of the life cycle you will need to compete harder for a traineeship, for your place at university and for your first job. At every moment in your economic life you personally may be poorer than people in smaller cohorts. You may have fewer children – so driving the cycle in which big cohorts are followed by small ones.

We have seen, however, that you actually gain enormous advantages from being in a big cohort. Your slice of the pie might be smaller but the pie will grow faster than in the lifetimes of other cohorts. And if you shift your behaviour compared with the generations immediately before you so your partner goes out to work, you can achieve a once-off improvement in household income even more. But the benefits for the baby boomers seem to have gone much further than this. Be it the effects of globalization on wages, the shift to lower inflation, the impact of improved life expectancy, or the house price boom, the baby boomers seem to have had all the luck. Or is there more to it than that? Being a big generation gives you a lot power. Your large cohort will dominate marketplaces. You will be kings and queens amongst consumers. Elections will be pitched to you. In fact your values and tastes will shape the world around you – you will be able to spend your life in a generational bubble, always outvoting and outspending the generations before and after you. That is what it means to be a baby boomer – unless of course you see yourself as part of a wider network of obligations that tie you to other generations. It is to these which we now turn.

Chapter 5

The Social Contract

The ultra-individualism with which we began Chapter 2 was not some chance event: we showed in Chapter 3 that it could be traced back to a series of demographic and economic changes driven above all by the baby boom. We then showed in Chapter 4 how this big cohort were also shifting power and wealth to themselves and away from the young generation coming on behind. These changes are one reason for the widespread belief that the inevitable trajectory of any modern society must inevitably be towards ever greater fragmentation. The trends towards more atomization look unstoppable.

But, and it is the biggest but in this book, this will not do. There is nothing inevitable about this development. Every man for himself (and every generation for itself) is not a well-founded account of what it is to be fully human and to lead a good life. It does not even accurately describe what our own society is really like. Many thinkers have been trying to find a contemporary way of expressing the deep human instincts for co-operation. It has been called social responsibility, social justice, communitarianism, civic conservatism. David Cameron has given powerful voice to these sorts of argument, understanding very clearly that the human hunger for freedom, choice, and opportunity needs to be reconciled with the equally deep human need for roots, belonging, and commitment. Religious leaders like Sir Jonathan Sacks and the Archbishop of Canterbury and thinkers of the Left such as David Selbourne have also made distinguished contributions to this debate, as have philosophers such as Alasdair MacIntyre and Michael Sandel. The Nobel Prize for Economics was awarded in 2009 to Elinor Ostrom, whose book *Governing the Commons: The Evolution of Institutions for Collective Action* is a path-breaking example of this genre of thought.[1]

Co-operation is a good thing and it is easy just to call for more of it. But that does not get us very far. We have to understand where co-operation comes from and how it works. I myself believe that co-operation between the generations is the most important form of co-operation and that its weakening is key to the widespread sense of social breakdown. But we will be able better to judge the importance of relations between the generations when we have a deeper understanding of how a society is held together. And we are fortunate that there is at the moment an extraordinary surge in research on how co-operation works. Even better, it starts with us as free individuals, not with airy appeals to a common interest.

We can start by going back to our hunter-gatherers. Two great political thinkers, David Hume and Jean-Jacques Rousseau, were close friends until a terrible falling out (it was, by the way, Rousseau's fault).[2] Both tried to root their political thought in an account of how primitive societies could have evolved.

Rousseau formulated one of the classic versions of the problem of co-operation – the stag hunt.[3] The story is briefly told in his *Discourse on Inequality*: 'If it was a matter of hunting a deer, everyone well realized that he must remain faithful to his post; but if a hare happened to pass within reach of one of them, we cannot doubt that he would have gone off in pursuit of it without scruple...'[4]

If we hunt on our own we have a good chance of catching a hare, if we hunt together we might get a stag, a much better return for our effort, but if everyone else gets distracted by pursuing individual hares, hunting on your own for a stag is the worst option of all. So what stops us chasing after hares individually and instead co-operating to hunt a stag?

David Hume wrestled with a similar problem and described it rather pessimistically:

Your corn is ripe today; mine will be so tomorrow. Tis profitable for us both, that I should labour with you today, and that you should aid me tomorrow. I have no kindness for you and you have as little for me. I will not, therefore, take any pains upon your account; and should I labour with you upon my own account, in expectation of a return, I know I should be disappointed, and that I should in vain depend upon your gratitude. Here then I leave you to labour alone. You treat me in the same manner. The seasons change; and both of us lose our harvests for want of mutual confidence and security.[5]

Hume's response was a deliberately naturalistic account of society and morality – very different from the appeals to external divine or ethical obligation which appear to solve such tricky problems by some *deus ex machina*. Now leading thinkers are following in his footsteps and try to understand co-operation and morality as natural human behaviour, using evolutionary biology, neuroscience and game theory.[6] Game theory has suffered from some terrible PR. Two geniuses of game theory star in famous films. The inventor of game theory, John von Neuman, was the model for *Dr Strangelove*, acted by Peter Sellers as a mad Nazi who can barely restrain his arm's indiscriminate urge to give a Hitler salute. John Nash does slightly better with Russell Crowe in *A Beautiful Mind* but the film's one attempt to define a Nash equilibrium gets it completely wrong. Perhaps it is not surprising if people are baffled by this strange discipline which seems to be dominated by tortured geniuses. And as for evolutionary biology, it has had nasty hints of the devil-take-the-hindmost. But we need to break free from these caricatures because these are some of the most exciting areas of intellectual advance today: they help us understand how humans interact, institutions emerge and co-operation flourishes. We can tell it as a story of human progress, which is incidentally how David Hume himself did it.[7] He calls it a move from natural to artificial virtues and now the standard theory does, in a more sophisticated way, show how primitive impulses can lead to complex and pro-social patterns of behaviour.

We are trying to explain pro-social behaviour not just assume it at the beginning of the argument to guarantee we get to the right conclusion about what society must be like. We are starting with minimal assumptions to see how far we can get in explaining our pro-social behaviour without solving the problem just by appealing to our better natures.

A good place to start therefore is with what Richard Dawkins famously called the selfish gene. The doctrine was formulated with classical precision by J. B. S. Haldane in what may have been a joke – 'I will jump into the river to save two brothers or eight cousins.' Now it has been tested with an ingenious if rather odd experiment: participants knew that the longer they remained in an uncomfortable ski-training-type position the more money would be given to a beneficiary. In each case they knew the beneficiary but they did not know that the key variable being tested was their genetic link to the beneficiary. And they did hold the position for longer the closer they were genetically to the beneficiary. The length of time did not depend on whether you liked the relative. There were broadly similar results in England and with Zulus in South Africa, though with some differences in sensitivity to distant relatives, which may be to do with our account in the opening chapter of different family structures so culture matters too; it is not just genetic determinism.[8]

We could just leave it there. That would risk repeating the mistake of those nineteenth-century Social Darwinists who thought there was just a brutal struggle for survival everywhere and at all levels, so Darwin's explanation of the evolution of the finch could justify the colonial powers massacring natives in the Congo because they believed they were winning out in the competition between nations. There is far more to human nature than just 'Genes-R-Us'.[9] One way out is to appeal to some external moral or religious obligation to overcome these selfish genes. But what if there is no *deus ex machina* or so-called 'sky-hook' we can appeal to? Or what if there are so many such beliefs in a diverse modern society that appeals to them are not the basis for a wider social contract?

———

We need an explanation of how we develop obligations to others without using particular religious or ethical assumptions but as part of a wider account of human behaviour.[10] This is quite a challenge. The classic example of game theory, the famous 'Prisoners' Dilemma', can give a rather bleak interpretation of the human condition. Imagine that two bank robbers are charged with their crime and held in separate cells. If they both confess each gets nine years. If one bank robber confesses and the other bank robber refuses to do so, the snitch gets off scot free and his partner gets ten years. If they hold out and refuse to confess they face a minor tax evasion charge and each gets one year. Suppose that our partners in crime had an understanding that if caught they will remain silent and will refuse to confess. Will they honour their agreement? Suppose that your partner has confessed. If you stay quiet, you will end up in prison for ten years. In that case, the best thing to do is to confess so you only get nine years. Now suppose your partner has stayed quiet. In that case, if you stay quiet you will get one year in prison. But if you confess, you can escape the charge. It does not matter what your partner has done, the structure of the game is such that you will always be better off confessing. Confessing is the best strategy to choose whatever the other player has chosen to do. According to game theorists there is only one possible outcome: both players betray their partners. They both confess and both receive a prison term of nine years. This makes it what the evolutionary biologists call an evolutionarily stable strategy. The game theorists call it the unique Nash equilibrium. It is a set of solutions in a game where no one player can improve their position by changing their strategy. It is a *unique* Nash equilibrium because, in this case, there is only one such equilibrium.

The choice between confessing and remaining silent has become a metaphor for our ability to co-operate, share burdens, and generally be a good citizen. The implication that we will not be good citizens and that the two partners will not co-operate with each other is what all the fuss is about. The outcome of the Prisoners' Dilemma might seem 'nasty' but this is a consequence of the payoffs built into the structure of the game. Change the payoffs and you change the game and its outcome. The Prisoners' Dilemma does not tell us anything very profound about human nature except that in some circumstances co-operation is difficult to sustain. You can also use the tools of game theory for the opposite effect – to show how co-operation can be sustained. To see how this is possible we need to go to a place where such behaviour seems inconceivable.

We can imagine few places more hellish than the trenches of the

First World War. But they have helped us understand how human co-operation can emerge. Even in those terrible circumstances co-operative strategies emerged between soldiers in the two front lines to make life more bearable. There were of course extraordinary acts of bravery. But there is evidence of co-operation too. Snipers would shoot to miss because otherwise neither side would ever be able to get out of their trench. They would not fire at certain areas marked out by flags. Bombardments would not happen at certain prearranged times. You did not shell supply trains coming to the front line. One account from a British soldier captures it very well:

I was having tea with A company when we heard a lot of shouting and went out to investigate. We found our men and the Germans standing on their respective parapets. Suddenly a salvo arrived but did no damage. Naturally both sides got down and our men started swearing at the Germans, when all at once a brave German got up and shouted out, 'We are very sorry about that; we hope no one was hurt. It is not our fault, it is that damned Prussian artillery.'[11]

Tony Ashworth calls these arrangements the 'live and let live' system. They show how co-operation can emerge even without explicit agreements because frequent interaction permits us to adopt strategies that reward co-operation, and punish a failure to co-operate. This is an example of reciprocal altruism. Each individual act by one of the soldiers refraining from firing may, on its own, seem altruistic but it was part of a system in which reciprocity was assured. It was sustained as it was in everyone's rational self-interest. It shows how co-operation can emerge without anyone appealing to a sense of community – in fact all the appeals were the other way. Even in these uniquely unfavourable circumstances repeated interaction meant that co-operation did emerge.

This is the crucial clue which transforms the classic Prisoner's Dilemma. Things look different if we change the game in one crucial respect; imagine that rather than this being a one-off decision, you face the same dilemma with the same partner in crime over and over again. In this new situation it is possible that co-operation between players can emerge and be rewarded. If the prisoners were brought back to a similar situation again and again, they would have the opportunity to 'punish' one another for confessing by confessing themselves in subsequent games. This means it becomes possible to enforce agreements. Robert Axelrod[12] arranged a tournament between computer programmes playing 'Prisoners' Dilemma'-style games again and again. He showed that the most effective strategy was a programme called 'TIT FOR TAT'. TIT FOR TAT would co-operate with the computer it was playing against, but if you betrayed it, it would punish you on a subsequent turn. If you reverted to co-operating, it would revert back too. In effect, it would mirror you one turn later. The Prisoners' Dilemma can be resolved if instead of playing the game once we find ourselves repeatedly playing the same game.

This is how institutions work – they are places where people interact with each other sufficiently frequently for co-operation to emerge as a rational strategy. Values are not worth much unless they are embodied and sustained in real live institutions which shape how people behave. The generals in their chateaus behind the lines in the First World War deliberately moved the troops around from trench to trench so as to destroy co-operation between them and the enemy.

Exchange and reciprocity are very powerful – so powerful they can be exploited by people like the philosopher Schopenhauer, who is supposed to have left a tip on the table at beginning of a meal and removed it at the end.[13] It lies behind many of the fascinating examples of persuasion which Robert Cialdini has analysed. A lot of persuasion works by creating a sense of reciprocity – it is what the followers of Hare Krishna are doing when they give us a flower for free but promptly expect something from us in return. It is the point Margaret Thatcher was trying to make in her notorious remark that there was no such thing as society – her actual words are in the footnote.[14] David Hume put it very neatly: 'I learn to do a service to another, without bearing him any real kindness, because I foresee that he will return my service in expectation of another of the same kind and in order to maintain the same correspondence of good offices with me and others.'[15]

Sometimes the co-operative behaviour institutions sustain is not necessarily for a good purpose. Classic psychological experiments have shown their power to make us behave badly as well as their power for good.[16] As Michael Oakeshott observed, 'We do not first decide that certain behaviour is right or desirable and then express our approval or disapproval of it in an institution; our knowledge of how to behave well is, at this point, the institution.'[17] Areas dominated by gangs where people refuse to speak to the police are a nasty equilibrium, largely based on the fear of future contact with local criminals. One role of government is to break up these unpleasant arrangements.

So far we have seen how reciprocity generates co-operation. But direct reciprocity isn't enough. That is the awkward issue behind the homely advice: 'If you don't go to his funeral, he won't go to yours.' We need to escape being dependent on repeat encounters. Direct exchange is the equivalent of a barter economy.[18] We need a currency. That currency is reputation – how we are regarded by others. Reputation allows us to enjoy indirect reciprocity. And if we go further and punish another person by refusing to help them because they refused to help another person, we can build a virtuous circle. This requires that their reputation be known to me, hence we need memory and gossip too. Adam Smith rightly identified how we are regarded by others as a key source of human well-being: 'What are the advantages which we propose to gain by that great purpose of human life which we call bettering our condition? To be observed, to be attended to, to be taken notice of with sympathy, complacency, and approbation are the advantages which we can propose to derive from it.'[19]

Small institutions are particularly effective for generating these sorts of behaviour. US college students are the lab rats of the social sciences so it is no surprise that one of the best pieces of evidence on this comes from American student dorms. You drop an addressed letter and measure what percentage of letters are picked up and returned. The score is 100 per cent returned in a small dorm, 87 per cent in one which is medium-sized and 63 per cent in a large one.[20] My own researches showed much worse problems of discipline and behaviour in larger English schools.[21]

We put a lot of effort into identifying defectors and impose lots of minor punishments for doing that. We spot cheaters in social contexts better than if the same situations are presented as pure logical problems.[22] This is what humans are particularly good at. Infant children at two and a half years have similar cognitive skills to chimps and orang-utans of that age but already have better social skills.[23] Reputation, good and bad, works because of willingness to approve or punish people whose behaviour has not directly affected us. And failure to punish must itself be punished. This may sound unpleasant but it is the subtle expressions of approval and disapproval that convey a sense of what we think of people's behaviour and even the most non-judgemental of us would be hard put to avoid these. It is how social values are protected. If you doubt this why not pause to enjoy Jane Austen's *Pride and Prejudice*.[24] The malefactors are a philanderer, Mr Wickham, and the youngest of the Bennet sisters, Lydia. They set up house together, 'living in sin'. The family is of course shocked and faces the dilemma of ostracizing them or being ostracized themselves: '... this false step in one daughter, will be injurious to the fortunes of all the others... who will connect themselves with such a family... Let me advise you to throw off your unworthy child... and leave her to reap the fruits of her own heinous offence,' says Mr Collins to Mr Bennet.

Then, later: 'This unfortunate affair will, I fear, prevent my sister's having the pleasure of seeing you at Pemberley today,' says Darcy to Elizabeth Bennet.

The reader's sympathy is directed towards her sisters and the obvious injustice involved in the need to punish them: '*who will connect themselves with such a family?*' Unless of course they in turn punish their sister: '*Let me advise you.... to throw off your unworthy child.*'[25]

There frequently is a strong reciprocator in these novels, somebody who derives pleasure from enforcing society's rules. In *Pride and Prejudice*, it is Mr Collins, the vicar. However, he is the least sympathetic character in the novel. His unseemly enthusiasm for punishment is treated with derision and contempt. Elizabeth is if anything rather pleased that she will no longer enjoy his company. Mr Darcy on the other hand complies only with the greatest reluctance. He obeys out of a sense of duty, a duty that derives from the importance he attaches to his standing in society (which he has every right to defend). The reader is left in no doubt who has the more important role in enforcing society's rules, Mr Collins or Mr Darcy.

Jane Austen was profoundly ambivalent in her attitude towards the subject of her novels: the moral codes by which society is governed. This ambivalence results not because she is a twenty-first-century liberal who thinks that sex outside marriage is OK. Her greatness lies in her subtle treatment of the role we all play, and the dilemmas we face. The world of the nineteenth-century novel may seem to be far removed from society today and sounds severe, but Austen's genius is to capture something timeless about human nature even if society's particular moral codes vary over time; we enforce our contemporary morality – be it about racism or drinking and driving – with similar disapproval.

We are trying to construct an account of how we co-operate with others drawing on limited assumptions about human nature. So far we have got from selfishness through reciprocal exchanges to indirect reciprocity and the importance of how we are regarded by others. The next stage is to consider how competition rewards different patterns of behaviour. We will go back to our hunter-gatherers and this time we have uncomfortable news. Nearly two thirds of hunter-gatherer groups for which records existed waged war at least every two years.[26] Archaeological data suggest 15 per cent of people in primitive societies died violently.[27] Darwin describes what he thought would be the effect of such competition: 'When two tribes of primeval man, living in the same country, came into competition, if the one tribe included (other circumstances being equal) a greater number of courageous, sympathetic, and faithful members, who were always ready to warn each other of danger, to aid and defend each other, this tribe would without doubt succeed best and conquer the other.'[28]

This idea of group selection is controversial. Some experts do not believe this step in the argument is correct or necessary.[29] But we can see how a competitive environment can create the conditions for co-operation, regardless of whether or not you think it goes beyond rational individual self-interest. A very good example is the behaviour of vampire bats. As we know from all the best horror movies, vampire bats need regular supplies of fresh blood. We now know that the vampire bats which come back from a night's hunting with lots of blood regurgitate some to share it with other vampire bats who were less successful. The vampire bat colonies which survive through tough times are the ones which are capable of this pooling of risk. So competition for limited resources rewards co-operation. Maybe vampire bats are caring, sharing creatures after all, or as Professor Binmore puts it: 'Although vampire genes are selfish, reciprocal sharing turns out to be sustainable as an equilibrium in the vampire game of life.'[30] This works best if everyone in the colony keeps an eye out for vampire bat free-riders who take blood but do not give – so, who knows, they may have bat squeaks of gossip too.[31]

This is where group selection gets tricky. Some scientists dispute this account, claiming that vampire bat blood-sharing is just restricted to immediate relatives. And there is a subversive challenge from the feminists who say that it is female bats who do most of the sharing of blood. In fact, women seem historically to have borne more of the burden of maintaining such contracts, perhaps because they live longer and so are likely to be recipients of more informal care later.

But this account does seem to match the empirical evidence on our moral values. If you ask people to endorse one of several classic moral codes for living, reciprocal altruism scores highest. The one which gets the greatest endorsement, from over three quarters of adults, is 'Do to others as you would have others do to you' (77 per cent). Next is 'Be true to yourself in all things' (72 per cent). Only 41 per cent endorse 'Always do what you want as long as you don't hurt anybody'.[32]

There is a paradox behind this model – we are trying to explain good features of human behaviour like empathy or co-operation. But we are deliberately making it hard for ourselves by not assuming what we are trying to explain in advance – so we are operating with a very limited set of assumptions about human behaviour which may put some people off the whole exercise. They may feel we are 'taking the altruism out of altruism'. We are trying to explain altruism without appealing to altruism in the first place. There is not some social glue to be poured over us to make us more co-operative: it is how institutions and incentives work.

A good example comes from Mediterranean trade in the Middle Ages. To an outsider it must have looked very trusting indeed – merchants sent goods around the Mediterranean not necessarily paid in advance, sometimes to people they did not know and had never met and all without an enforceable law of contract. How did they do it? Were they just more trusting? We now know how it worked from an extraordinary cache of eleventh-century documents found in an ancient synagogue in old Cairo. It all depended on a network of agents. An agent who defrauds one trader loses business with all of them as the traders have a reciprocal network in which they all exclude an agent who defrauds any one of them. It is in the interests of the traders to preserve the coalition as all contracts are short term and so they can be penalized by other members of the coalition if they do not enforce action against a delinquent agent.[33]

This is a case study in how ingenuity in designing an institution creates 'trust'. We do not need to rely on personal moral improvement, desirable though that would be, nor worry that we are somehow worse people than we were. We need to give institutions the space to emerge and to function and create their own networks of reciprocity. Governments can be like those First World War generals, disrupting the inner life of an institution and stopping co-operation. And the demographic disruption wrought by the baby boomers has eroded the contract between the generations which is at the heart of a healthy society.

Politics is not therefore about pouring social cement over atomized citizens to try to stick them together so they co-operate with each other. Instead we can think of co-operative behaviour as being like drystone walling held together by its inner structure – Hume's image was the stones held together in a well-designed stone arch. In the words of Ken Binmore's powerful book *Natural Justice*, 'social capital isn't a thing, it is just the word we use when talking about the properties of an equilibrium that has evolved along with our game of life.'[34]

Reciprocity involves empathy, being able to put yourself in someone else's shoes even when their feet are a different size. Sympathy is feeling for someone else. Empathy is making the leap to understanding someone else even if your emotions are not directly involved. When Adam Smith puts sympathy at the heart of his *Theory of Moral Sentiments* he means what we would now call empathy: this is the key that unlocks the argument in that great book – otherwise it is just about being nice to each other.

Other mammals with sufficient social structure and mental powers to practise reciprocity also have some capacity for empathy. Rhesus monkeys do. One experiment involves monkeys in two separate cages side by side. 'One would have a chain and a trough. If they pulled the chain, food would be delivered to the monkey. However, at the same time, the other monkey would receive an electric shock. Having realised the connection, monkeys in these cages refused to ask for more food for five days and for 12 days. They starved themselves to avoid shocking a peer.'[35]

The scientists have even tracked down the chemical which governs this behaviour. Paul Zak has shown that infusing the human brain with moderate doses of oxytocin can induce people to trust strangers with one's money.[36] It is sometimes called the lust and trust chemical. Or if you prefer the same thought in a rather more spiritual way, Thomas Jefferson put it beautifully: 'The Creator would indeed have been a bungling artist had he intended man for a social animal without planting in him social disposi-tions.'[37] And if you want to put it in the language of modern neuroscience, there is a concentration of processing power in those parts of the brain we need for empathy. It takes a lot of high-power neurological activity to act empathetically. We have to be able to distinguish between what we want and others want. Nicholas Anthony argues this is where self-consciousness comes from – we have to be able to think ourselves into other people's heads to func-tion socially and that generates a sense of what is different about what is going in our own heads. Our empathetic interaction with others creates our sense of who we are.

Instinct and emotion fit in here too. We are not desiccated cal-culating machines. Apart from all the other problems with it, it wouldn't work. We would endlessly be doing intricate calculations about what other people might do; life would be like playing an elaborate game of chess. We would be incapable of actually doing anything until our computations were complete. So we need short cuts, instinctive rules of thumb. Apparently irrational anger also has a place – it is a good way of showing we will protect our recip-rocal understandings and not be patsies who can be exploited.[38] Professor Binmore argues emotion is to help police, more rapidly than rational calculation, primeval social contracts. It protects co-operation.[39] The emotions which police and sustain these particular arrangements and understandings are linked to our most physical responses – disgust and nausea. The evolutionary biologists suggest that we took the most basic aversions which had developed to protect us from eating stuff that would kill us and used what were literally powerful gut feelings to protect and enforce our social contracts.

Our emotions are particularly engaged in defence of fairness: anger makes us irrationally committed to deals we think are fair. The Ultimatum game captures this very neatly. In its simplest form there are two players. One, the proposer, is given a sum of money and distributes some of it to the second player. If the responder rejects the offer then there is no deal and the money is lost to both of them. The experiment has been played in many forms and there is a clear pattern – a responder offered less than about 30 per cent of the money rejects the deal and both players lose everything. It is hard for conventional economics to explain this behaviour because economists assume something is better than nothing. It is telling us that fairness matters so much to us that we will make sacrifices for it. One explanation is that we are behaving as if the negotiation is to be repeated even if it is not – so we kind of over-shoot, thinking we can generate reciprocal altruism even when we can't. Neuroscientists have also identified the part of the brain that controls our behaviour in the Ultimatum game and can tem-porarily disable it with waves of the right frequency aimed at the specific part of the brain so that when we then play the game we accept lower offers.[40] This does not just apply to humans. Capuchin monkeys can learn the value of a token which they exchange for barter at different values, so a low-value token gets a cucumber and a high-value one gets a grape. Capuchins who had observed their peers receiving a high-value item for a given token or price would ignore the reward or refuse to make the exchange if offered a lower-value one.[41]

We are beginning to see how our hunter-gatherers got to hunt stags not rabbits. They would need a deal about sharing out the stag which they would believe was fair. A convention for sharing consumption was essential for co-operative production. And it would be policed by knowing that someone you betrayed would be so angry about it that he would be willing to stop everyone else having the stag.

———

We have got a long way in understanding co-operation, empathy and fairness. It is an exciting and productive research programme, which has not yet been properly absorbed into our wider culture. I believe this naturalistic account of morality is increasingly going to contribute to public discourse about the many ethical issues in public policy. It does not resolve all our dilemmas but it helps us understand them. And it enables us to talk about them in a way which reaches across the different religious or ethical views now represented in open Western countries.

The most profound dilemma arises from what has been called the move from tribal brotherhood to universal otherhood.[42] It is the tension between the intimate experience of a community and the abstract rules of a modern market economy. We have seen how we develop our understandings and reciprocity within a particular community and within an institution. What about people who are outside our group? How do we co-operate with them? Is it fairness just for us or does it include them too? What happens when the local and the universal collide? Institutions provide the framework in which we co-operate – and that often involves defining others as outsiders, hence what has been described as the 'Antagonism between social tribes who must maintain their internal solidarity – through bonds of loyalty, religion, language and so on.'[43] And how do other generations count in all this – are they part of our community or outside it?

There are deep philosophical issues here. But rather than tackle them head on we can look at the evidence of how our moral attitudes are actually formed. One survey showed the top influences on people's moral values were parents (95 per cent) and family (91 per cent), way ahead of teachers (75 per cent) or religion (46 per cent).[44] The family is the first place where we experience these reciprocal exchanges, particularly between the generations. The good news is that early experience of strong reciprocity yields a belief in universal values. The evidence suggests that strong families (where children were particularly close to their parents) are unusually effective at generating a willingness to reach out beyond the particular group. One researcher studied the Germans who had the courage to shelter Jews in Nazi Germany and found that they had one key thing in common – they all came from strong families. The same is true of people who were willing to stand up against discrimination and the Vietnam War in America in the 1960s.[45] Low levels of father contact also appear to lower altruism.[46] Interaction with siblings also appears to be a good way of learning how reciprocity works. Individuals' behaviour is not of course determined by these factors and a community can be rich in other types of ways of experiencing reciprocity and altruism. But the good news is that the experience of family life suggests that strong, tightly focused reciprocity can provide the basis for wider moral understandings too – the dilemma which looms so large in theory does not appear to be so bad in practice.

One reason why families matter so much is that many family exchanges are across different generations. This has been one of the great weaknesses of social contract thinking – it treats the contract as between a group of middle-aged men, like those illustrations of the American founding fathers or members of a Victorian club. The challenge is to extend it across generations. Indeed we may think that what makes nationhood and family so important to us is that both are communities which extend across generations. (Universities, transmitting a critical understanding of a body of knowledge from one generation to the next, are also very strongly represented in lists of those very special institutions which have lasted more than 500 years. By contrast it is striking evidence of the sheer dynamic turbulence of the marketplace that very few companies last more than a hundred years.)

If we want to understand contracts going across generations the family is a good place to start. Here are four implicit contracts between members of successive generations:

i   if we care for our children when they are young, they will care for us when we are old (a direct exchange);

ii   if we care for our parents now they are old, our children will copy us, and similarly care for us when we are old (replication of our behaviour to our benefit);

iii   if we care for our children, they will copy us, and care similarly for their children, our grandchildren (replication of our behaviour to the benefit of future generations);

iv   our parents helped care for our children so we have got to

UNIVERSITY OF WINCHESTER
LIBRARY

copy them and help our children when they have children (we have to replicate behaviour from which we have benefited).

It is this cat's cradle of relationships between the generations, half exchange and half obligation, which makes the world go round. They do, however, come with very different emotional overtones, captured in the proverb:

> When the father helps the son they both laugh.
> When the son helps the father they both cry.

Before we get too misty-eyed about the intergenerational contract within families across many different types of society, we should recognize that it was women who did most of the work keeping it going whilst men earned most of the money. Those four key commitments between the generations are still more likely to be discharged by women than men. Indeed, the blindness of conventional social contract thinking to what have been the distinct roles of men and women may be one reason why it has also been so weak on the contract between the generations.

The list comprised examples of reciprocity or exchange but we think that this is not what morality should be like – it should just be absolute injunctions. Look at the Ten Commandments. They take this unconditional form – *thou shalts* and *thou shalt nots*. If they say anything about consequences, they are in the next world not this one. But the commandment on relations between the generations is unique. It alone explains what should happen in this world as a result of complying with it: 'Honour thy father and thy mother that thy days may be long upon the Earth which the Lord thy God giveth thee.'[47] It is saying you will do better and live longer yourself if you have cared for the older generation. There will be a benefit back to you from honouring your parents, presumably as you are more likely to be so honoured yourself. So even the Bible is implying some kind of reciprocity between the generations, even if it is not direct exchange.

The four relationships in our list are all examples of reciprocity, but only one is a direct exchange between the same two generations. Behaviour is copied or cascades across the generations.[48] These exchanges across the generations are not necessarily between the same people. They are less like a conventional exchange than like someone passing the baton in a relay race. The pattern of obligations can become so complex they look more like the links in a TV soap or a particularly elaborate family line. But all of us start benefiting from an enormous investment of care and education and if we are not betrayed we should not betray the next generation. We know where babies come from but even more important is where adults come from. And they are shaped by their experience of these intergenerational exchanges.

Moral philosophers are much better at neighbourhood ethics, obligations to fellow citizens now, than they are at obligations across the generations. And we can see why it is much harder for them. They are not a classic set of contracts entered into at one moment in time. We can think of it as a special case of the Prisoners' Dilemma where co-operation is even harder to obtain as the iterations occur across time with people who may not yet exist. And even if you do not think in terms of contracts, the problems still remain. Nowadays much of our moral reasoning is based on the assertion of rights – captured by the cartoon showing the lawn with the notice: 'Please respect the rights of the grass'. But it is hard to think of the rights of people who do not yet exist.

Such questions understandably trouble the philosophers.[49] But perhaps our original model of the interests of the selfish gene can help for our purposes. Let us go back to Haldane's neat remark about our genetic interests. How would the calculation of the interest of a selfish gene look like across four generations? Your child has half of your genes, your grandchild a quarter, and your great-grandchild an eighth. 4/8 + 2/8 + 1/8 adds up to 7/8 in total. After one more generation it adds up to 15/16ths and carries on getting closer and closer to 1. So even if all you care about is your own gene's future you soon find that the interests of the aggregate of descendants in the future weigh very heavily indeed – more heavily than any one contemporary, however close they are to you.[50]

There is strong empirical evidence for these sorts of intergenerational exchanges. Imagine that you are a harassed middle-aged woman with an elderly parent as well as children. If you think of these as conflicting claims then you would expect that the more time you have to spend on your parents or parents-in-law then the less you have for your children. But the evidence shows the opposite. The more you do for your parents then the more you do for your children as well, and this is after allowing for class, income, etc.: 'British women who provided help to a child were twice as likely to help a parent as those who were not helping a child (and conversely those helping a parent were twice as likely to be helping a child).'[51] The best way to explain this is that the intergenerational contract suggests these are complementary activities. What you give to the next generation depends on what you received from the previous ones.

Simulated games in which volunteers are put into situations where they have to decide how to act in dilemmas involving future generations confirm that our behaviour to future generations is influenced by how previous generations treated us. For example, they are running a commercial fishing company and have to decide how to respond to a request voluntarily to reduce their catch to protect fish stocks for the future but sacrificing income now. When these dilemmas are modelled we are more willing to make cuts ourselves if we are told that previous generations themselves had ensured fish stocks survived by making voluntary cuts, but are much less willing to do so if told that previous generations had not. The sacrifice of income called for now was the same in both cases but those who were told that previous generations had made sacrifices were far more willing to make cuts themselves – by 84 per cent to 37 per cent. This is a potentially powerful way of 'nudging' our behaviour – our decisions about how to treat future generations are shaped by how we believe past ones treated us.[52]

We are moving way beyond transfers between generations within the family – they are across generations as a whole. Can we think of the whole social contract as being intergenerational?

The social contract has a long tradition in political thought: its greatest recent exponent is John Rawls in his book *A Theory of Justice*.[53] He asks us to imagine that we are choosing in advance a set of political and economic arrangements from behind a veil of ignorance. We do not know whether we will be rich or poor, man or woman, talented or not. In fact, for his thought experiment to work we do not really have anything distinctive about us at all – we cannot have a culture or a religious faith. If you assume away all those things then you end up with the classic modern state – tolerant of an extraordinary diversity of lifestyles and beliefs but licensed to intervene to reduce diversity of income.

The classic objection to this type of social contract theory is that it invites us to think of ourselves as somehow existing outside society, history, and culture. We cannot even have a language, which does after all embody a set of values. We are just bearers of some genes, 'selfish' ones. Rawls might as well ask us all to imagine that we are sheep. But Rawls, to his credit, is one of the few political philosophers who has seriously wrestled with inter-generational fairness. Even more to his credit he recognizes that the problem of justice between generations 'subjects any ethical theory to severe if not impossible tests'.[54]

The idea of obligations across the generations radically changes the implications of Rawls's account of justice. He argues that any particular difference of outcomes would need to be justified as helping the least well-off in society – the so-called difference principle. But he says that this should be applied to 'the longer-term prospects of the least-favoured extended over future generations. Each generation must not only preserve the gains of culture and civilization, and maintain intact those just institutions that have been established, but it must also put aside in each period of time a suitable amount of real capital accumulation.'[55] That opens up a host of arguments for saving, enterprise, and cultural traditions that are often ignored. And it happens as a direct result of his brave attempt to include future generations in his model.

Rawls is saying we have to look to the future and that might limit what we feel able to spend on ourselves today. He is going out of his way to avoid the criticism of so much liberalism that it does not understand our obligation to transmit a culture and capital from one generation to the next. This attitude was captured by J. M. Keynes who dismissed concern about the long-term consequences of his economic theories by saying, 'in the long run we are all dead.' As his model broke down in the 1960s and 1970s the riposte came back: 'now Keynes is dead, and we are in the long run.'

Rawls does not want to be open to the same line of criticism.

That means he has to explain why these long-term consequences for future generations should matter for the liberal individuals entering into his social contract behind the veil of ignorance. He solves his problem by an extraordinary move – he describes the contracting parties behind his veil of ignorance as 'heads of families'. 'The parties are thought of as representing continuous lines of claims, as being so to speak deputies for a kind of everlasting moral agent or institution.' He expressly says this is necessary so that they will think of the consequences of their actions for 'at least two generations'.[56] This enables him to include obligations across the generations. But it comes at the price of sacrificing the integrity of his theory. These people behind the veil of ignorance who are not allowed a language or a religion or a nationality are supposed to have children. And these children are not just products of chance sexual encounters and abandoned at birth.

They are part of something called a family – and one suspects that the kind of family Rawls has in mind is the classic nuclear family, which itself is part of a rather unusual social and economic structure, as we saw in Chapter 1. Rawls, even though he is willing to shed every other feature of our lives as a social animal, cannot abandon the family, otherwise our obligations to future generations would not have a firm foothold in his theory. Rawls has to put people into some kind of institutional framework after all in order to create the moral obligations without which his theory of justice would collapse – and what drives him to it is the need to include obligations to future generations. This shows that any worthwhile social contract has to be between the generations.

Just as the Old Testament has to make an exception for the intergenerational contract in the otherwise unconditional structure of the Ten Commandments so the greatest contemporary liberal thinker, Rawls, has to make an exception in his theory too. It tells us how important these contracts between the generations are even if they are hard to pin down in conventional form. These intergenerational transactions are deeply embedded in our nature. Intergenerational exchange is at the heart of the social contract. And they are as natural as it is possible to be – if we want to understand what ties us together in a way that bridges the gaps of culture and age then a commitment to the future of our children and grandchildren is the most powerful appeal we have. The social contract is, at root, a contract between the generations.

Chapter 6

Ages and Stages

The little old lady on her own in her flat is genuinely anxious about what she fears is the threat from a gang of youths outside her window. The police are called. Sometimes it is very serious indeed but other times they find a disconsolate gang of youths hanging around who feel they are being harassed by older people when they are just bored. The youths can be dispersed for good by installing a Mosquito, the device which emits a high-pitched note that can be heard by teenagers but not older people, so as to drive them away from areas where they are not welcome. It is in effect a declaration of intergenerational warfare. Imagine the outrage if the sound could only be heard by pensioners and was being used to exclude them.

Such misunderstandings erode a nation's sense of trust and well-being. This breakdown of trust between the generations lies behind much of our anxiety about social breakdown which we conveyed in Chapter 2. We described in Chapter 3 the disruptive demographic changes since the War that lie behind this break-up. In Chapter 4 we provided the economic evidence of what has gone wrong: we are indeed spending the kid's inheritance. We could just pack up and go home, conceding that deep social and economic trends are moving inexorably against us. But that won't do. It is not inevitable that the intergenerational contract must break down. We tried in Chapter 5 to show how even a modern secular society can still understand and value a social contract, at the heart of which is a contract between the generations. We can now go further and look at what our attitudes and values really are, not just what we assume they are, so we can see to what extent there really is a generation gap and how it could be bridged.

We have to start, as always, with the baby boomers. The boomers have led a big change in attitudes towards work and domestic life. Of people aged 65 or over in 2006 55 per cent agree with the proposition that 'being a housewife is just as fulfilling as working for pay'. The big change came with the boomers: only 42 per cent of early boomers, people aged 50–64 in 2006, agree with the proposition, and the proportion agreeing then remains just about identical at 40 per cent for subsequent cohorts. Of the oldest cohort 43 per cent agreed that 'A job is all right but what most women really want is a home and children.' That falls to 26 per cent for early boomers and again remains pretty much the same for subsequent generations.[1] So the boomers led a change in attitudes which has remained stable for subsequent generations. Even if they have led the way, this change goes way beyond the boomers, sometimes affecting even the attitudes of people older than them. (So, for example, all age groups have become far more tolerant of gay people.) A change in the culture affecting all age groups is called a 'period effect'. That is why one way of thinking of these changes is a general trend to greater individualism led by the boomers but affecting all of us. That means our connections to each other are looser. As so often in life, good and bad are intimately linked. We are more tolerant (a good thing) but also more disengaged (a bad thing). But it is not the whole story.

The first clue is the TV series *Absolutely Fabulous*. The central joke in *AbFab* is very simple – Edina and Patsy are fun-loving, liberal-minded baby boomers but Edina's daughter is earnest and straitlaced. She has little time for the irresponsibility of the older generation who as children of the sixties seem to have had life far easier. And as we look at the way in which the younger generation assemble their CVs, make the most use of their gap years, and are so driven by moral concerns, we might think that *AbFab* is on to something. It is possible that this idea of a dramatic shift to individualism is based after all on the behaviour of a particular cohort, the baby boomers. Maybe once again the baby boomers have constructed a world in their own image and claim for it the status of a universal truth.

There is some empirical evidence from attitude surveys of a special sixties generation, far more liberal in its attitudes than its successors as well as its predecessors. The cohort whose formative years were in the 1960s might have a different view of the world because of the exceptional events of that decade. The flood of the baby boomers into early marriage and then out to divorce may have been deeply disruptive for them. The evidence bears this out. The cohort whose formative years were in the 1960s have even more liberal attitudes than previous or succeeding cohorts. Thus, for example, 49 per cent of the cohort of those who were young in the 1960s disapprove of extramarital sex, as against 56 per cent of people who are ten years younger and 63 per cent who are ten years older.[2] Another survey showed that it was the youngest age groups who were most likely to agree that life in Britain would improve if people were more sexually faithful.[3] Another question also suggests that the baby boomers are different. Researchers ask when was the last time you completely changed the way you style your hair or the way you dress. This is, if you like, a question about how fixed our identities are. You might expect a clear pattern with the youngest generation those who are most likely to be changing all the time. But the evidence is subtly different. Pensioners do indeed live up to the stereotype. The average older person has not changed his or her hairstyle since the age of 41, the way they dress since the age of 36, or their diet since the age of 38. The early baby boomers, those born between 1948 and 1957 are the opposite. Of all the different cohorts studied they are the ones who are most likely to have completely changed their hairstyle or the way they dress. The younger generation are more likely than them never to have changed.[4]

It was said of Winston Churchill's book on the First World War that he had written a book about himself and called it *The World Crisis 1911–1918*. The baby boomers have done something similar for our cultural and political understandings. As the key generation in the breakdown of social institutions in the 1960s and the transformation of our economy in the 1980s they have created a picture of the world which is their experiences applied to everyone else as well. They are behind this assumption of a simple trend to ever greater individualism. But you could see things very differently. Think instead of each generation as distinctive, imprinted with the experiences of its youth, and carrying them through life. Generations are more like slices in one of those ice cores they drill in Antarctica – for ever imprinted with the unique features of its period. That was Mannheim's way of thinking which we applied in Chapter 3 as we described different cohorts.

There is some evidence of particularly important years when these attitudes are shaped. What happened when you were aged 17–25 is likely to be reported by you for the rest of your life as a very important event. The major national or world events recalled by Americans as especially important 'refer back disproportionately to a time when the respondents were in their teens or early twenties'.[5] Another researcher finds that savers' decisions about what to invest in were shaped for twenty or thirty years by the performance of different assets when they started saving in their youth.[6] Similarly an early experience of unemployment is a scar whose effects can be found with higher risks of unemployment and lower wages twenty years later.[7] So these years in your teens and early twenties are as formative as the early years on which so much attention is focused.

This idea of distinctive generations each with its own character is a very fruitful one. It liberates us from the idea that there is an inexorable trend in one direction. Each generation could be shaped by rather different events and respond to them. So, for example, in a world of economic slowdown, Islamic extremism, and environmental damage there might be a hunger for more security, community, and a recognition of the ties that hold the West together. Instead of an inexorable trend towards greater individualism perhaps we should instead think of a society of successive generations, each imprinted with its own values and carrying them through life.

This model, however, raises a new set of problems. Are there no experiences which link us to the generations before and after us? If the past is a different country and so is the future, then what obligations do we have to the different generations who live in those different countries? What do we share with the people coming before or after us? To answer that question we need to think instead about the life cycle.

The classical model, the seven ages of man, was dominant before generational thinking came along. It assumes that what matters above all is not which cohort you belong to but where you are in relation to the big experiences of life. It is also similar to the way in which economists explain individuals' patterns of income, borrowing, and saving over time.[8] This thesis says it is the real experiences of getting a job, becoming a parent, becoming a grand-parent indeed that shape attitudes. The old rather rigid concept of the life cycle is being overtaken by the idea of the life course. This allows for a much greater range of experiences such as first sexual encounter; leaving home; the first death of a significant elder; the first death of a contemporary; widowhood. These are fundamental human experiences which change us as we go through our lives.[9] Personal learning and growth, often around the big events of one's life, are what many novels are about. If economists and novelists agree on this way of viewing the world, it just might be true.

There is evidence of the life cycle shaping people's attitudes. Take, say, attitudes to sex, especially outside marriage. We have already seen there is quite an interesting cohort effect with the 1960s generation apparently more tolerant of extramarital sex. But also as people get older and get married, and see what damage can be done by extramarital relationships, they become more dis-approving – a clear life cycle effect.

Having children is the key event in changing people's attitudes. That is the point at which we stop just living for ourselves and sud-denly start connecting with others across the generations. It is our first experience of life repeating itself through the next genera-tion. We may get more self-knowledge as we reflect on our own childhood. And we get a personal measure of how the world has changed. The other event, whose significance is not properly appreciated, is having grandchildren.

Let us go back to the evidence at the beginning of this chapter, which suggested that the boomers led a big change in social atti-tudes that has affected subsequent generations. Geoff Dench has ingeniously analysed the data between parents and childless people.[10] He finds that the oldest generation of parents had rather less traditional attitudes than their childless contemporaries, who were very traditional, and younger cohorts of parents had less liberal attitudes than their more liberal childless contemporaries. The biggest swings in social attitudes occurred amongst successive cohorts of childless people; they were more susceptible to changes in the culture. When people had children this fundamental experience shaped their attitudes in similar ways, whichever cohort they were born into.

The significance of the family is shown when you ask people about crucial events that have happened during the previous year. Top of the list are family events, with 23 per cent of first mentions and 41 per cent of total mentions. Second is work, with 11 per cent of first mentions and 24 per cent of total mentions. Leisure and holidays are third, with 10 per cent of first mentions and 23 per cent of total mentions.

Table 5. Highly mentioned life events and happenings (per cent)[11]

Life events	first mentions	total mentions
Family	23	41
Employment	11	24
Leisure	10	23
Health	9	19
Education	6	14
Consumption	4	10

Politicians should note that national and world events get 0.5 per cent of first mentions and 2 per cent of total mentions.

This evidence does not just tell us how important the family is for people; it also reveals a lot about the significance of life course events. The family events that were then described are births, weddings, and deaths. In the words of a character in T. S. Eliot's verse play *Sweeney Agonistes*: 'Birth, copulation, and death. That is all the facts when you come to brass tacks'.[12] Moreover, events apparently unrelated to family life may actually derive their significance from the life course, such as holidays. Consumption comes a low 4 per cent on the table. We know from separate research for General Motors that purchases of cars are often linked to life course events – 80 per cent of people who have recently married or divorced, become parents, or suffered a beareavement buy a car within one year.[13] There is one other important piece of evidence from this research which tells us something important about how we change as we go through the life course. Younger people are much more likely to mention events affecting themselves (81 per cent of 16- to 24-year-old men and 76 per cent of 16- to 24-year-old women mention something that has happened to them).

But above the age of about 40 references to oneself decline. And only 47 per cent of men and 39 per cent of women aged over 65 mention events affecting themselves. They are beginning to live through the younger generations coming after them. There is an important paradox here. It is older people who are the most future-oriented. They are thinking about the world their children and grandchildren will inherit. It is young people who have the luxury of living in the present because when you are young you think that the present will carry on for ever. That is why it would be entirely wrong to think this issue of justice across the generations is some kind of appeal targeted on younger people. If anything it is the opposite – it is an appeal to the baby boomers. It is an appeal to the old world to redress the balance for the new.

We must not get carried away, however. As we get older we do not become completely altruistic. There is clear evidence of a life cycle impact on attitudes to public spending. In general older people support public spending more, perhaps because they depend more on public services. This is shown in, for example, a very clear increase in support for public spending on health care as people get older. When it comes to education spending, if anything, it is the other way around. It is one of the few areas of public spending that is strongly supported by younger people and where support declines as people get older.[14]

There is also one other very significant life cycle effect. One of the most fruitful areas of research at the moment is happiness. There are a host of influences on our happiness – from the state of our marriage to our income. But happiness is also heavily influenced by the stage we are at in our lives. If you draw a graph of how happy people are it is a very strong U-shaped curve. You are happy when you are young and you are happy when you are old but it is when you have all the burdens of middle age that your happiness level plummets. These are the people who bear the burdens of the intergenerational contract, with obligations to children and older people.

So the life cycle matters. It is not just a matter of which generation you were born into. The events that matter in your life, what you think of public spending programmes, even how happy you are, depend on the stage you are at in your life.

Our social attitudes are like an intricate Bach fugue with three distinct strands. First, as our society changes, all of us are influenced by the same trends. But each cohort has a different character because of its different experiences. And then, the different stages of the life cycle shape our values. We can make more sense of our society if we understand these three effects. One estimate is that two thirds of changes in social attitudes are due to change within the cohort as they go through the life cycle and one third are due to successive cohorts having different attitudes.[15] This is a much richer view than a simple model of an underlying trend towards social breakdown as each generation succeeds the next. There is no law of social entropy that the beliefs which successive generations hold must diverge or that the ties which bind us must break. In fact as we go through our lives we create and understand more of these ties, both with friends within our own generation and across generations within the family.

Now we can use these tools to get to grips with what is happening to the connections between us. Robert Putnam, the leading expert on the subject, describes social capital as 'the networks, norms, and trust that enable participants to act together more effectively to pursue shared objectives'.[16] It is the trust and social co-operation we analysed in the previous chapter when we showed we could think of it not as a social cement but instead as the sum of our co-operative strategies. A good starting point is the classic question: 'Would you say that most people can be trusted?' 'Yes,' said 44 per cent in the UK in one survey, compared with 38 per cent in the USA 'How often would people try to be fair or would they take advantage if they got the chance?': 53 per cent in Britain and 57 per cent in the US said most people try to be fair most of time.[17]

Those who say most people can be trusted also belong to voluntary groups. Of people who belong to no organizations 44 per cent say people can be trusted most of the time, compared with 48 per cent of people belonging to one and 75 per cent of people belonging to two or more organizations. There is a similar pattern when it comes to willingness to ask a neighbour to collect a prescription when out shopping. So involvement in institutions builds trust, confirming the account we offered in the previous chapter.[18] Younger people appear to be less trusting. But is this telling us that successive cohorts are less trusting or that we start off not very trusting and then become more trusting as we become older? Robert Putnam explains it as changes between successive cohorts. He says that the younger generations are less trusting: 'the decline in social trust in America is entirely generational, that is if you look at any birth cohort, average trust has not changed over time, but each successive birth cohort over the last thirty–forty years has become adult with a lower level of social trust.'[19] Of people who were born before 1914 45 per cent agreed most people can be trusted as against 31 per cent of those born after 1959.[20] It is as if this hole in society opened up with the baby boom.

Putnam believes this decline in trust in successive cohorts is a result of changes in the contract between the generations. He argues that the GI Bill providing a massive expansion of places at colleges and universities paid for out of taxes was a fantastic investment in the young men who came back from the Second World War – fighting for your country in your youth is a powerful way for your generation to stake a claim. The claim was honoured with a transformation of education opportunities for young Americans. This in turn gave them a sense of obligation which has left them the most civic generation in America's history. It is a potent piece of evidence of the power of the intergenerational contract. When I see a disconsolate 20-year-old I imagine him wading ashore on D-Day and the debt we would then owe his generation. Do we have any less of an obligation to the young man today?

The trouble is that, especially in the USA, the battles fought by the next generation, the boomers, were much more divisive than the battles fought in the Second World War. The boomers' civil rights campaigns and cultural wars divided people by age and attitudes whereas the soldiers of the Second World War had fought on behalf of whole nations and united different generations. So the boomers' battles, however justified, were more destructive of social capital. Indeed, one of their deliberate aims was to open up institutions to greater diversity: they wanted less conformity and for institutions to be more porous. This made it easier to join them and also to leave, but at the price of generating less trust.[21]

We showed in Chapter 5 how important institutions are in generating reciprocity and hence altruism. But there is some rather uncomfortable evidence of what happens to reciprocal altruism when institutions become more diverse. One ingenious experiment involves two partners in a game; the first player is given an opening stake; he can then give any proportion of this to the second player; this amount is doubled by the experimenter, and the second player then decides how much to return. He sends back less if the first player is of a different race or nationality so, in the words of the experimenters, 'heterogeneity may reduce trust' perhaps because there is less expectation of reciprocal altruism. In particular white Americans return little to Asians – cynics might say this appears to have become American economic policy. The better news is that the amount returned rises more than one for one with the amount sent, which is good evidence of reciprocal altruism.[22]

Trust appears to be in decline in Great Britain as well as in the USA. There is a reversal of attitudes going on: in 1959 young people were actually more trusting than the old but by 1990 this had reversed, with older people more trusting than young.[23] Membership of clubs and organizations has fallen. It appears to be a cohort effect too: 60 per cent of men born in 1946 belonged to at least one organization in their thirties, as against 15 per cent of men born in 1958 and 10 per cent of men born in 1970 in their thirties.[24]

So far we have looked at the loss of trust as an example of a cohort effect, with successive cohorts less trusting. There is evidence to support this explanation. But something else could be going on too – a life cycle effect with people becoming more trusting as they become older. Indeed, Peter Hall's survey of social capital in Britain suggests that 'levels of social capital generally seem to have remained reasonably high in Britain', this being disguised by the tendency of social capital to appear low amongst the young.[25] As we go through stages of the life cycle so we build up social capital – at least until we become very old, when we may be more isolated. So young people may appear to be less trusting than older people, but as they settle down and become rooted in a community we might expect their levels of trust to grow. Marriage increases civic engagement, for example, as measured by voting behaviour.[26] Parenthood is a key moment too. Having children can increase the civic engagement of their parents as they become more involved in the local community and create new networks though the play group and sharing the school run. A key figure in all this is the grandmother. She may be the custodian of a family's roots and traditions and a source of wisdom and advice , as we will see in Chapter 12.

This is a reason to hope successive generations will indeed put down roots and rebuild social capital. The only trouble is that our move through the life cycle is slower and messier than it used to be. Education is a good example. The evidence suggests that the longer you are in education the more friends and acquaintances you build up. More people are in education for longer so this should be good for social capital. But the amount of extra social capital you get out of each year of education is not as great as it was, so you need longer in education to accumulate the same network of friends; for example, Americans used to acquire 0.15 of a confidant for every year of education, but now this figure is down to 0.08.[27]

The trouble is that we are finding it harder to move through the stages of the life cycle. Our aspirations remain surprisingly conventional. Most young people say they want to settle down with someone they love in a marriage with kids, a decent job, and a home of their own. The evidence from attitude surveys shows how resilient and widespread marriage is as an aspiration. A survey of the attitudes of 25-year-old women revealed thoroughly modern attitudes to sex. They had an average of eight partners: two thirds had had a one-night stand. But 90 per cent said that they would like to get married and that they then expected their marriage to be faithful.[28] (One explanation sometimes put forward for delayed marriage is that weddings have become more expensive, but cause and effect may be the other way round. Weddings have become more expensive as a commitment device to show how serious we are about our relationship.)

There is no revolution against these bourgeois values. What is happening is that we are finding it harder to achieve them. What was previously a normal rite of passage to adulthood has instead become like scaling a distant peak that can only be conquered after years of effort and preparation. We find it harder to navigate the stages of the life cycle. Then we interpret what is really a delay in doing the big things of life as a wholesale abandonment of them. We misinterpret a slower process of moving through the life cycle as somehow a decline in commitment to them.

We think modern life is fast and urgent, but when it comes to the things that really matter, modern life is very slow. Getting started in the housing market, for example, is much harder than a generation ago – if it isn't high house prices it is the sheer difficulty of getting a mortgage. That means you are more dependent on your parents. Then there is the jobs market and the slow process of getting a job paying a family wage. The earnings of young people have fallen relative to older workers, even before the recession, which is already hitting young people hardest.

These tough conditions for getting jobs and houses in turn affect relationships. One reason is that it takes longer to work out what kind of life you might have with your partner. So you cohabit as neither partner quite feels they know enough to commit. Cohabitation can be a route to marriage but the relationship can easily break up and you boomerang back to your parents. This in turn means extra dependence on your parents for longer – the company advertising Lynx the deodorant to young men on the proposition it made them sexy have discovered that it is actually bought by mothers for their 20-something sons who are still at home. All this pushes back the average age of marriage, which has risen steadily, reaching 31.9 years for men and 29.8 years for women.[29] If things carry on as they are we will become even more dependent on our families for longer. So parents with more money can afford to support you and then pay for you to go out into the big wide world. It means a more divided society. We do our best for our own children even whilst our society gives a raw deal to young people as a whole – this is a reason for the decline in social mobility.

It is not that marriage has been rejected. If anything we have higher hopes of marriage than ever before. We are taking longer than before to find the right partner, but we are still searching for that person with whom we want to spend the rest of our lives – just ask Bridget Jones. Or how about Carrie, Samantha, Miranda and Charlotte from *Sex in the City*? Here is Rosie Boycott's take on the series:

The real secret of the show's appeal was that it gave confidence and reassurance in spades to the... growing world of singletons... being single is just a brief state to be got through as best you can so make the most of it. But beneath this well polished liberation... At the end of the day, the girl wants the boy and she wants him loyal, faithful and – preferably – bearing a ring.[30]

We are beginning to see what has reduced social trust. Younger cohorts who may feel the intergenerational contract has not been honoured may be less trusting. And although as we move through the life cycle we build up trust, this process itself has become slower and messier. There is something else going on, too, which helps explain these shifting patterns of trust and the disruption wrought by the boomers – changes in the relative size of successive cohorts.

We saw in Chapter 3 how thinkers such as Comte and more recently Richard Easterlin saw the different sizes of successive cohorts as giving a fundamental pattern to human affairs. They thought this gave them their different characters as they were imprinted with different economic experiences. We need not go as far as them but the shift in balance of ages in a population shapes the character of a society and changes relations between generations. We can measure changes from small to big cohorts through the way they change median age, the age of the middle person in a population. Imagine there has been a surge in the birth rate, creating an unusually big cohort. When this extra large cohort is young your society as a whole feels younger even whilst the steady processes of improving life expectancy is underway – that is one reason we look back to the 1960s as a time when the country was young: 1968 was when the first post-War baby boom peak got to 21. Such youthfulness is intoxicating. It also brings turmoil and even war.

What do Afghanistan, Iraq, Yemen, Congo, and Somalia have in common? They are all teenage countries. They all have a median age of 19 or under. Afghanistan is one of the youngest countries in the world: its median age is 16. This makes it far harder for tribal elders to exercise authority over the youthful Taliban. The other median ages estimated by the United Nations are Iraq (19), Yemen (17), Democratic Republic of Congo (16), and Somalia (18). Just above them are Zimbabwe, Nepal, and Sudan, all with a median age of 20. It is a list of the world's trouble spots.[31] The CIA attach a lot of importance to this demographic analysis and estimate that of the world's twenty-five youngest countries, sixteen have experienced war and civil bloodshed in the past decade. These young countries in particular have massive surges of teenage males. These young men will need food and worthwhile jobs – a challenge in itself. And how will they secure a position in society? One theory is that they will fight for it – either within their countries or by being sent abroad to fight – Europe's solution to its similar demographic challenge in the nineteenth century.[32]

China's population growth meant it was at its most youthful at the time of the Cultural Revolution. For Iran it was the time of the fall of the Shah. The median age of Russia in 1917 was 15. France was going through this sort of demographic turbulence at the time of the 1789 Revolution. Riding such a demographic surge of young people is the greatest single challenge to any social and political system – most do not survive it. Now the world faces just such a surge: 'Young people aged 10 to 19 are the largest age group in the world, making up close to 20 per cent of the 6.5 billion world population estimated in 2005, 85 per cent of whom live in developing countries and account for about one third of these countries' national populations.'[33]

So unlike our own dear country now, you may think. If you look at the median of advanced Western nations the picture is indeed very different.

Table 6. Median ages[34]

	1950	1980	2009	2050
UK	34.6	34.4	39.7	42.5
USA	30.0	30.1	36.5	41.7
China	23.9	22.1	33.8	45.2
World	24.0	23.0	28.9	38.4

The table shows that China's extraordinary demographic slow-down caused by its one-child policy will make it by 2050 one of the oldest countries the world has ever seen. After India, the world's second-largest population will be Chinese pensioners. The UK is also growing older with our median age rising. But this isn't the whole story. We have been clustering in places with people the same age as ourselves, a tendency reinforced by social housing allocation policies. We have about 12 million children out of a population of about 60 million. On average, therefore, across the country, there is approximately one child to four adults. But we are not evenly spread by age. On the tough estates, however, there are such large numbers of children relative to adults that demographically they are closer to some of the poorest and youngest parts of the World. Some of our social housing projects have ended up with three children to every two adults – six times the national average. Research by a leading housing expert suggested that changes in the age mix of an estate were crucial in explaining the growth of anti social behaviour: 'There is considerable evidence that the ratio of children to adults on estates affects the amount of bad or anti-social behaviour experienced.'[35] Although the two bodies of research, one on instability in the developing world and the other on anti-social behaviour on housing estates, have developed entirely separately from each other they have reached the same demographic explanation.

The best account of the impact of all these teenagers is not to be found in the works of the demographers but in William Golding's novel *Lord of the Flies*. It is a vivid and all too credible account of children turning feral when they find themselves trapped on an island without an adult after a plane crash. It was a deliberate counterpoint to the Victorian idyll of R. M. Ballantyne's *Coral Island* in which youngsters on their own are shown as being intrepid and co-operative. But even *Lord of the Flies* reaches a kind of happy ending when it only takes the arrival of a few adults to stop the savage blood-letting and to restore order. It is a tough job socializing successive generations of children, especially when there are lots of them. Even in sober law-abiding Britain we saw the turmoil that resulted when the baby boomers were coming to adulthood. The two most violent riots in post-War London were the Grosvenor Square riots of 1968 and the Brixton and Broadwater Farm riots of 1985. They occurred around twenty years after each of the post-War baby boom peaks.

———

Strengthening civil society means strengthening contact and the contract between the generations. But we are increasingly segregated by age. In 1991 just 3 per cent of 18- to 19-year-olds would have had to move in order to distribute themselves evenly across local authority boundaries. By 2001 this had gone up to 8 per cent. For 20- to 24-year-olds it went up from 8 per cent to 12 per cent.[36] This is partly driven by 'studentification' but it doesn't stop there. We work with our contemporaries too. One survey showed 9 per cent of employees in workplaces were aged between 16 and 21 but

15 per cent of workplaces had at least one quarter of their work-force in this age group... employees aged 50+ made up 20 per cent of the workforce but were at least a quarter of the workplace in 32 per cent of establishments.[37] Our friends tend to be contemporaries too. The family is one of the few places where this sort of intergenerational experience is still possible. We socialize as they do in *Friends* and live in families like the Simpsons. One reason why *The Simpsons* is so much deeper and more satisfying than *Friends* is that *The Simpsons* does show people of different ages interacting. *Friends*, by contrast, is focused narrowly on one 20-something age group. Individual age cohorts may have a strong sense of collective identity, shaped by shared formative events, but it is not quite a full, real community. Something precious is lost.

There does appear to have been a decline in social networks both of family and of friends. But networks of friends are shrinking faster, so the family is becoming relatively more important. Researchers have compared confidants with whom Americans discuss important matters in 1985 and 2004. Mean network size, including both family and friends, has fallen from 2.94 to 2.08. The number saying they have no confidant has trebled. And the number speaking regularly to at least one non-relative fell from 80 per cent to 57 per cent.[38] Both kin and non-kin have declined but as non-kin has fallen more this increases the relative importance of kin.

One piece of British research asked respondents to whom they would turn with the sorts of problems that can happen to anyone.[39] The results were striking.

Table 7. People turned to for various problems (percentage of respondents)

	Job	Help while ill	Borrowing money	Marital problem	Depression
Spouse/partner	58	61	21	9	47
Parent	8	13	20	15	8
Child	13	11	6	17	7
Sibling	4	3	4	12	6
Friend	7	5	2	27	21

Then researchers went on to explicitly to ask about comparisons between family and friends.

Table 8. Attitudes towards the family (percentage of respondents)

	Agree	Disagree	Neither
People should keep in touch with close family members even if they do not have much in common	70	18	10
People should always turn to their family before asking the state for help	48	19	29
I would rather spend time with my friends than my family	13	23	59
On the whole my friends are more important to me than members of my family	7	12	76

When asked about who they would turn to for advice or to borrow money, most people put fellow members of the family, often from a different age group, ahead of friends, who are often contemporaries. It is ties across the generations through families which matter to us above all. Indeed if anything the family is becoming more important as trust in others declines. It is partly because if you spread out across the generations there is much more you can do to shift money and the burdens of care, whereas within your own generation everybody is facing the same struggles and the same problems at the same time. So the intergenerational cover provided by the family makes it better as an insurance scheme. Indeed, this is why economists think of families as an imperfect annuities market. They have calculated that even small Anglo-Saxon families can do more than 70 per cent of the job of an annuity in enabling you to spread the risk of living longer than your savings.[40]

There is an important paradox here. In the rest of our lives we are divided more horizontally by our age group, working with and living in communities of people our age. But the shrinking of the family is taking it in the opposite direction to a beanpole with fewer siblings and cousins. If, to take one extreme example, Italy's fertility rate of 1.2 continues for two generations then, Nicholas Eberstadt has calculated, 'Almost three fifths of the nation's children will have no siblings, cousins, aunts, or uncles; they will have only parents, grandparents, and perhaps great-grandparents.'[41] The future is tall, thin families in a wide, flat world. This is why the family is becoming so important for delivering the intergenerational contract.

Strong families are very powerful ways of passing on advantage from generation to generation. It is a genuine and legitimate source of deep fulfilment for many people. Studies of changing values also show us the ability to provide for one's family is a key driver of self-worth. In four surveys from 1968 to 1981, 'family security' came in second or first as a life goal, leading 'companionship' or 'a comfortable life'. It is surely no coincidence that the people most likely to be unhappy are divorced or unemployed – both events sever that sense of keeping a family and discharging our obligations across the generations.[42] These are very powerful findings. They are just as powerful as the earlier evidence from a different research project on the events that matter to people. Again, it is these deep and real ties across the generations that matter to people. In the 1960s and 1970s there was a lot of worry about the generation gap, the rows and tensions above all within the family as different generations could not get on. That gap has largely gone, to be replaced by an economic gap between the generations.

The best single advantage you can have is parents who are committed to the project of investing in you and your future. That probably means they have got married, an important form of commitment to this project. That advantage tends to go with many others. Poor families are far more vulnerable to breakdown than well-off families. Kay Hymowitz has analysed this phenomenon in America and shown that family structure is creating what she calls a new caste society.[43] The well-educated and well-off stick together whereas poorer families find it harder. New British evidence from the Millennium cohort study shows that 5 per cent of degree-educated mothers split before their child's third birthday compared to 42 per cent of mothers without qualifications.[44] This is not simply an education effect – the biggest factor influencing whether couples stay together was marriage, followed by age; then came education, income, ethnic group, and being on benefits. A separate study showed that by a child's fifth birthday, 8 per cent of married parents have split up, 57 per cent of cohabitees and 25 per cent of those who married after the birth.[45] Whatever the exact pattern of cause and effect the conclusion is clear: families powerfully transmit advantage from one generation to the next. We are better at providing for our own children than looking after the interests of the next generation as a whole. We are indeed better parents than we are citizens. We shall pursue the implications in Chapters 9 and 10.

Chapter 7

Why Bother About the Future?

He was a liberal-minded aristocratic reformer who played a big role in the early stages of the French Revolution but, like the reformers in Russia in 1917 or Iran in 1979, he himself was then consumed by the Revolution. He was condemned by Robespierre and went into hiding before being captured and dying in mysterious circumstances whilst in detention. Knowing he did not have long to live, he scribbled notes on the back of revolutionary posters in which he dreams of humanity moving to perfection. And what is this utopia? He envisages a world where people become ever more prosperous, freedom and democracy are assured, foreign colonies gain self-government, free secular education spreads equality of opportunity, there is no discrimination by race, class, or gender, and a benign government insures you against the risks of poverty, ill-health, and old age. Of all the eccentric utopias envisaged by political thinkers, Condorcet's *Sketch for a Historical Picture of the Progress of the Human Mind* has the distinction of being the one that got closest to the hopes and in many ways the reality of the modern world. At the same time William Godwin, an English radical, was writing his *Enquiry Concerning Political Justice and Its Influence on General Virtue and Happiness*. He envisaged a world where it was understood that vice and evil were not individual failures but a consequence of social problems, and as we improved social conditions so vice would be eliminated and we could achieve ever more freedom and happiness.

A young Anglican parson with a formidable mathematical mind read these two revolutionary texts and concluded that their utopias rested on a simple fallacy. Thomas Malthus replied in his *Essay on the Principle of Population*[1] that the population would grow much faster than the resources, notably the food, which they needed. He thought their utopias were mathematically impossible: the population would grow geometrically (multiplying every generation) but the food supply would only grow arithmetically (adding a fixed amount per generation).[2] The result of such population growth would not be human perfection but misery and vice. By misery Malthus means starvation. By vice he means sex outside marriage and without children: indeed, you could argue this is what has happened as contraception with earlier sex but later childbearing has lowered the birth rate from what it was in his day.

All three books were published in the 1790s and in a way we are still arguing about them now. By and large the optimists have won – even conservative economists now subscribe to a world view closer to those eccentric utopian revolutionaries. Worries about the future are denounced as Malthusianism. Malthus himself is accused of the fallacy of failing to realize that if the human population could multiply so might the resources of the natural world, such as for example domesticated animals. And even when there are constraints on natural resources, advances in technology can overcome them – hence the observation that the Stone Age did not end because they ran out of stones. Moore's law that the number of transistors which can be placed on an integrated circuit doubles approximately every two years captures modern attitudes. It takes the original Malthusian model of multiplying growth of population and turns it round by applying the same mathematical relationship to our technological capacities.

This optimism about long-term growth has a profound effect on the contract between the generations. The Iroquois were supposed to have a rule in their tribal council that they should consider the impact of any decision on the next seven generations. But imagine that each generation of our tribe of primitive hunter-gatherers became more skilled at making straighter spears better for hunting and sharper scythes better for gathering berries and wheat. Then each generation would believe its successors were going to be better off. The deliberations of the tribal elders would be very different. They might be willing to take larger contributions from the younger generation coming along behind, expecting they would have more to live on when they were older.

In a country growing at 5 per cent per annum, GDP is doubling every fifteen years. A 20-year-old would expect that at the age of 50 he or she would live in a society four times as wealthy and by the age of 65 it would be eight times so. Any attempt to help future generations appears to be a shift from the poor (us now) to the rich (them then). Instead of worrying about our grandchildren we think we can take from them some of the extra wealth they are going to enjoy. Disraeli may have denounced an opponent because 'He thinks posterity is a pack-horse, always ready to be loaded.' But we have to face the response that in the future the pack-horse will be far sturdier than anything we have now so we should worry about the here and now, where there are quite enough problems thank you very much.

Conventional market economics has a powerful mechanism for putting a value today on future income and costs. The social discount rate is the way economists describe how much a pound in a year's time would be worth to you now. Imagine a world with no inflation and no risk. If you were due to receive £105 in a year's time, how much would you settle for right now instead. If, under these conditions, you attach the same value to £105 in a year's time as £100 today then you have got a typical social discount rate of 5 per cent. It is an essential tool for any economist trying to work out what the payback is from any kind of investment. If you set a discount rate at 5 per cent then costs and benefits more than twenty or thirty years out do not have much value today. It tells us that the future more than a generation or so ahead counts for little.

Environmental economics with its powerful concept of sustainability is changing all this. In his report on climate change Nicholas Stern explicitly sets a very low social discount rate of 0.1 per cent.[3] Indeed, he argues that really we should value costs and benefits in the future at exactly the same value as they have today – there is no rational basis for pure time preference. It is only 0.1 rather than 0 because, being the rigorous economist that he is, he wants to allow for the modest risk of the extinction of the human race. The 0.1 per cent is to allow for the slight chance of there being nobody around in the future to enjoy it. It is as if he looks at the distant future through a powerful telescope so it suddenly looms much larger. That means £1bn of cost then is as expensive as £1bn today. The critics of Stern argue that he should assume a more typical higher discount rate so future environmental costs on future generations do not look so expensive. He argues that conventional economic analysis might work for appraising particular investment projects but it does not work when we are assessing fundamental issues such as scarce natural resources and indeed the cultures we have created with them – be it Venice or the Maldives. It is the same thought as Margaret Thatcher's: 'No generation has a freehold on this earth. All we have is a life tenancy with a full repairing lease.'[4]

We may admire Nick Stern's moral judgement that we cannot value future generations any lower than ourselves. It does not sound very moral for us to say that we should prefer our pleasure now to the pleasure of our great-grandchildren. But we have to recognize our own inconvenient truth – distance in both space and time does affect the claims people have on us. Stern's unusually low discount rate is indeed like a telescope, offsetting our natural tendency to focus on the here and now. Dickens mocks such an attitude in the famous portrait of Mrs Jellyby, the 'telescopic philanthropist' who devotes all her energies to 'Borrioboola-gha' and ignores the wretched children around her.[5] And if we are to stick with the naturalistic morality we described in Chapter 5 this may be one area where we find our local loyalties do not stretch so far out into the future. There are good reasons why we do not behave as Stern wants us to – we would be paralysed by endlessly having to attach the same value to everything and everybody however far away in the future. So the criticism of Stern is that he is not describing how we currently value the future but proposing a very different standard, far removed from everyday life.

We have a dilemma. There is a conventional economic device of the discount rate which basically says we do not need to attach much weight to anything more than a generation or so out. And we have an attempt to argue that we should calibrate it so we attach equal value to the future, which appears to be implausible. But this smart dismissal of Stern leaves us uneasy that future generations might curse us for our insouciance. Even John Locke, the ultimate classical liberal, had the principle that enough and as good should be left for future generations and we do appear to be breaching that principle. Is there a way out of the dilemma?

One way is to go back to the realities of human psychology and look at how we actually behave. Then we liberate ourselves from the tyranny of the straight line. We see that when it comes to short-term decisions over the next few years we do indeed have quite a high discount rate, so money now is worth quite a bit more than money in, say, four years' time. These are the typical short-term decisions for which conventional discount rates work quite well. But then we appear to attach continuing value to costs and bene-fits ten or twenty or more years out – we do not continue discounting them at the same rate. So we can draw a discount rate not as a straight line but as a hyperbola with the value of the future falling sharply at first and then flattening out. This enables us to combine conventional discount rates for normal purposes and also to attach some value to what our grandchildren face. (This in turn leads to some imaginative proposals for nudging our behaviour – for example, it might be hard to get people to save more out of their current income but they are more willing to commit to save a significant part of pay increases a few years out.)[6]

Stern still has the challenge that we will be richer in the future. Even if we value £1,000 in the future the same as £1,000 today, he still accepts they will be better off in the future so they will command more resources than us now and so be able to do more. But he replies that 1 per cent of GDP in the future will only yield the same amount of happiness to people in the future as 1 per cent of GDP today, so they will be not really be better off than we are. It is combining this assumption with his ultra-low discount rate that has really generated the controversy amongst economists. If we believed that future generations would not really feel any better off, and that it would take greater resources then for them to achieve any given level of happiness, we would do an enormous amount of saving for future generations. But that isn't how we behave. Stern has not just offered a neutral economic analysis; he has in effect called for us to attach more value to the future than we do at the moment.[7]

The Stern Review accepts we will still enjoy strong economic growth but also wants to argue we should spend money on protecting the environment now, not in the future when we will be richer. The assumptions he uses to generate these conclusions are what have proved so controversial.[8] Instead we could just challenge the assumption that the next generation is bound to be so much richer than us. That is what they do in an episode of *South Park* – 'Goobacks'. Time travellers start arriving from the future because life is tough then and they are looking for work. Everything Americans say about Mexican immigrants is run as an argument about whether to let in these impoverished time travellers.[9]

Such fears immediately face the charge of neo-Malthusian pessimism. We certainly have to recognize that the innovative power of the almost 7 billion humans alive today is a resource which dwarfs all others. And the future may be a world transformed for the better, just as Condorcet expected. But some of the very same critics who are keen to stress the uncertainties in the science of global warming seem to be sublimely confident that post-War economic growth as enjoyed in the West can carry on automatically. We do not need to speculate about the distant future. If we just look out over the next fifty years we can already see the problems facing advanced Western nations like our own. These are not speculations but trends which are in train now. We know that the bulge of post-War baby boomers in many advanced Western countries will grow old and will reach a point when they want to command a lot of resources without working to generate them any more. We know that the environment is changing fast and avoiding or, more likely now, adapting to these changes is going to be very expensive. We also know that we are currently seeing a massive increase in public debt which will have to be paid for out of our taxes then. These are good reasons why the next generation may not be as much better off as we like to think.

The focus on the environmental threat has very much been on climate change. This may indeed have massive effects. But even this is only one of a series of interacting pressures on the environment.[10] The rate of growth of the world's population is levelling off but the UN's central forecast is still that it will rise to about 9 billion in the next fifty years.[11] The growth of total demand for food may slow a bit as population growth slows. But if people enjoy rising incomes, as we hope, then that means much greater demand for meat and dairy products – as we have already seen in China. One forecast is a doubling of demand for meat by 2050. That means more land for livestock and more animal feed for them. That can be achieved with another green revolution in agriculture driven by higher prices encouraging investment in agriculture. But the price signals themselves are painful.[12] Big increases in agricultural output in turn mean big increases in water needed for agriculture. Already 1.2 billion people are affected by water scarcity and that could get much worse. Much of the water we are using in some key agricultural areas is being extracted from depleting acquifers. It is hard to predict total water demand but one model forecasts increases in the range of 35–60 per cent between 2000 and 2025.[13] Desalination is one obvious technology to tackle water shortages and again one instinctively trusts human ingenuity to develop it and other solutions. But desalinating water, like making fertilizer, is energy-intensive so it will put yet more pressure on energy demand. We can look to ingenious solutions here too. A recent example is America's encouragement of bio-ethanol. But using agricultural crops as a source of energy in turn puts more pressure on land use and has a knock-on effect on food prices. It is the sheer interconnectedness of these pressures – population, food, water, energy – which makes the global challenge all the greater.

All this is before factoring in climate change itself. It threatens some of the world's most productive agricultural areas, such as California. There are gainers from climate change as well as losers – Canada and Russia seem to do well in most scenarios. Opening up Siberia as it thaws (releasing enormous amounts of greenhouse gases in the process) is potentially of enormous significance for Russia and China but it will not come cheap. And meanwhile we will be having to divert resources into adapting to climate change, with, for example, massive investment in flood defences.

This is not an attempt to make your flesh creep. It would be very unwise to endorse any particular forecast of what might happen. And one can reasonably hope that human ingenuity will see us through and world GDP will continue to grow. But it might not feel much like growth as we know it. Imagine that you were told your income was going to increase by half as much again by 2030 – pretty good you might think. But then you are told that a lot of that extra income will be going on higher energy bills, higher food prices (with meat especially affected), and higher levies to pay for flood protection, and that the water meter in your house will rattle up costs like a taxi meter in central London. Then you would not be quite so sure that this growth automatically meant greater prosperity. And you might wish that a bit more had been done sooner to prepare for all this. But we aren't doing that.

Saving for the future in Britain and America shrank to catastrophically low levels during the boom years when we should have been setting money aside for a rainy day, as we saw in Chapter 4. This has affected levels of investment. You need a lot of basic infrastructure to enable a modern economy to function effectively.

It is key to the technological innovation we are relying on because people have to be able to cluster together and organizing that is expensive. But in the UK our level of business investment has plummeted to historic lows. The official figures have been flattered by high levels of investment in software and other short term investment which gets a high return but only lasts a few years. We have not been so good at the long-run investment in infrastructure.[14]

We can now see how financial innovation has eroded the commitment devices needed to save and invest for the future. Imagine an island where there is a goose that lays a golden egg every month. By selling the gold every month and investing some of the proceeds they gradually become more prosperous. Then some innovative bankers sail into harbour and everything changes. For them the flow of golden eggs is a guaranteed income stream. You do not have to wait for anything as vulgar as the goose actually to lay the egg before you enjoy the income from it. You can write contracts promising to pay an income out of future golden eggs and sell those contracts today. The goose and her eggs can be priced, leased, mortgaged, and securitized. They say to the goose's owner that the family should be able to control their own flow of income to meet their own needs, which are quite independent of the goose's egg-laying habits. It is all very plausible.

But it has a consequence which we are confronting now. David Laibson has shown, using sophisticated calculations which he calls, of course, the golden eggs model, how an economy could move from above the amount of savings needed to sustain its growth to below it by the simple expedient of increasing credit availability. Increasing liquidity effectively diminishes the effectiveness of savings vehicles as commitment devices and so reduces personal welfare. He shows that when access to credit rose dramatically in the USA in the 1980s and 1990s, savings fell from an average of 7.3 per cent in 1946–83 to 5.3 per cent in 1985–94.[15]

Borrowing against your goose's future egg-laying worked fine for a time. You enjoyed higher living standards as you borrowed against future golden eggs. And you might even have persuaded yourself that you were spending the extra money on really worthwhile things that would make you more prosperous in the long run. But the losers if your gamble goes wrong are your children and grandchildren because they inherit the family goose and find that its income is allocated to pay off various bond-holders who appear now to have a bigger stake in your goose than you do. The next generation find that they have to work harder for longer to pay their debts. This is why future generations are the real losers from the current financial crisis.

An implacable sceptic might concede that perhaps future generations are not going to be so much better off after all but still say, 'So what? Stuff happens.' Different generations born at different times get dealt a good hand or a bad hand by history. Life is hard enough for us without bearing the burden of providing for future generations who may not even be born yet. Future generations have no claim on us, any more than we have a claim on generations that came before us. Even if the baby boomers are getting a particularly good deal and their successors a raw deal that is their problem not ours and does not put us under any moral obligation to do anything about it. In the famous words of one Irish MP: 'Why should we do anything for posterity; for what has posterity done for us?'[16] The answer is of course that we are the posterity of previous generations and they did do things for us – from fighting for us to building schools and churches. That is why it was so important to establish in Chapter 5 that there is indirect as well as direct reciprocity. The argument in earlier chapters that the social contract is a contract between the generations is one answer to this challenge. But we can go further in explaining how valuing the future is fundamental to us as humans and how our society works. It helps to look at it in three stages.

First, there are the claims of future generations as yet unborn. There are tricky philosophical issues about attributing rights to people who do not yet exist, though the implicit contracts which we listed in Chapter 5 could still apply. We are not, after all, talking about legal documents but the social contracts that keep families and nations going. You might, for example, think it was wrong to borrow against the buy-to-let flat which you hope to give to your potential grandchildren, some of whom are as yet unborn. Nevertheless this is the most ambitious claim.

Then there is the second stage – our obligations to the next generation, young people who are already born. For them the intergenerational exchanges we set out in Chapter 5 have certainly begun. We are assuming that in future they will produce wealth and pay taxes to pay for services we will need. For example, the pensions we hope to live on are claims on future resources which they will have to create for us at the time. We are not squirrels setting aside nuts now. The bread we will eat in the future does not exist now. Ultimately we just have claims on the bread that the younger generation will be baking. Some of those claims rest on the state's power to tax future income and others rest on our shares in businesses giving us a claim on their future earnings. Either way we need to behave fairly towards them now so that they will share their bread with us then. The reciprocity is becoming clear.

Thirdly, just think of us in the future. The median age in Britain today is 40. Rather neatly, a person of that age can expect to live for roughly another forty years. So the middle person in Britain is at the mid-point of their lives. As a nation we are on the cusp, perfectly balanced between past and future. The big challenges we face – the costs of adjusting to environmental change, demographic burdens as the boomers age, and the taxes to service massive public debt are all issues that arise well within the next forty years. The key date is 2050, when the middle person in Britain today might be getting to the end of their life and the youngest boomer will be 85. Up to then the future probably includes the majority of us. Even a selfish majority should care about our circumstances to 2050. Perhaps we cannot expect people to look forward for the rest of their lives so we can just look twenty years ahead to 2030. That is less than one generation ahead. It is the pinch-point when many of the pressures we have identified come together. It is when the million people born in the first peak year of our baby boom get to 83 and may be needing more care. It is when the challenge of global population movements from areas of environmental distress looks potentially quite serious. But it is too soon for transformational technologies like nuclear fusion to be harnessed for us. Even if valuing other people's future is too much, the boomers might be expected to care about their own. At least the boomers need to confront the risks they are running with their own futures – unless of course we are all going the way of Phineas Gage.

Phineas Gage was by all accounts a sober, prudent, gratification-deferring working man, blasting a route for the American railroads in the 1840s. That was until he had a horrific industrial accident in which a spike went into his head, destroying some of his brain. He survived but thereafter he was totally impulsive, his capacity to plan for the future had been lost.[17] A lot of our problems arise from our difficulty in valuing the future, deferring gratification. As

Avner Offer argues in his important book,[18] our ability to think prudently about the future has eroded. We worry about growing childhood obesity. It is just so seductive to eat those sugary foods, and to keep on eating them. In the past ten years the number of girls aged 2–15 who are obese has risen by 51 per cent and the number of obese boys is up by 65 per cent.[19] Then there was the explosion of personal borrowing: it was just so tempting to use that credit card, and keep on using it. It is hard to say no to that extra borrowing. It seems just as difficult for teenagers to say no to early sex or at least to be sensible about contraception: 35 per cent of 15-year-old boys and 40 per cent of girls reported that they had had sexual intercourse, one of the highest rates in Europe.[20] Childhood obesity, high rates of personal debt, and teenage pregnancy are not really different problems, but are the same problem – the difficulty we all face trying to resist our appetites of today in the cause of something better in the future.

What we are talking about here is prudence. Here is Adam Smith's account:

The qualities most useful to ourselves are, first of all, superior reason and understanding, by which we are capable of discerning the remote consequences of all our actions and of forseeing the advantage and detriment which is likely to result from them and secondly self-command by which we are enabled to abstain from present pleasure and to endure present pain in order to obtain a greater pleasure or to avoid a greater pain in some future time. In the union of those two qualities consists the virtue of prudence, of all the virtues that which is most useful to the individual.[21]

We have more choices and more temptations than ever so our capacity for such self-command matters: it is the ultimate soft skill. Gray's 'Elegy' is treated nowadays as an ode to social mobility.

As the poet reflects on the lives that are marked in that churchyard he does think of the missed opportunities – an appeal that particularly touches our modern sensibility. But he goes on to make a rather different point – about evil averted because of the absence of temptation. Modern life is full of new temptations. Our self-control is tested in a way that was not possible until Britain emerged from austerity after the War – when one of first responses was of course a baby boom.

There is a permanent battle for self-control in a modern consumer culture. With all these temptations we need to signal that we have self-control. One reason for our obsession with being thin is that we want to offer evidence of self-control in an age of temptations.[22] It would be very convenient if self control were like a muscle which got stronger the more it was used. Sadly the evidence is that it resembles more a scarce natural resource – like water in a flask, you can use it up. Researchers ask a group of people to regulate or suppress some thought whilst watching a film clip and a control group are given no such instruction. Then you ask them to squeeze a handgrip hard for as long as possible. The group asked to regulate their thoughts give up much sooner on the hand grip.[23] So self-control may be in limited supply. Resisting temptation once does not appear to make it easier a second time.

One of the most famous tests of our capacity for self-control is the experiment conducted by Walter Mischel in the 1960s.[24] He offered children aged 4 the choice between one marshmallow now or two in twenty minutes' time. The ones who were able to wait for the second marshmallow subsequently massively outperformed the other group in America's Scholastic Aptitude test. It is a key element of what we now think of as emotional intelligence. The value children place on the future has also been measured in a study engagingly entitled *Economic Experiments You Can Perform at Home on Your Children.*[25] A child loses a tooth and leaves it under their pillow night after night. Each day they delay handing it over to their parents an extra dime accrues for them. So you start off with high percentage returns but they fall relative to the amount you have built up in your tooth deposit. The research shows children do indeed have very high discount rates, 3 per cent per day, which fall as they get older.

The capacity to defer gratification is clearly very important. But instead of just telling people to pull their socks up we need to think about the circumstances in which this capacity flourishes. How do we resist these temptations and exercise prudence? Dieters provide a useful clue. Dieters need a plan for the future which makes it all worthwhile. People who find it hard to diet lack a sense of how it is all part of a long-term plan, so the sacrifice seems meaningless to them. Evidence for this came after 9/11, when Americans were deeply uncertain about their future and many gave up their diets, observing, 'Life is too short to suffer again through... celery sticks.'[26]

This is the clue that enables us to get back to the tricky philosophical question that has been hovering over our discussion since Chapter 5. It is the most metaphysical of all the challenges to this concern about the future – from the philosopher Derek Parfit. He deploys some of the most trenchant challenges to the idea of obligations across the generations, arguing we cannot have obligations to people who do not yet exist. But he goes further with his scepticism. He would not even be satisfied with our more modest appeal to our own futures twenty or forty years out. Parfit's radical challenge to our conventional notions of personal identity is to ask whether me in twenty years' time is really the same person as me now.[27]

His ideas have now been tested empirically by asking people of different ages how similar they are to what they used to be like and how similar they expect their future selves to be. One thing old and young have in common is greater expectation of change in the next ten years. It is the middle-aged who are most connected to their other selves. They are also the ones who are most linked into the different stages of the life cycle and bear the greatest burden of other generations.[28] As we saw in Chapter 6, the young live in the present, and although older people do worry about the future they are sadly not going to be around for so long to shape it. The baby boomers are at the stage of the life cycle when they should be most susceptible to these appeals to the future. (And separate research shows that we make the most rational calculations of future risk when we are aged around 53.[29]) The key issue in our ability to control ourselves may be connectedness – the links between us now and how we think we could be in the future.

The narrative we need to link us to ourselves in the past and the future is not that different from the one linking us to other people. Indeed, it might be like our evidence on empathy and consciousness – we first learn to value the future in relation to others and then apply it to ourselves. We can see this if we go back to that evidence on deferring gratification. That classic study by Mischel appeared to show East Asians in Trinidad were willing to forego a dollar today for a dollar fifty cents tomorrow but the black population preferred the dollar today. What lies behind this? It isn't ethnic. His research showed the key was father absence – if you had lacked an authority figure you trusted to do things for you in the future you found it much harder to have your own plans for the future and make sacrifices for them. So once again the intergenerational exchange within the family proves to be crucial to shaping our character. Inability to defer gratification is not a psychological, let alone moral, defect in a child; it is an understandable response to particular circumstances which make it difficult to trust in a project for the future.

Ability to plan for the future is very closely linked to the reciprocal altruism we focused on in Chapter 5. Reciprocity depends on being able to value future benefits in return for sacrifices today. And the neuroscientists have indeed established that the same bit of the brain which makes decisions on inter-temporal choices is used for altruism and fairness. It is the limbic system which lights up for immediate rewards, whereas the lateral prefrontal cortex is lit up by inter-temporal choices. This is also the bit of the brain which protects our sense of fairness (and which the scientists temporarily disabled in the Ultimatum game experiment we described in Chapter 5). This tends to confirm our explanation of our behaviour then – we reject the unfair deal because we think we are part of a set of long-term exchanges.[30] The capacity to engage in long-term reciprocal exchange with others and our ability to have a long-term plan for ourselves are linked.

We need an environment rich in commitment devices, and that includes institutions with long and stable histories where we can be confident of rewards and indeed penalties out into the future. These will work to protect not just our own futures but those of future generations too. It is hard to imagine a society where individuals are good at deferring gratification for themselves but uninterested in others. Indeed, future generations can be the project which causes us to exercise self-control.

The link can also be thought of as operating through the stages of the life cycle. Those exchanges we analysed in Chapter 5 are also between us now and us in the future – the contracts are between us at different stages of the life cycle. Perhaps Charles Dickens can help us bring all this together. In *A Christmas Carol* Scrooge is forced to observe himself at other stages of his life (and after) and that leads him to change his behaviour now.

Alfred Nobel, the inventor of dynamite, had an experience not unlike that which Dickens created for Scrooge. His brother died but a French newspaper got them confused and reported it was Alfred who had died, so he found himself reading his own obituary, entitled 'The Merchant of Death is Dead'. It was this which led him to change the direction of his life and give away most of his fortune to endow the Nobel Prizes. We give meaning to our lives by trying to leave something for future generations coming after. Reflecting on our mortality encourages this. If you conduct interviews with people near a funeral parlour about how much they would give to charity, without making any explicit connection, they will volunteer to give more than when in a more neutral environment.[31]

Thinking about future generations, instead of being like a particularly superhuman exercise in virtue, may actually be so strong that it encourages us to be altruistic. An interesting experiment to test this asked people to imagine they were running a logging company which makes bigger profits this year the more trees it cuts down. But there is a choice about how many to cut down. In fact there are three different trade-offs, each of which invites a sacrifice of some income and profit this year. One says that if the participants cut down fewer trees this year they would make more profits in the future as the forest will continue to generate income for them – a trade-off between personal prosperity now and in the future. The second trade-off is that if they do not chop down so many trees more of the forest could be made available to the community to enjoy now. This is a trade-off between self-interest and altruism now. The third trade-off is that if they do not cut down so many trees future generations could enjoy them. When people played these roles they were most susceptible to an appeal to restrain their logging to protect the interests of future generations. If people have to make sacrifices, they are most willing to do so if it is for future generations.

Chapter 8

What Governments Do

A nation is, along with the family, a way of transmitting a body of knowledge and culture from one generation to the next. We may do our best as individuals to pass on something worthwhile to our own children: it is a powerful and benign instinct. But we cannot rely on individual families to do it all and indeed too much dependence on family inheritance weakens progress to a more open and mobile society. We cannot just respond to the challenge of justice across the generations individually, family by family. Governments matter too. They have the power to sustain or break the contract between the generations.

If our account of the pattern of people's lives is on the right lines, then it should help us make sense of how the modern welfare state does this. We don't need a complicated account of tax rules and benefit entitlements. Such detail can all too often obscure any sense of the structure that lies behind them. We won't start with finance or politics either. We can grasp the basics from the tribes of the Amazonian rainforest.

We will start with the food our hunter-gatherers obtain and consume. They do not yet have money or government so we can look behind these to the fundamentals of calorie consumption. Humans spend much longer than chimpanzees dependent for their calorie intake on parents and other adults. The family is a commitment to share food; indeed, sharing meals still remains at the heart of family life and its decline into serial grazing is a trend we worry about.

Studies of surviving groups of hunter-gatherers show that until the children reach the age of 5 they are heavy consumers of the energy generated by others – which any parent could have told them. They then have a long period when they are semi-independent but are not making any net contribution. Much more than other mammals humans go for food which is hard to obtain but high in nutritional value. It takes a long time to learn the skills to get this. That is one reason why we have always been dependent on our parents for an exceptionally long time. The calorific value of the food youngsters produce takes a long time to catch up with and overtake the value of their food consumption: when that happens they reach adulthood. They then contribute through a long life of hunting and gathering in which they reach their peak net contribution quite late on, especially the more skilled hunters. Then old age starts reducing their performance and they become once again net recipients of calories generated by others. One study of three surviving foraging groups, the Ache and the Hiwi of South America and the Hadza, the last remaining hunter-gatherers in Africa, calculated when these transitions occurred. You might just recognize the key ages for these shifts in surviving hunter-gatherer tribes to being a net producer and then once more becoming dependent – they were 18 and 65.[1]

These late ages of transition may be surprising because child labour has been widespread in primitive societies and in the developing world. Some researchers might indeed place the age when a youth becomes a net contributor a bit earlier, perhaps 15. But one study of a contemporary developing country, the Ivory Coast, also showed a surprisingly high age when young people became net producers in the rural economy (over 20 years old). It was even higher in the town than the countryside (closer to 30 years old) because their urban consumption was higher when they were young. Even though young people are producing, it is less than what they are consuming. This tells us something very important. In most societies families deliver big net transfers to young people which carry on well into their teens and quite possibly beyond. These transfers predate modern government. The general pattern across these societies has been for a substantial flow of resources in the family down to the young people. Older people carry on working but with less efficiency so they eventually also become net recipients. But the scale of these receipts is modest compared with what young people receive.[2]

We like to think of the modern state as redistributing from rich to poor. But that doesn't really give us a full sense of what it is all about. The welfare state is also supplementing or even displacing the family as a device for transmitting resources across the generations. It takes money from us at times when we are earning a lot and provides for us at times when we are not; that means transferring money from the middle-aged to the young and old.[3] The key ages for transfers of resources in the modern welfare state match broadly the calorie transfers of our primitive hunter-gatherers, though the trend is for the age you start full-time paid work and the age you retire to shift later. You get educated up to about the age of 18 or more. Then you become a net taxpayer. When you are older you are once more a recipient of public resources, delivered both as your pension and also as health care.

Education is what we owe our children. Much of health care and all pensions are the debt we owe our parents. In Britain we devote about £50bn of public spending to educating the under-18s. Child Benefit and Child Tax Credits add another £30bn or so. The total

NHS budget is about £100bn. One estimate is that we devote less than £500 a year of public spending on health care for a person of working age, £1,500 on people aged 65–74, £2,400 on those aged 75–84 and £4,000 a year on health care for those aged over 85.[4] So perhaps £50bn goes to the over-65s. We also spend about £75bn on benefits for pensioners.

Modern government in the industrialized world appears to operate differently from these transfers within families in primitive societies. It may be the consequence of industrialization or the democratic power of older voters, but in modern Western welfare states the flow appears to be much more towards the older generation. Think of your own family. How much care and attention has been devoted to children as against older parents – probably more to the children? But then think of what the welfare state does. The value of the pension and the health care exceeds the cost of schools and Child Benefit. Modern government shifts resources upwards to older people. It works very differently from family flows.

We can confirm this account by looking at how money is redistributed by government – the income tax we pay and the benefits we receive. It is a neat comparison because total income tax revenues of approximately £158bn in 2007–8 were not too far from total spending on benefits and tax credits of approximately £136bn in the same year.[5] Income tax is above all a tax on middle-aged men – men aged 35–55 pay £63bn, two fifths of the total from men and women. (The table at the end of this chapter gives the full breakdown.)[6] Some men may think it proves that they bear the heaviest burden. Others may think it is powerful evidence that women's earnings are still far too low compared with men's. But the message from the figures is stark.

Now let's look at who receives the main social security benefits.

There is a transfer across the generations – most benefits are paid to old people or for children. In fact, over-60s account for three quarters of benefit spending (£74bn out of a total of £99bn of spending).[7] There is also a transfer to women particularly as mothers or those, be they widows or lone parents, who are not living with a man. Men get more per person from, for example, the contributory state pension, but as there are many fewer men than women pensioners, the total pensions budget is still skewed towards women – 62 per cent of pension spending goes to women. The only exception to these general rules is compensation for people of working age who are not able to work, notably unemployment and working age disability benefits, which does go disproportionately to middle-aged men. But overall the tax and benefits system shifts resources from the middle-aged to the old and to the young and from men to women. Sometimes critics say that the tax and benefits system just robs Peter to pay Paul – it churns money around for no real purpose. That is one of its problems. But it also does something else – the system takes from Peter to pay Kylie and Edith.

Education, health care, and benefits together account for over 60 per cent of all public spending. The overall pattern is clear. The modern welfare state provides services to you when you are young, extracts a large amount of income tax from you when you are middle-aged, and then once more provides you with services and cash when you are old. John Hills calculates that, in 2001, a middle-aged person received on average education, health, and benefits worth about £2,000, someone in their seventies about £8,000 a year, and someone in their eighties about £10,000.[10] At any one moment it may look as if we are paying them but really we are both contributors and beneficiaries at different stages of our lives. In the wise words of Nick Barr, we should think of much of the modern welfare state not so much as Robin Hood but more as a piggy bank.[9] The best estimate of the balance of these roles is that it is three quarters piggy bank and one quarter Robin Hood.[10] (The piggy bank does not need to have a separate fund; it just has to be a programme that we have a reasonable expectation of receiving from as well as paying for.) Most Western countries distinguish explicitly between social security, which is contributory, and means-tested welfare for the poor, which is not. Britain's debate about social policy gets unusually muddled because we have lost sight of this important distinction, perhaps because of our confusing history in which first health care was financed on a contributory basis and then pensions instead.[11]

One research project measured how much poverty and inequality affected the size of the welfare state in advanced Western countries. If the welfare state had a Robin Hood function you might expect it to grow when there were wider disparities of income. But they did not find any such correlation. It is the piggy bank which matters more.[12] Of course, there are very important arguments about how the welfare state could do the job better and not undermine key values such as work or saving or family. There are also arguments about whether this redistribution across the life cycle has to be done by the state. You could imagine a society where this smoothing out of income across the life cycle was achieved differently. You would borrow lots of money when you were young in order to finance your education, repaying the loan in your peak years of earning, and then, after you have done that, setting money aside to pay for your pension and the social care you need. That is increasingly how university education is financed. But by and large toddlers cannot walk into a bank and borrow £100,000 for their education, paid for out of future earnings. In the language of the economists, capital markets are not perfect. There is another twist as well. Men by and large earn more than women and partly for this very reason women tend to receive more than men. But men are not as reliable at providing this support through families as we used to be. The modern welfare state has developed because sadly it is not just capital markets that are imperfect – so are marriages.

Our account does not of course capture everything that the government does. There are also the classic functions of the nightwatchman state – maintaining our security through the police, the legal system, and the armed forces. Nevertheless it does describe a lot of what government does now. Even though it has not loomed so large in political theory it certainly matters to real people. Education and health are consistently high on voters' list of priorities for government action, suggesting that this shifting of resources across the life cycle is crucial for them. You do not have to be a socialist to think that these are quite useful functions.

We have described them as shifting resources across the life cycle. But at any one moment, if you take a snapshot of what government is doing, it is shifting resources between generations. It is sometimes compared with a chain letter or a Ponzi Scheme but that is misleading because, provided each generation keeps its side of the deal, it can usually be sustained. A classic paper by the Nobel Prize-winning economist Paul Samuelson set out the conditions for this model to work: it includes the key statement, which ties in with the argument in our previous chapter, that 'giving goods to an older person is figuratively giving goods to yourself when old.'[13] This is a powerful example of the contract between the generations.[14] You can think of it as shifting an individual's resources across the life cycle. But that is only possible because at any given moment it is also an exchange between different generations. In a stable world it comes down to the same thing. But the world is not stable. It comes under a lot of pressure when there are big differences in the sizes of successive generations. And governments as custodians of this contract can exploit their power to favour one generation over another. They can pursue a policy which appears neutral but which actually favours a particular generation. Governments have to understand the contract between the generations and be committed to it if they are avoid the temptation to raid the piggy bank. This power is all the more significant because modern welfare states seem to operate a different pattern of flows between the generations than do the other types of society we have studied. Instead of the historic pattern of flows from old to young, in advanced Western welfare states the flow appears to be from young to old. Governments are more than offsetting the effect of family transfers, which tend to go the other way.[15]

We can estimate how successive cohorts have done out of the welfare state. The generation born early in the twentieth century gained from getting the benefits of it without a lifetime of contributions. British people born between 1901 and 1921 are estimated to have taken out of the welfare state between 115 per cent and 122 per cent of what they put in. Then it balances out more evenly until once more it is the boomers who are the biggest gainers. In particular the cohort in the middle of the boom, born between 1956 and 1961, are forecast to get out from the welfare state 118 per cent of what we put in.[16]

A good example of how a big generation can enjoy palpable economic gains, without even realizing it, comes from the impact of changes in the balance of tax and spending. Imagine a government has a simple rule that it must balance the budget across the economic cycle. That sounds quite prudent. And imagine as well that public spending policies just respond to changes in demand. So there is higher pension expenditure when there are more old people, less spending on education when there are fewer children, but spending per pensioner or per child just grows with the economy. If you have cohorts of equal size working their way through the system then there is fiscal equity across the generations. There are times when a cohort is a beneficiary from the system, for example when children are receiving education or older people are receiving a pension. And there are other times when, as middle-aged workers, they are putting in more than they take out. But overall it is in balance.

Now what happens if you stick to your balanced-budget rule but the big baby boomer cohort works its way through? When this big cohort are all children you will be spending more on services for children than before and public spending will rise. As you have got a balanced-budget rule, taxation will rise to pay for this, paid by the working population. Then that big cohort gets to working age. There is a reduction in demand for public services because there is a smaller cohort behind them, with fewer youngsters in schools, for example. At the same time tax revenues are buoyant because there is a surge in the number of taxpaying workers. So you can save on public expenditure, cut taxes, and still balance the budget over the economic cycle. This is the fiscal and economic sweet spot when a big generation are in the middle of their lives. But then they get older, claim their state pensions, and become heavy users of the NHS. This pushes up public spending and hence taxes. These effects are then magnified as there are fewer workers behind them, so tax per worker goes up even more. This example shows how the balanced-budget rule would actually work very neatly to the advantage of the baby boomers' generation and the disadvantage of their successors. They could enjoy low taxes when they were working taxpayers and then demand higher taxes from the next generation. The baby boomers enjoy the benefits of good public expenditure programmes when they were young and when they were old. But in their middle age they also enjoy the benefits of 'prudent' tax cuts. This is how the boomers can gain at every stage from apparently responsible management of the public finances. If you have got big changes in the relative size of cohorts then an apparently neutral balanced-budget rule is not enough to deliver fairness across the generations.

Let us see what happens to public spending over the next fifty years just as a result of demographic changes alone. We will not assume any changes in policy unless already implemented; we will just assume that programmes change in line with demographic change and the rest of the economy. So if there are fewer children then that brings down the education budget. If productivity goes up so does pay. If there are more pensioners that puts up the pensions budget. In the 2008 Budget the Treasury gave its estimates of the impact of such demographic changes on the total of public expenditure over the next fifty years. Here is the key table.[17]

Table 9. HM Treasury's long-term public spending projections (percentage of GDP)

	2007–8	2017–18	2027–8	2037–8	2047–8	2057–8
Education	5.0	5.6	5.8	5.6	5.5	5.6
State pensions	4.9	5.1	5.6	6.3	6.3	7.2
Health	7.4	7.9	8.6	9.2	9.6	9.9
Long-term care	1.2	1.2	1.4	1.7	1.8	2.0
Public service pensions	1.5	1.8	2.0	1.9	1.8	1.8
Total age-related spending	20.1	21.7	23.4	24.7	25.0	26.6

We can see what happens to age-related public spending if policy remains the same but these demographic changes are fed in. The answer is that public spending rises by a massive 4.9 per cent of GDP in the next forty years or over £60bn in today's money. Over the ten years to 2017 demographic change alone pushes up public spending by 1.6 per cent of GDP or over £20bn in today's money. That would mean tax increases just to carry on delivering programmes which don't change to a population which does. This is a heavy burden for the young generation to bear as they go through their working lives.

It is striking that the official projection is that the biggest increase in the next ten years, bigger, just, than either pensions or health care, is education spending. This comes from a combination of high immigration and high fertility. Net immigration is forecast to continue at the high rate of 130,000 a year, which sustains our mini baby boom. This means more education spending early on as there are more children. But then a bigger economy with more taxpayers dilutes the cost of the extra pensions for the baby boomers as they grow old. In fact, this means that, together with steady improvements in life expectancy, Britain's population is projected to grow by 17m over the next fifty years. The Treasury does not appear to have fully factored in the infrastructure costs of a population more than 25 per cent bigger than it is now. And it is not clear such a massive increase in our population is either desirable or likely. If we went for an assumption of no net migration then our population peaks in 2031. Our economy is, of course, smaller. That means that the promises we have made to the boomers when they retire have to be paid out of a smaller economy, which pushes up public spending by 1.2 per cent of GDP by 2047. Either way, these official forecasts understate the demographic challenge we face. They understate the infrastructure costs of a large population. And if we do not grow so big the pension costs of the boomers will be a bigger proportion of a smaller population. The Treasury uses high immigration to solve one set of problems without recognizing that it brings a new set of its own.[18]

Hidden in the forecasts of future pension spending is a key assumption which matters more for us than for most other advanced countries. For most Western countries the future cost of pensions depends on the contributory pension entitlement people have built up over their working lives. But as we have a lower contributory state pension than most countries our pensioners are more dependent on means-tested benefits. The cost of these is very sensitive to the value of the private pensions and savings of older people. The Treasury has long had a tendency to make implausibly optimistic assumptions for funded pension savings, which makes their estimates of long-term public spending on pensions implausibly low. A boost in private occupational pensions as enjoyed by the current generation of pensioners holds down public spending, but if the pensions crisis means future pensioners have less income from their funded savings then spending on means-tested state benefits will rise. The independent Pensions Policy Institute estimates that income from private pensions which was 5.8 per cent of GDP in 2007 will peak at 6.3 per cent of GDP in 2017 and then fall to 6.0 per cent in 2027, divided as well of course among more pensioners.[19] This forecast that we will see a fall in income from funded pensions even as the boomers age shows the long-term damage done by the pension crisis. We will see how much public spending on benefits for pensioners has to pick up the bill.

The Treasury also assumes that the basic state pension rises by earnings but that benefits for people of working age only rise with prices. That means that over the next fifty years benefits for families, for the unemployed, and for disabled people of working age are forecast to fall by half relative to the incomes of the rest of the population. The Treasury is assuming the boomers enjoy higher benefits for themselves when they retire but that the generation coming along behind has to settle for benefits growing with prices. It uses this to offset the higher spending on age-related spending shown in the table with a big fall in non-age-related spending.[20] This assumption holds down the growth of projected public spending by 3.3 per cent of GDP. Without it the projected increase in aggregate spending by 2047 on the Treasury's projections is much larger – 5.9 per cent of GDP.[21]

This is the fiscal environment within which British governments are going to have to operate for decades to come. We will be in an environment where the apparently neutral option of sticking to individual public expenditure programmes would mean increasing public expenditure as a percentage of GDP.

We have seen how even an apparently prudent financial rule like balancing the budget over the cycle can deliver big shifts between different generations. We have also seen how the cost of these commitments is going to grow in the future. But so far we have ignored the burden of debt. This can offset these trends or magnify them. Government debt shifts the burden of paying for today's public expenditure on to the next generation. A big cohort that is at the height of its prosperity should repay debt so as to reduce the burden when it is a heavy user of the welfare state. That is the responsible thing to do. But if even in the demographic boom times it builds up debt then it really can impose a heavy burden on others. Perhaps a forensic media inquisitor can get to the bottom of what is happening. It was the first TV interview ever given by a Governor of the Bank of England, and a lively young reporter called Robin Day was selected to conduct it. It was 1958 and people were worried about the size of the national debt, so Robin Day asked what it was. Here is Governor Cobbold's reply:

Cobbold: The National Debt represents the sums of money which the Government have over the years borrowed from the public, mainly in this country and, to some extent, abroad. That is really the amount of expenditure which they have failed over the period to cover by revenue.

Day: Have we paid for World War II?

Cobbold: No.

Day Have we paid for World War I?

Cobbold: No.

Day: Have we paid for the Battle of Waterloo?

Cobbold: I don't think you can exactly say that.[22]

So these are deep issues – and incidentally we finally repaid our remaining Second World War debt to the USA in 2006.

The burden of debt has shot up. It is claimed it was all due to the recession, when the automatic stabilizers mean that spending and borrowing go up. In reality it now looks as if we were living beyond our means in the good years. That means that the next generation will find itself having to service a lot of expensive government debt, which even on the Treasury's own figures and excluding the costs of the bank bail-out rises from 36 per cent of GDP in 2007/8 to 76 per cent in 2013/14. This is a massive increase in the national debt, tantamount to the burden of fighting a major war. It will leave a debt burden to be paid by younger generations for decades. You can argue, as we saw in the previous chapter, that they will be richer and can afford it. But they will be bearing this extra burden at a very bad time, when the boomers are retiring and generating further pressures on public spending. In fact prudently managed economies were trying to run budget surpluses in the good times so they were better prepared for these burdens. We should, as George Osborne puts it, have fixed the roof when the sun was shining. The consistent and principled position is to be worried about imposing on future generations both the cost of government debt and public spending on the boomers as they get older. That is before we add in other extra costs such as adjusting to environmental change.

Edmund Burke believed we are all bound by mutual contracts between the generations. Thomas Jefferson had a very different philosophy. He was a believer in the autonomy of each generation: 'Each generation is as independent of the one preceding, as that was of all which had gone before. It has, then, like them, a right to choose for itself the form of government it believes most promotive of its own happiness.'[23]

Ironically, the US Constitution which he himself helped to shape is one of the most powerful refutations of his belief – successive American generations have not dissolved their government and started again. But Jefferson is at least consistent and applied his principle to debt born by successive generations:

The earth belongs in usufruct to the living... No man can, by natural right, oblige the lands he occupied, or the persons who succeed him in that occupation, to the payment of debts contracted by him. For if he could, he might during his life, eat up the usufruct of the lands for generations to come, and then the lands would belong to the dead, and not to the living... The conclusion then, is, that neither the representatives of a nation, nor the whole nation itself assembled, can validly engage debts beyond what they may pay in their own time, that is to say, within thirty-four years of the date of the engagement.

If there is an intergenerational contract we can pass on both assets and liabilities from one to another. If there is not, by the Jefferson argument you leave each generation unencumbered to make its own way, free to remake a political settlement but also free of debts taken on by the dead. So if there is an intergenerational contract then we can leave debts for the next generation, provided of course we do not exploit it and we leave assets too. In the remaining four chapters we will look at practical examples of how this contract between the generations is changing as we go through the different stages of our lives.

Chapter 9

Time for Childhood

For many people raising our children is the most profoundly satisfying thing we do. It can give dignity to work and purpose to a marriage. It rests on deep-seated and admirable human instincts. It is what we do for the future. Rites of passage such as weddings or funerals are often a celebration of that achievement. It is deeply democratic as well – you can mess up despite great privileges or you can do brilliantly despite facing great adversity. Having parents committed to this project is just about the greatest single advantage a child can have.

Nowadays we seem to be making heavy weather of it. Parents worry about how we are doing. A UNICEF report showed Britain at the bottom of the league table of advanced Western countries in the well-being of our children: it touched a raw nerve. The charge is that we are failing to pass on to the next generation the values, the knowledge, and the skills which will enable them to thrive. If we cannot do this then we are indeed in deep trouble.[1] For parents it can feel as if you are battling in a hostile environment. Alison Pearson's novel *I Don't Know How She Does It* captures vividly what it is like to be a parent of young children in Britain today. You feel harassed, pummelled, and pressured like never before. And being affluent is no protection from these pressures.

Some simple economics can help us understand what is going

on.[2] As productivity improves so returns to an hour of work increase. The cost of leisure time, the income we forego by not working, therefore increases. That means we cut our leisure time until once more it is yielding as much return as our paid work. It also means that we change the way we spend our leisure time so that it is more intense, yielding a higher return. Indeed sometimes we become so focused on trying to extract the maximum output from every hour that we lose any ability to distinguish between work and leisure time – neatly captured in one man's description of modern family life as like running a small business with an ex-girlfriend.[3]

It used to be assumed that as we earned more per hour, so we would need to do less work – what the economists call the income effect. But if we earn more per hour we also have an incentive to work even longer hours and cut out less rewarding activities – what they call the substitution effect. What has happened for many well-paid people is that, contrary to what was expected, the substitution effect has turned out to be more important than the income effect. This is a key reason why modern life feels so pressured and the quality of life suffers. Earning more money does not solve this problem. In fact it can make it more acute: as we become better paid we need to get higher returns, not just out of an hour of work but an hour of leisure or an hour in the home. (Think of the issue as what taxi drivers do when it rains. If they head off home early as they have achieved their target takings for the day then it is the income effect that matters. If they keep on the road as an extra hour's work is earning them so much it is the substitution between work and leisure which matters. Reasonable people differ on this crucial issue.[4])

Because we all feel busier it is easy to assume that time for children has suffered. One survey showed that 80 per cent of adults think parents spend less time with their children than in the past.[5] This is one reason parents get blamed, even though for parents it can feel like they are working very hard indeed. We used to worry about the generation gap, but now we worry about the parenting deficit and fear that harassed parents are not able to devote enough time to their children. These anxieties are reinforced by the belief that a child's experience in the early years determines its future.

One reason we worry about the time we devote to our children is that now we understand how malleable the brain of a young child is. If a songbird has not learnt how to sing in the crucial months of its development as a fledgling then it will never be able to. Eric Knudsen of Stanford has shown wise old owls cannot learn things that young owls with more flexible brains can learn.[6] Before about 12 months babies brought up in the USA can detect the difference between certain sounds common in the Hindi language which after 12 months they cannot distinguish: this is when the first synaptic pruning takes place.[7] Then there is emotional development as well – secure attachments help a child to develop the capacity for empathy or self-control as well so as to develop a robust sense of his or her own identity. The early years do matter, especially for children who are deprived then and find it hard to catch up afterwards. Some theories of child development are, however, rivalled only by cosmology in the determining power they attribute to such early events. Then we fall into what has been called infant determinism.[8] In the past people used to think our fate was determined by the stars or the gods; now we believe it is determined in the playpen. As a result 'parent' is no longer just a noun but a verb. Parents feel under ever more pressure. One survey found that the key words used by parents to describe child-rearing were 'demanding, thankless, and exhausting'.[9] Whenever there is

UNIVERSITY OF WINCHESTER
LIBRARY

a social problem, from obesity to knife crime, there is one obvious group in the firing line – it is the parents. It is parents above all who are supposed to be failing to discharge their obligation of raising children who will grow into mature adults. But are parents all doing such a bad job? And is the problem too little parental supervision or too much?

We need to look at what parents are really doing with their time. Over the past forty years 66,000 people in the UK have filled in a diary recording minute by minute how they have used their time. It is an excellent way of mapping social change.[10] We will use the raw data to compare time use in 1974–5 and in 2000–2004. We will focus on parents in couples with children under the age of 5, looking at time devoted to various activities in minutes per day, averaged over a seven-day week. Both working and non-working parents are included. We are simply comparing the average time that mothers and fathers in two-parent families were able to devote to children in those two periods.

The evidence is dramatic. The average amount of time a mother devoted to caring for a child under the age of 5 has increased over the past thirty years from 73 minutes to 151 minutes, an extra hour and a quarter per day. For fathers the increase in time was from 17 minutes to 63 minutes, a smaller absolute increase of three quarters of an hour per day, but a bigger percentage increase. This confirms what experts such as Professor Gershuny and Frank Furedi have reported and conflicts with the conventional wisdom that somehow parents are too busy to devote time to their children. Parents are spending more time with their young children than before. Whereas nearly a quarter of mothers of young children devoted less than half an hour to childcare in the 1970s, only around a tenth devote so little time now.

When we look at how mothers with young children have found

that extra hour and a quarter a day, it is clear that investment in domestic labour-saving equipment has been crucial. The following list identifies all the items where time has been saved.

Table 10. Saving in time of mothers of young children between 1974–5 and 2000–2004 (minutes per day)

	Time saved
Housework	25
Cooking, eating, and washing up	51
Relaxation	43
Time watching TV	13
Sewing and darning	10
Total time saved	142

The time remaining from that 142 minutes which did not go into childcare went mainly of course into more paid work – mothers with young children work on average six hours forty minutes longer per week than they did in the mid-seventies.

So far we have been averaging across a whole range of different types of family and of course there has been a big change in the composition of different types of family over that period. So let us compare the changes for working and non-working parents and also by educational background. (Less educated means having left school at 16 whereas well-educated means having a qualification beyond A level. These are the comparisons we will make, though there is of course a significant group in the middle.)

Table 11. Amount of time devoted to care of young children by different categories of mother (minutes per day)

	1974–5	2000–2004
Well-educated working mother	58	162
Less-educated working mother	31	122
Well-educated non-working mother	96	204
Less-educated non-working mother	73	59

This shows that the transformation in the amount of time for childcare is spread across working and non-working mothers, be they well-educated or not. In fact it is such a dramatic increase in time for children that a well-educated mother who is in paid work now spends almost twice as much time on childcare than she would have done as a non-working mother thirty years ago. We can see how she has managed it:

Table 12. Time saved by a working well-educated mother (minutes per day)

Activity	1974–5	2000–2004	Difference
Cooking	107	63	−44
Eating	67	53	−14
Housework	96	75	−21
Shopping	43	30	−13
Relaxation/hobbies	75	45	−30

This yields an extra 122 minutes a day which is mainly devoted to more childcare. Babies and young children are gaining from an investment of parental time on a scale which very few young children appear to have had a generation ago.

This overwhelming picture of an increased amount of childcare by parents, especially mothers, be they working or not, is further supported by very similar evidence from other advanced Western countries. In America the argument that parents were not spending enough time with their children was advanced by Sylvia Ann Hewlett in *When the Bough Breaks: The Cost of Neglecting Our Children*.[11] The empirical refutation came out five years later and got much less attention. Actually average hours per day spent in childcare by white married mothers in the US went up per child from 32 minutes in 1924–31 to 49 minutes in 1975 and one hour in 1981. The conclusion of the researchers was clear: 'The public as well as many policymakers perceive that modern families have failed their children and that their mothers and grandmothers did more. Our analysis provides evidence to the contrary.'[12] In the Netherlands it is a very similar story with the increase for the time of mothers up from 61 minutes to 147 minutes (an increase of 86 minutes) and for men up from 22 minutes to 63 minutes (an increase of 41 minutes).[13] We are dealing here with nothing less than a transformation of the amount of time that Western parents are devoting to the care of their young children.

There is, incidentally, no equivalent increase in the time that British parents devote to teenagers. The evidence is less clear because the time use survey asks about time devoted to childcare and that may seem odd applied to older children, so the data is not so reliable. But it does suggest that parents devote very little time to direct engagement with their teenage children. This is reinforced by the evidence from teenagers themselves, who report very little time in direct contact with their parents. Indeed, British teenagers spend more time with their peers and less with their parents than in other European countries.[14] It may be a consequence of the focus on the early years, which can undervalue parenting as a longer-term commitment extending to the teenage years. And as parents' earnings rise as they get older so the opportunity cost of time for teenagers may be higher than for young children. Whatever the reason, it means we have a widening gap between intense parental investment in the early years and then a dramatic fall, with much more importance for peers whose influence peaks at the age of 15. The challenge to parents to do better is not when our children are young, small, and cuddly but when they aren't.

So far we have focused very much on the evidence for mothers with young children. Let us now look at what has happened for fathers. It is a good test of the widespread expectation that as we got richer we would work less. Our alternative account says that the more you earn per hour the greater the rewards to spending your time that way so you will work more. What has happened? In 1970 less skilled men with jobs and with children under 5 worked on average 6 hours 55 minutes a day, whilst well-educated men worked for 6 hours a day. (These may seem rather low but our averages do include weekends.) By 2001 the more educated man with children under 5 worked more (6 hours 32 minutes), but the less skilled worker had cut his work to just less than that, to 6 hours 26 minutes. If we categorize our men not by education but how well-paid their jobs are, we get a very similar pattern. Using admittedly rather patchy data it looks as if in the mid-eighties less well-paid fathers with young children used to work 54 minutes a day more than the highest paid quarter of fathers. Now they work 68 minutes less. This is real evidence for the aphorism that the leisured classes have less leisure and the working classes less work.[15]

There is also some modest evidence for the 'new' man. The average father of a child under 5 has also moved from doing around 7 minutes of cleaning each day to 23 minutes a day. (This contrasts with the reduced time for personal grooming, which suggests the metrosexual new man who moisturizes may be a myth – or perhaps he cannot manage it if he has young children.) They also spend more time cooking and less time eating with the family.

Table 13. Time devoted to household activities by fathers of children under 5 (minutes per day)

	1974–5	2000–2004
Housework	6	21
Cooking	10	29
Relaxation/hobbies	53	34
TV/Radio	143	130

Before men get too pleased with themselves about this modest increase in housework, separate research shows that married women do the housework that is time-inflexible such as preparing meals and doing the laundry and which can affect their employment prospects: men still tend to do more flexible weekend jobs such as gardening or home repairs.[16]

Once you add in the time saved by fathers sleeping, relaxing, and grooming themselves less this adds up to a big increase in time for childcare from fathers. In the early 1970s fathers spent on average around a quarter of an hour with their young children each day. They now spend an hour. This trend covers all fathers but it is distributed across the week very differently. During the busy weekday, the more educated man only manages 30 minutes and at the weekend two hours. By contrast the less well-educated fathers, whose time pressures are apparently less uneven, spend about one hour a day with their very young children every day.

There is one uncomfortable implication of all this. We have been focusing on couples with children. Insofar as we have got a 'new' man who contributes a modest increase in time cooking, doing housework, and being with his children, then the cost of being a lone parent has increased. Lone parents do their best in difficult circumstances, investing enormous quantities of time into their children, but this evidence suggests that a father does not just contribute his pay-packet but increasing help with childcare as well.

What we are seeing here is a doubling of parental investment in their young children within one generation. And that investment should be paying off in better cognitive and emotional development for our children. One of the most hotly debated issues in human development is the so-called Flynn effect, named after Professor James Flynn from New Zealand, who first observed that IQ was rising across advanced Western countries.[17] Many different explanations have been offered for this. But there is a clear pattern in which the improvements in IQ scores measured by Flynn seem to match the increase in parental time for their young children, which in turn is influenced by the spread of labour-saving household appliances. We may have found a new explanation of the Flynn effect – it is the spread of household goods, increasing the time available for parents to devote to childcare, which is crucial. The microwave oven has raised IQ.

We have got very encouraging evidence that parents are actually investing more in the younger generation and we are seeing the payoff in higher IQs. But it is not the whole story. All those reports warning about the quality of childhood in Britain are on to something. To understand what is going on we have to see what is happening to trust within and between the generations.

———

Children can generate trust; 70 per cent of parents said they had met people or made friends through their children.[18] Walking through a park is a far more social experience if you have a child (or of course a dog). Children can also be the victims of a loss of trust. This loss of trust takes many forms.

For a start, the level of confidence we have in other adults playing any role in raising our children has fallen. Other adults are less trusted in Britain than in many other Western countries. (The latest figures for the percentage believing 'most people can be trusted' is 31 per cent for Great Britain as against 19 per cent for France, 37 per cent for Germany, 39 per cent for the USA, 45 per cent for the Netherlands and 68 per cent for Sweden.)[19]

The evidence from voluntary groups suggests that, not least because of worries about paedophiles, it is harder to get other adults to take a role in supervising children. There is a waiting list of 30,000 youngsters who would like to join the Scouts but cannot because of a shortage of adult volunteers. The commitment that men make to the Scouts has also subtly changed. It is less likely to be long-term commitment and more likely to be a commitment to helping out during the short period when one's own child is involved. The pressure to be better parents has also made us worse citizens as parents withdraw from civic activities. Time pressures mean parents do less voluntary activity. One estimate showed a 25 per cent fall in the time devoted to voluntary activity simply in the five years 1995–2000.[20] The process may go the other way too: as we lose trust in other adults so we take on more of the burden of raising children ourselves.

It is not just a loss of confidence by adults in other adults. There is also a growing distrust and wariness of other adults by children. This is deliberately encouraged by the authorities. Police visit schools warning of 'stranger danger' and telling children not to speak to any stranger as they are a potential threat. However, the reality is that children may feel threatened by other children and want to turn to an adult as a source of protection and support. As Margaret Atwood observes in her novel *Cat's Eye*, 'Children are cute and small only to adults. To one another they are not cute. They are life-size.'

Thirdly, as we track down this breakdown of trust within and between generations, we can see that adults have lost confidence in other children. Again, there is powerful evidence showing this is more acute in Britain than in the rest of Europe. One survey asked adults in different countries if they would intervene if they saw 14-year-olds vandalizing a bus shelter: 65 per cent of German adults would; 52 per cent of Spanish adults would; the British figure is 34 per cent.[21]

It all comes together in a loss of confidence in public space. They are seen as places of risk and danger. There is some empirical evidence behind this: 43 per cent of gangs actually gather in children's play areas.[22] Parents do not want their children playing in places where graffiti, bottles, and syringes all show territory belonging to teenage gangs. (There are, however, subtle ways of fighting back. One council has found teenagers do not like sandpits as they are bad for their trainers, so play areas that include sandpits are less likely to be taken over by gangs.)

This all adds up to very powerful evidence about how the contract between the generations is changing. It is more intensively focused on this particular relationship between parents and children, especially when they are young. There is much less confidence in other adults or other children. So each individual family feels they are on their own. Other adults are not trusted, and other children are seen at least as competition and perhaps even as a threat. This breakdown of contact and trust between the generations is a key element in the fear of social breakdown. Whatever has happened to the level of crime as recorded in police statistics or crime surveys there is no denying the perception that places are more dangerous. One and a half million Britons thought about moving house to escape young people hanging around in 2005.[23] Similarly, young people are far more likely to suspect that a man whose behaviour is in any way out of the ordinary is somehow a threat to them. When people fear that our country has become more dangerous it is often a threat from a different generation which lies at the heart of their anxiety. This loss of trust in others in turn erodes the quality of childhood.

Tim Gill, who has thought deeply about childhood and play, invites adults to look back on some of the magic moments of their childhood. One hopes there are good family times – Christmas or holidays, or moments of particular kindness and closeness with our parents. But often we have other sorts of memories as well – incident and excitement when we were out on our own or just with a group of other children. These are what he calls the everyday adventures that help give childhood much of its special meaning. I think of cycling around the suburbs with my friends. My parents did not know where we went; we just had to be back for our mealtime. It was not an idyll from an Enid Blyton adventure – it was Birmingham after all. But, at least, looking back, I was incredibly lucky to enjoy such a mixture of freedom and security. A childhood like that, enjoyed by many boomers, is what is disappearing.

We are moving from free-range to supervised childhood. And toy consumption is not the same as play.

We have also become far more demanding and restrictive when it comes to the behaviour of children. As the president of our local Scouts in Havant, I opened an exhibition at our local museum to mark a century of scouting. Some of the Scouts had kept diaries of their activities. Here is an extract from an account of a Scout trip in the 1920s:

On Easter Monday a very large party of our Scouts and Rover Scouts paid a most enjoyable visit to Kingley Vale... arriving at the Vale about 11.30. We then started the day's sport in earnest. Six of us started a battle: suddenly we discovered we were pursued by several others. We hid amongst the bushes and pounced out on them as they came along. After this a fierce battle ensued: trousers and shirts were torn: a few cuts and bruises and the battle was won. We then sat down to a good meal and rested a bit.

Later the patrol leader describes a fight with another group: 'one was armed with an ugly scalping knife and the other with a catapult'; then he adds, 'so there was no serious damage done.' This description of a Scouts trip now constitutes a list of criminal offences for at least some of which campaigners now want a mandatory jail sentence. Three boys from the West Midlands, none of whom had ever been in trouble before, were arrested in 2006 and DNA-tested for building a treehouse in a cherry tree on public ground. Another group of boys were building go-karts from bits of junk; neighbours contacted the boys' families to complain and to move them on. In the words of Tim Gill, 'Activities and experiences that previous generations of children enjoyed without a second thought have been relabelled troubling or dangerous while the adults who permit them are branded as irresponsible.'[24] This is matched by a failure of the authorities to distinguish between everyday children's activities and serious anti-social behaviour which is not tackled effectively either. These are examples of the behaviour of boys. Boys in particular need to be able to let off steam or they will be more violent later on. For girls the expression of these pressures is different. For girls it is sadness – and there is nothing sadder than a sad child. 'Boys externalize their problems as bad behaviour, girls internalize them as sadness.'[25]

Children spend more and more of their time being supervised and managed. In fact we have reached the stage where a good parent has to be permanently on the look-out for risk and danger. Even if a child is not directly in our view we need to know where he or she is. Parents worry if their child is out without their mobile so that they can be in touch all the time. New products feed this anxiety. A company is launching children's clothes fitted with tiny transmitters linked to a geo-stationary satellite so that a parent will always know where a child is. The following table[26] shows how the age when a child is allowed out unsupervised has increased in a generation.

Table 14. Age when a child is allowed out unsupervised

	Age at which adults now went out as children (per cent)	What adults think for our children (per cent)
Under-8	16	3
8–10	23	14
11–13	27	36
14+	32	43

Children are more supervised and managed by their parents than ever before because their parents feel the outside world is dangerous and other adults are not trusted to do it. At the same time all the other adults are worried about other people's children; nearly 80 per cent of Britons and 99 per cent of those over 55 thought that 'young people today have too much freedom and not enough discipline'.[27] Bentham famously designed a model prison, his panopticon, so that prisoners could be kept permanently under watch; we seem to be doing something similar for our children.

Children respond by finding new ways of escaping parental supervision. One thing to do is to retreat to your bedroom. A child's bedroom has become the new territory that belongs to them and enables them to escape supervision; 90 per cent of children from poor families have a TV in their bedroom and half of children in middle-class families do.[28] And children may be more at risk online than out in the playground – one in three children have received unwanted or nasty sexual comments online but only 7 per cent of parents are aware of this.[29]

The decline in confidence in public space also increases the importance of organized outside activity instead. Parents drive their children to sports matches, and join organized outdoor activities. This may mean they are sometimes over-supervised and over-organized but at least it is an opportunity for children to get physical exercise. It is likely to depend on access to a car, parental commitment, and perhaps going to a school where there is more of this activity. In the past poor children were skinny and active, endlessly outside, even if they were cold. It was the rich kids who were inside and plump. But now it is the poorer kids who are more likely to be inside watching TV in their bedrooms whilst the more affluent kids are out playing competitive sport. We can test this hypothesis against our evidence on time use. Twenty years ago[30] male teenagers from the poorest quarter of families watched 169 minutes of TV per day as against 201 minutes, far more, for male teenagers from the most affluent quarter of families. But twenty years later this relationship has been reversed. Teenagers from the poorest families are watching about the same amount – 163 minutes – but for teenagers from the most affluent families it is down to 118 minutes. Television viewing by teenagers from poor families has fallen over the last twenty years from 21.5 hours to 20.5 hours per week, whilst for rich teenagers it is down far more – from 27.5 hours to under 18 hours.

This reduction in time when more affluent children watched TV may be partly offset by more time on computers. But there is another significant change as well. Twenty years ago poor children were more likely to spend more of their time engaged in sport than children from more affluent backgrounds. In 1985–9 male teenagers from the poorest households spent 20 minutes every weekday playing sport, mostly at school. They still do. But the time they spend playing sport at weekends, when volunteers matter, has fallen from 56 minutes per day to 47 minutes. The most affluent teenagers have increased their time playing sport at school from 12 minutes per day to 28 minutes. And at the weekend it has shot up from 12 minutes per day to 60 minutes. Boys from wealthier families used to do under 2 hours of sport a week; they now do more than 4. For poorer teenage boys it has gone down from 3.5 to about 3 hours per week. Now teenagers from poor back-grounds do less sport than their middle-class contemporaries. And playing outside, including in team sports, is one way you learn the soft skills which are so important not just for a job but in order to study effectively.

This is a case study of how a change in relations between the generations (an intergenerational shift) can also change the distribution of advantage within generations (intra-generational). The loss of confidence that adults have in other adults and in public space is much more of a blow for a child from a poorer background than for one whose parents have the money to organize alternative activities instead. This is delicate territory. It is not that poor families are incompetent and useless. Nor is it a sin for a family to drive their children to a sports club or a ballet class or do anything else they can to invest in them. But it does show the impact of the different constraints and environments facing different families. We are beginning to see one of the reasons why it is important to re-create a sense of adventure and enable more children to enjoy outdoor activities.

———

Jean Piaget realized that experiencing the world in three dimensions is what enables us to develop even some of our most abstract concepts. Kicking a football, throwing stones, standing at the sink helping with the washing-up, or jumping on hopscotch squares all helped develop these cognitive skills. If children increasingly retreat from a three-dimensional to a two-dimensional world it is much harder to develop these capacities. Thomas Friedman wrote a bestselling book in praise of globalization entitled *The World is Flat*. But in a child's world that is bad news: when the world is flat, the child is fat. But it goes beyond that. Children may have digital dexterity and eye/hand co-ordination that is faster than ever. They may be adept at manipulating the symbols flashing up on their screens. These skills even show up as higher IQs. But meanwhile their wider ability to interact with the world in 3D may be declining. We end up with what have been called screenagers.

Professor Michael Shayer of London University has for the last thirty years been recording how children have mastered the fundamental concepts they need to understand the world around them. For example, you pour water from a tall, thin beaker into a short, squat beaker and ask if it is the same volume or not. After decades when responses were broadly stable there appears to have been a downturn since the mid-1990s, when children's conceptual grasp has deteriorated dramatically: 'my findings show that 11- and 12-year-old children in year 7 are now on average between two and three years behind where they were 15 years ago in terms of cognitive and conceptual development.'[31] This evidence appears to contradict Flynn and suggest children today may lack the basic conceptual equipment to master living in a three-dimensional world.

How is Shayer consistent with Flynn? This gets to heart of the conflicting messages we receive about childhood. As well as Sue Palmer warning us about a toxic childhood there is Steve Johnson saying our kids are smarter than ever and all those flat screen computer games we worry about are good for you.[32] Our explanation of what parents are up to shows how both observations can be true. Parents have been liberated above all by domestic appliances to spend more time caring for their children when they are young. This extra investment has yielded good results. The bad news is, however, that they have lost confidence in other adults so their children are spending more time indoors and under closer supervision. This combination of extra time supervised by parents but less free-range experience of the world in 3D may explain both why IQ appears to be rising but grasp of fundamental physical concepts appears to be declining.

This is reinforced by international evidence. The Flynn effect is a universal phenomenon across all developed countries. The Shayer effect is a British problem – there is no equivalent decline in the USA for example. The spread of household appliances liberating parental time affects all Western countries, but the loss of trust in other adults, and hence the restrictions on children, is a much more specific British problem. Another international analysis after the 2007 UNICEF report on the quality of childhood showed British children doing particularly badly for sexual behaviour, alcohol consumption, and relationships with parents: these are all problems particularly affecting teenagers.[33]

Moreover we saw earlier there has been no increase in the amount of time parents spend with teenagers. Whilst early years are important for neurological development, the teenage years are just as neurologically significant. One reason why, despite all the misery it showed, we loved the optimism of the film *Slumdog Millionaire* was that it was about how you could escape appalling childhood adversity. Some brain areas, in particular the pre-frontal cortex, continue to develop well beyond early childhood. Kevin the teenager's brain is rebooting, or at least installing new software – 12-year-olds do literally have more grey matter than 15-year-olds. The adolescent brain can function oddly as a result. One experiment presents adults and adolescents with an option such as swimming with sharks and asks them to click on good idea or not a good idea – it takes adolescents rather longer to work out it is not such a good idea.[34] Our upbringing of children is now focused very much on early years. We leave teenagers to their peers.

This opens up an unusually wide gap between teenagers and adults in Britain. It might affect their cognitive development. The latest evidence from Professor Flynn does suggest a loss of progress for IQ in 12- to 15-year-olds. For 14.5- to 15.5-year-olds he shows a loss of 1.88 IQ points between 1979 and the present.[35] The unusual dependence of British teenagers on their peers could well be behind this; indeed Professor Flynn hypothesizes this is linked to teenage subculture not being cognitively demanding. 'Up until the age of nine and ten the home has a really powerful influence, so we can assume parents have been providing their children with a more cognitive challenging environment in the past 30 years. After that age children have become more autonomous and they gravitate to peer groups that set the cognitive environment.'[36] He concludes with a powerful warning: 'I look forward with some trepidation to what the next century has in store.'

This warning from the researcher who has given his name to the extraordinarily optimistic finding of rising IQs is very salutary. It means we have not just been riding a favourable demographic trend but a favourable cognitive trend too. We do not know to what extent our post-War GDP growth has depended on demographic growth let alone IQ growth. We have not yet begun to contemplate a world where these trends could go into reverse. Parents are doing their best but as citizens we are making life tougher for the next generation.

Chapter 10

Schools and Social Mobility

Nowadays we all believe in a society which is open and mobile. You should be able to get qualifications and a job and make your way in the world because of your own abilities. Of course we want to do the best for our own children, but we also want a society where what you do is not determined by what your parents did. This argument was first put by Benjamin Franklin, 250 years ago, when he said that America would be a 'land of opportunity'. Then he was drawing a bold contrast with what he saw as the stale, hereditary systems of Europe. Now every politician promises to spread opportunity.

We want to give the best chance to the next generation as a whole, through, for example, access to a good education, not just one by one within the individual family. This is not only a moral argument. In a modern market economy we are part of intricate networks of specialized labour. We depend on many other people delivering goods and services: it matters to us that they should be well-suited to their jobs and do them well. We cannot expect to be a successful, dynamic economy if we waste talent. Indeed, one study suggested that the Western countries with high social mobility have enjoyed an economic growth rate over the past century of 2.43 per cent a year as against 1.77 per cent for the low-mobility economies.[1] Blocking opportunity is worse than a sin – it is a mistake.

It is a good thing that families invest in their children, but we have to balance it by opportunities for everyone. Defining the right balance between these alternative principles of heredity and opportunity is not straightforward. After all, most of us are British citizens by right of inheritance. Ten per cent of British graduates follow the career of their father. If their performance were below that of their fellow professionals it would suggest nepotism, but if anything their earnings grow by more than those of their fellows, suggesting some genuine transmission of skill and human capital. Whatever one may think of the survival of the ninety-two hereditary peers in the House of Lords, at 12 per cent of the total they are close to the national average for heredity determining occupation. They are some way below the extremely hereditary activities of farmers (25 per cent of farmers' sons go into farming), medicine (17 per cent), and the law (14 per cent). Self-employed entrepreneurs are also strongly hereditary, suggesting access to capital is an issue. There are also twenty Members of the House of Commons who had an MP for a parent. There are businesses that are proud to call themselves '& sons' and increasingly, one hopes, '& daughters'.[2]

We can now measure how strong these ties are. Researchers estimate the strength of the economic connection. The answer is about 0.35.[3] Imagine two children born in the same year. If one had parents who earned 100 per cent more than the other then thirty years later that child would on average be earning approximately 35 per cent more than the child of the less affluent parents. It is what economists call the elasticity of income with regard to parental earnings. It includes every possible method by which parents can help their children – from the genetic inheritance of ability to buying an expensive house near a good school. We may think some of these ways of transmitting individual affluence to the next generation are better than others. And of course there is a lot of luck involved. That is what makes the debate on social mobility so fraught.

A society where there were no family ties whatsoever would be so rootless it would be almost as unbearable as the opposite, a caste society. This may be why popular attitudes are quite mixed; 69 per cent believe parents' income plays too large a part in children's life chances. But 50 per cent of people believe opportunities for social mobility are about right with a third believing they are too low.[4] This is heavily affected by where you are on the class scale – 58 per cent of people in social classes A and B believe it is about right as against 41 per cent of people in social classes D and E. We have stronger views on inequality, with 74 per cent believing income differences are too great. Perhaps people will accept less mobility if there is more equality. They might also accept more inequality if there were more mobility too. The trouble is the world does not work like that: if anything, the Western societies with less mobility are the ones with less equality too. The reason is that social immobility means a pernicious process of passing disadvantage from one generation to the next, which increases inequality. And greater inequality means you have further to travel to catch up with the people ahead of you, so it makes mobility harder.

Even if the inequities you worry about are within generations, they are transmitted across generations. We live in a society where your weight at birth is a powerful predictor of how long you will stay in education.[5] As soon as we look seriously at poverty and deprivation we have to face the powerful effects of inherited disadvantage. So the vertical transmission of disadvantage across generations helps to shape its horizontal distribution within one generation.

We used to think that there was an inevitable trend to increased mobility in modern capitalism. The author of Labour's 1945 manifesto, Michael Young, coined a word for it – 'meritocracy' – in his book *The Rise of the Meritocracy*, published in 1958.[6] He defined merit as IQ plus effort. He thought it was inevitable that in the future merit would rise to the top. He mischievously argued, however, that when personal inadequacy was the only reason for lack of achievement, failure would be more cruel than before and this meritocratic society would not be a happy place. Hayek's humane response was that there was no reason why the pattern of rewards in a market economy should be seen as a judgement on merit or moral worth.[7] That reminder is even more relevant today, with our worship of worldly success.

Michael Young predicted meritocracy would be achieved but we would not like it. But things have turned out exactly the other way round. Now the word he coined to mock it has come to stand for something desirable but unexpectedly difficult to achieve. Let us look at the evidence of what happened to the children born in the year his book appeared.

———

We used to assume social mobility would steadily improve. That is why it was such a shock when in 2005 evidence came out that social mobility had declined. Steve Machin, Paul Gregg, and Jo Blanden compared children born in 1958 and 1970 and looked at where they were on the income scale thirty years on, compared with their parents.[8] The tables below summarize their evidence, focusing on the children with parents in the poorest 25 per cent of the income scale (or quartile) and then children with parents in the richest 25 per cent. They measure the chances of a child born to parents in these quartiles of the income scale then ending up him- or herself in each quartile of the income scale. In a completely frictionless society where outcomes were completely unaffected by where you started, you would find that 25 per cent of the children from the poorest quartile were themselves in the poorest quartile and so on with 25 per cent of children ending up in the richest quartile.

Table 15. Income mobility for children of parents in the poorest quartile (per cent)

Year of birth of child	1958	1970
Chances of staying in poorest quartile	31	38
Chances of moving to the richest quartile	17	16

Table 16. Income mobility for children of parents in the richest quartile (per cent)

Year of birth of child	1958	1970
Chances of staying in richest quartile	35	42
Chances of moving to poorest quartile	17	11

That single piece of research has had a massive impact on the debate on social mobility because it showed the trend going in the wrong direction.

The evidence has been challenged and questioned. For a start, two points do not make a trend. Moreover, it looks back at people who are now middle-aged – we are like astronomers studying the light from a long-dead star. In response the researchers have tried to carry forward their findings and found that social mobility appears to have stopped declining. But nobody is seriously claiming that social mobility in Britain has suddenly massively improved again. If anything the consensus amongst the researchers is that the higher mobility in 1958 was exceptional. The children born in the year when Michael Young wrote his book were the products of a society more meritocratic than before or since. The result for children born in 1970 is thought to be more typical of British society.

The evidence of falling and low social mobility caused such a stir because it is easy to assume that there must be more and more social mobility as the traditional working classes shrink and more people join the middle class. This is where the sociologists come in. They look at social class, not just income. The economists' measure with which we began ensures that social mobility must be a zero sum game, because there is always going to have to be a quarter of the population in the bottom quartile of income. Unlike fixed slices of the income scale the size of different social classes can change. Indeed, one of the most significant changes in post-War Britain is that many more of the population are in middle-class white-collar jobs than there used to be (even if there is a strange reluctance to describe them as middle class).[9] These changes in the social structure have therefore themselves delivered apparent improvements in social mobility as the sons of manual workers become white-collar office workers. But John Goldthorpe, the doyen of such researchers, allows for this by measuring how people have done relative to the changes in the social structure around them. His research suggests that people have floated up as the types of occupation have changed but there has been no further social mobility on top of that. So social mobility has just been driven by changes in the types of job people do. This explains why it feels like we have been enjoying upward social mobility – it is because there are more white-collar jobs. But it is also telling us that we have not been able to achieve anything beyond that. And if that expansion in higher-status white-collar jobs were to slow down, which is possible given the hollowing out of middle-management posts, then changes in social structure would no longer generate even those improvements in social mobility. There is also new evidence that access to the leading white-collar jobs, in the professions, is itself becoming harder for young people from less affluent backgrounds: 'Younger professionals, born in 1970, typically grew up in families with incomes 27 per cent above the average family compared to 17 per cent for today's older professionals who were born in 1958.' Lawyers born in 1970 grew up in families 64 per cent above the average family's income; doctors 63 per cent; journalists 42 per cent; accountants 40 per cent; and bankers 32 per cent above average. These gaps are often far wider than they were only a decade or so earlier (for a fuller breakdown see the endnote).[10]

There is one response to all this which is not talked about in polite society. It is a widely shared but unspoken belief about heredity. Let us put the argument starkly: it goes like this: 'in a flexible market economy bright people tend to earn more; they also tend to have bright kids who in turn earn more; so what the critics denounce as social immobility is really genuine meritocracy plus genetic inheritance.' How do we know that we are not living in a genuinely open and meritocratic society with inheritance of ability? The biologists reply with evidence about regression towards the mean: bright parents or tall parents tend to have children who are closer to average intelligence or average height. But smart parents can then invest in their less smart children so as to preserve the gains the parents have won. That is why if you are from a poor background you need an IQ 15 percentage points higher to succeed.[11]

That still does not rule out a meritocratic explanation of the decline in mobility between 1958 and 1970. What if society got better at sorting us by our intelligence and as this was partly hereditary we would get less mobility as a result. The evidence, however, is very clear – cognitive skills do not explain the fall. Our society did not spot or reward intelligence better and so inadvertently rewarded heredity as well. If anything the relative importance of ability in predicting educational attainment actually declined.[12] Instead it was soft skills which mattered more.

Mobility declined because soft skills had a powerful double impact.[13] First, soft skills bypassed education to have a greater direct impact on your earnings – in a service economy being good at dealing with people might matter more, for example. But secondly, softer skills like application became more important relative to IQ in predicting your educational attainment. These softer skills are good qualities. They include empathy and emotional intelligence but it is misleading to call them all soft. Grit is a better name for the key attribute.[14] Michael Young did specifically include effort in his definition of merit. But he probably did not expect that effort would become more important relative to IQ. It means you study and stick at things even if you do not get good results straightaway. It is about valuing the future and deferring gratification, as we saw in Chapter 7: 'Under-achievement among American youth is often blamed on inadequate teachers, boring textbooks and large classes. We suggest another reason for students failing short of their intellectual potential: their failure to exercise self discipline.'[15] This is not hereditary – even though it is shaped by our experiences of family life as well as the world around us.

We have still, however, not quite got to the root of the popular belief in the inheritance of ability. Clearly genetic inheritance matters, but it may loom particularly large because our view of the world is shaped by our experience within our peer group: it takes a leap of imagination to think outside the group. Compare your height with that of your friends. It is very possible that the main explanation of the difference in height between you as individuals is genetic. But why are you taller than your parents were at the same age? Or people in a much poorer area? The explanation of that is not genetic; it is environmental. Imagine living in a community where the environment was so bad that it restricted growth. You would observe that in general taller parents had taller children and shorter parents had shorter children. Then your diet is transformed and people grow to be much taller as adults. You would still see directly the genetic influence on people's height, but everybody might be six inches taller and that would be explained by a change in the environment. This is the clue that helps us understand how a society can both feel competitive and meritocratic yet also not be genuinely open and mobile.

If, for example, you are working in the City it might look like a world of intense meritocratic competition with some inheritance of ability. But if you shift from the micro to the macro, the City may be part of a wider society which is far from open. Travelling the distance from being a child in East London to working in the City skyscrapers you can see from the school playground may require a journey of almost epic proportions. The competition for jobs in the professions is like English tennis, a competitive game, but largely one the middle classes play against each other.

If there is one institution which we expect to make that journey easier it is the school. Education is the most important single way in which society as a whole invests in the future. We hope we can transmit a culture, ways of thinking, and a body of knowledge to the next generation. It is not for individuals through personal experiment to discover a tiny fraction of the world's knowledge for themselves. Instead schools work best when both teachers and students are confronting a body of knowledge and thought which is far greater than any one individual. This does not mean passivity and deference. It is so that each generation can then advance for itself. We are indeed dwarves standing on the shoulders of giants. Then we can draw on what Burke called the stock of wisdom of the ages, regardless of your background or that of your parents.

Spreading social mobility is not the only task of schools and they are not the only institution with this responsibility. But we do expect that social mobility should be one benefit of a strong education system. Instead, for a child from a modest background getting a good education is like a salmon trying to get upstream against a raging torrent. At every stage it is tough. In fact, far from offsetting the advantages of the investment in children by their parents in the early years, schooling seems to magnify these effects. There is a shocking destruction of talent as the cognitive skills of bright children from modest backgrounds steadily decline during their years at school compared with more affluent children who start off with lower cognitive skills. Our education system is actually entrenching social advantage rather than spreading it.

Professor Leon Feinstein has measured the basic cognitive abilities of children aged 22 months and tracked what happened to them.[16] He found that the cognitive skills of a low-ability child from a high-income background improved relative to the performance of a high-ability child from a low-income background. Imagine two curves with the performance of the high-ability low-income child declining over time while the performance of the low-ability high-income child improves. The two curves cross over long before the age of 11: bright children from modest backgrounds have already fallen behind less intelligent children from more affluent social economic backgrounds. This is also of course powerful evidence against the argument that it is all just to do with inheritance of ability – if it were only a matter of our genetic endowments our country would be far more mobile than it actually is.

The latest evidence from the Millennium study of children born in 2000 shows this effect is as powerful as ever and if anything starts even sooner. Children from poor backgrounds are already behind when they start school. And that is not because of some genetic inheritance; it is because they have been falling behind as soon as they come into contact with the outside world. Schools never manage to offset this. Even if you assume away that problem and take children of the same cognitive abilities at the age of 11, you then find that the children from more modest backgrounds are less likely to get to an academically good school than equally able children from a more affluent background.

One study analysed the likelihood of your going to your nearest school depending on how good the school is and whether you are on free school meals. Children from poorer families are more likely than average to end up at their local school if it is bad and less likely to end up there if it is good.[17] The Sutton Trust has assembled powerful evidence on the social background of children at our 200 state schools which are best academically. It does look as if sadly not many children from poorer families get to these schools. On average 14 per cent of pupils are on free school meals across the country as a whole. In the areas where these academically successful schools are located this falls to 12 per cent. But only 3 per cent of pupils in these schools are on free school meals so, whilst the standard of their education is excellent, it is not benefiting many poorer students.[18]

Some say it is the abolition of grammar schools which explains what has been happening to social mobility. But the loss of grammar schools was just part of a deeper problem as traditional pedagogy lost out to progressive teaching fads that let down a generation of children. There is an ironic twist to all this. Progressive teaching methods were pursued by middle-class educationalists who believed that they were going to transform the educational opportunities of children from poor backgrounds. But experimental teaching methods – many of which had no rigorous basis in children's development or education science – were tried out first in poor areas.[19] Meanwhile the middle classes kept them out of their own schools in the more prosperous areas. Just as middle-class professionals stayed in their terraced houses whilst building tower blocks for the masses, so by and large they kept their children in schools with traditional teaching methods, even while imposing a very different pedagogy on others. This is why empirical and rigorous evaluation of education initiatives is so important: it could have stopped the destructive fashions of the 1960s and 1970s in their tracks.

This dense interconnection of family investment and access to good schooling lies behind our low social mobility. The desire to be a good parent is a strange mixture of co-operation and competition. Being well-educated is not a zero sum game, in which your gain must be at someone else's expense. But being top of the class is a zero-sum game. Getting a place at, for example, an elite university depends on how your child does compared with others. So you get a kind of parental arms race in which the aim is to give your child a competitive advantage over others. This is all entirely understandable behaviour. Parents want to do the best for their children. It helps make the world go round. It is reinforcing the pressure for parents to devote more time to their children. If all time is now to be seen as an investment with a rate of return then we must expect this to be applied to childhood as well. The only way forward is for more children to have a chance of getting to good schools. There are three main options for doing this.

The first approach is to try to get more and more control over school admissions policies. The School Admissions Code now stretches to eighty-six pages.[20] We do need an admissions code, given the evidence about how schools use their powers on admissions. But there are common-sense limits to what you can do. You cannot micro-manage the admissions policies of 20,000 schools. You cannot have a government inspector sitting on the shoulder of the admissions panel as they decide individual cases. As with all central plans, a government finds itself embroiled in very tricky ethical issues. Can you give preference to the children of your teachers to make life much easier for them, or is that social selection? Can you give preference to siblings in a partially selective school, or does that spread social selection too? The trouble is that the admissions code is a device for allocating a fixed number of places at good schools. It fails to get to the root of the problem. What we need is more school places in total. It would be so much better if the whole issue of which school your child is admitted to became less life-shaping and hence less fraught for so many parents.

If one approach is to try to fix schools' admissions policies from above there is another approach which has great appeal because it trusts parents – introduce school vouchers. The idea is to empower parents to choose the good schools by giving them direct spending power. There is a subtle and more attractive form of a voucher in which you adjust the spending power for the social background of the student so that children from poor areas have, if you like, a higher price on their head. If a parent's request for their children to get to the school of their choice is written on the back of a cheque to pay for it then the letter is going to get far more attention. This is a powerful and important argument. We need to go further towards clearer, more predictable per capita funding of pupils, particularly with a premium for the poorer children being let down at the moment.

There are significant cross-boundary flows already. Ever since the Greenwich judgement, more than twenty years ago, local authorities have not been able to run little protectionist autarchies and only educate children from their own local authority areas. Indeed, it is one reason why the best schools are not actually representative of their catchment areas. There is some per capita funding and, supposedly, a system of school choice but these have not transformed educational standards as they should have done. School choice, which has done wonders for educational attainment in Sweden, the Netherlands, and some parts of the United States has not had the same impact here. One reason is because ability to travel and to exercise choice is limited. (Children of the poorest 20 per cent of parents travel on average one mile to school and their parents own on average half of a car. The most affluent 20 per cent of children travel on average 2.5 miles to school and their parents have two cars.[21]) But above all it is because there are no mechanisms in place to enable successful schools to expand, to take over failing schools, or for new schools to be created.

If we simply issued vouchers for an unreformed education system, that problem would be repeated in spades. It would be as if we were focusing on the details of exactly what free railway tickets we should hand out to people without tackling the problem that the trains people want to take are full to bursting already, health and safety regulations make it very hard to add extra carriages, and planning rules obstruct the building of new track. It is the failure to open up the supply side which is the reason why, despite years of ambitious attempts at education reform, Britain now lags behind many other advanced Western countries. We have already got parents who want to choose and a significant amount of public money that would follow them. Indeed, more parents are appealing against admission decisions than ever before. But we have not created the mechanisms to provide more of the good schools that they want to choose. We must make it easier for people, including parents themselves, to set up new schools. New school providers must be able to enter the maintained sector, responding to what parents want. That is crucial to a school system which provides fairer opportunities to the next generation.[22]

––––––––––

Getting a university degree has become an increasingly important condition for getting a well-paid job in a profession or in a leading company.[23] It is a rite of passage taking you into the middle class. There has been a big increase in the number of university places – indeed universities are the part of the education system which has expanded most in the past forty years. So far, so good. It was easy to assume that this massive expansion would improve social mobility. However, it did not work out like that. Let us go back to that decline in social mobility for children born in 1958 and 1970 and see what happened when they were going to university, twenty years later. In 1978 there were 160,000 male students and 95,000 female. In 1990 there were 170,000 male students and 145,000 female.[24] So there was a big increase in the number of students, almost entirely accounted for by female students, up by more than 50 per cent in just over a decade. And the trend carries on. Female students overtook male students in 1996. Now there is a gap of over 10 percentage points with 38 per cent of men and 49 per cent of women aged 18–30 going to university.[25] Men, like some of the industries for which they used to work, are losing market share and fast. The expansion of university education has helped both men and women. But it has had a far greater impact on women than on men.

It is of course absolutely right that women should have education and employment opportunities opened up to them which were closed even only a generation ago. But the women who benefited from this expansion came from more affluent backgrounds. The same percentage of girls from low-income families born in 1958 and in 1970 got to university – just 6 per cent. But the percentage of girls from high-income families going to university went up from 21 per cent for those born in 1958 to 36 per cent for those born in 1970. So the gap between the chances of a girl from a high-income background getting to university as against a girl from a low-income background widened.[26] For boys there was no significant change in relative chances over the period. The old-fashioned attitude of middle-class families was to put much more emphasis on the education of a son rather than a daughter and now those days, thank heavens, are over. But it does mean that the expansion of higher education, whilst quite rightly helping these women who had previously lost out, did not spread opportunity to people from poorer families. The spread of higher education is indeed a powerful factor in the decline of mobility because of this effect.[27] In fact it is estimated that overall 'educational upgrading' – more young people getting more qualifications – 'accounts for 21 per cent of the fall in mobility for sons and 40 per cent for daughters' between 1958 and 1970.[28] We should not fail to be shocked by this statistic: it says that the expansion of education was actually a major reason for the fall in social mobility over the period, especially for women. The way our education system works is the biggest single explanation of falling social mobility.

This is not the end of the story. These newly liberated women emerge from higher education and expect to marry men with a similar level of education or at least similar job prospects – so-called assortative mating. The change in the balance of male and female participation in higher education is why it is hard for Bridget Jones to find a suitable man. Female graduates but not male graduates are more likely not to have married by the age of 45. Indeed, at this age the individuals who are least likely to have ever married are men with no qualifications and women with university degrees.[29]

The process does not stop there either. We measure income and inequality not by individuals but by households. A well-off household may now have two people in well-paid jobs. The expansion of women's educational opportunities and women's earnings has opened up an even greater gap between well-off households and poor households. The tendency for well-paid, well-educated men and well-paid, well-educated women to marry is one reason why we have a more unequal and less mobile society.[30] And if advantage marries advantage then we must not be surprised if social mobility suffers too. No one could possibly wish to reverse these new opportunities for women. But it looks as if increasing equality between the sexes has meant increasing inequality between social classes. Feminism has trumped egalitarianism.

––––––––––

There are some countries where there really is a system which organizes your working life for you – you are assessed and directed to the job or career thought right for you.[31] If you try to plan your economy you understandably try to plan your workforce. Alternatively, where you have extended families there is likely to be an uncle or a cousin who will find an opening for you – indeed, it is regarded as your moral obligation to your family to try to find jobs for your relatives.

England has never really functioned like either of these models – our school to work system has always been far more diverse. Our academic qualifications like A levels were first created by universities to help them decide whom they should admit. There was a recognized vocational route from apprentice to journeyman and then master of a craft. We had a network of mechanics institutes and colleges financed by local employers which trained people for the local trades – our Further Education colleges, the Cinderellas of our education system, are heirs to that tradition. It also depended on independent accreditation bodies such as the City and Guilds giving you a vocational qualification which employers would value and recognize. It was not perfect but at least the routes were well understood and clearly marked. It was the world which my family came from, rooted in the different Birmingham trades of gun-barrel makers, glaziers, and silversmiths. It all ties in with the picture of our country with which we started – no authority and no relative allocated you to a job. Instead we had to look out to open institutions, and indeed we were leaders in open exams and meritocratic selection processes. It gave us what was widely admired as one of the Western world's more socially mobile societies. Those who look at this with a more sceptical eye might say we then used these institutions to protect the interests of their members and obstruct mobility and markets. But regardless of the history, it is not working as well as it ought now.

The conventional explanation of what has gone wrong is low aspirations. This says the problem is young people themselves who lack ambition or drive and end up hanging around on street corners. This may be part of the story. But there is a different sort of explanation. This says that now we leave a young person with much less advice and mentoring than ever before (not least because of that retreat of adults from engagement with them which we saw in the previous chapter). At the same time the routes from school to work are much more complicated than they used to be when a big local employer would probably take you on as an apprentice. The problem is the disengagement of adults from offering guidance for members of the next generation just when the choices they have to make became less straightforward. A fascinating series of interviews with young people not in education employment or training showed that these young people had remarkably normal aspirations: a job, a home, a car, a family. They wanted conventional jobs such as chef, solicitor, holiday rep, bar worker, plumber, soldier, etc. But 'it was also clear that they did not have a planned trajectory for achieving those aspirations' and they were pessimistic about where they would be in ten years' time. In the words of the researchers, 'The issue is perhaps less about raising aspirations, and more about providing the means to realise existing aspirations.'[32] Many young people believe in the light at the end of the tunnel, but they cannot find the tunnel.

What we might think of as the English school to job system worked because of its mechanisms for transferring knowledge, expertise, and advice from one generation to the next. Apprenticeships were a widespread and effective way of passing knowledge and skill from one generation to the next – the intergenerational contract in practice. Careers advisers in schools knew what was available and how to make your way through the system. Firms themselves took on young recruits for life and invested in them accordingly, steering a promising recruit through night school and developing their career. It was not nepotistic but it was, in the best sense of the word, paternalistic. These sorts of mechanisms have broken down but no modern equivalent has been put in their place. It has left adrift in particular teenagers who do not necessarily want the conventional academic route. There is a widely understood route through A levels to university which ensures around a half of young people can set off into adulthood like a jumbo jet heading straight down a runway. But for the rest the system is erratic and confusing.

Immigrant families with very different family traditions are an interesting contrast here. Whatever their children's performance in the early years it looks as if they make a real surge in performance at secondary school, especially in the crucial two years leading up to GCSEs.[33] This improvement is across most ethnic minority groups and most schools (though black Caribbean teenagers are still behind on absolute performance whereas Indian, Pakistani, and Bangladeshi teenagers come from behind to overtake white students between the ages of 11 and 16). The researchers speculate that the students and their parents may have their 'eyes on the prizes' and when they can see education directly opening up job opportunities they raise their performance. So their fate was not determined in their early years. In particular the Asian community with their stronger traditions of grown-up children supporting their parents may have a stronger incentive for parents to invest in their children's education. An extreme example of this is China.

In general we leave our teenagers unusually dependent on their friends and peers, as we saw in the previous chapter. The influence of peers peaks at the age of 15 – and is greater than in most other advanced Western countries, where parents have greater engagement with their teenage children. We are close to the bottom of the league for the number of 15-year-old girls who find it easy to talk to their mother but top of the league for the number of them who have three or more friends.[34] Forty per cent of 13-year-old boys spend four or more evenings per week with friends, which is well above the international average of 29 per cent. Netherlands ranks top for life satisfaction of 13- and 15-year-olds, perhaps because it is close to top of the league for ease of speaking with both mother and father.

The most powerful single message that comes across from survey after survey of young people asked about their ambitions and choices of education and career is a desperate hunger for more information advice and guidance. Only 44 per cent of all 17- to 18-year-olds felt that they had received sufficient guidance to support their decisions about what choices to make at 18.[35] Eighty-six per cent of 16- to 17-year-olds 'would have valued help in finding out which career suits my skills and abilities'.[36] Instead teenagers end up depending on their friends and peers. This dependence on people your own age can help those who come from rich networks but trap others. In deprived areas people's three best friends were twice as likely to live locally as in the most affluent areas.[37] The origins of the social network sites shows how these networks are created and reinforced. Facebook was specifically set up so Harvard students could keep in touch with each other after they left university. It was intended to be a way of reinforcing the networks you made at university.

———

Education is not just for children and young people. Even if things don't work out first time round there should always be a second chance. There is a particularly bleak neurological determinism which says the only way our intellectual capacity can go is down. We used to believe that we were born with a fixed number of brain cells – of which many thousands were supposed to be killed with every glass of whisky. But now researchers such as Elizabeth Gould are discovering that our brains can grow and regrow – what they call neurogenesis.[38] Another leading researcher is equally optimistic: 'research on neural plasticity suggests that the brain is well set up for life-long learning and adaptation to the environment and that educational rehabilitation in adulthood is possible and well worth investment.'[39]

We can perhaps draw some encouragement from the London taxi driver. His hippocampus – the enlarged section of the brain which is necessary for navigation – has gone into popular mythology. London taxi drivers were not all born with brains like that. It has developed that way in response to need and opportunity.

Stanley Baldwin, who was actually expelled from school, had his own rather quirky explanation of this: 'the English schoolboy, for his eternal salvation, is impervious to the receipt of learning, and by that means preserves his mental faculties further into middle age and old age than he otherwise would (and I may add that I attribute the possession of such faculties as I have to the fact that I did not overstrain them in youth)...'[40]

We can carry on learning and seizing our chances. But now we must turn to another stage in the move to adulthood – a job, a home, a family.

Chapter 11

Houses and Jobs:
Generation Crunch

Stanley Kubrick's film *A Clockwork Orange*, based on the novel by Anthony Burgess, remains one of the most powerful accounts of a nihilistic youth culture. We follow the exploits of a gang led by Alex (Malcolm McDowell in the film) as they attack, steal, and rape, to the music of Beethoven's Ninth Symphony. It has everything about youth culture which so shocks adults – random violence, an outlandish dress code, an exclusive language of its own, and a predatory attitude to women. The film generated great controversy when it came out in 1971. It still shocks today.

At the time all the attention was on the portrayal of the amoral behaviour by the gang. There was surprisingly little discussion of the crucial dilemma which both Anthony Burgess and Stanley Kubrick faced – how should it end? What was to happen to these 20-year-olds? We might easily assume they would turn out to be criminals and social outcasts for the rest of their life. But there are fewer 50-year-old tearaways than 20-year-olds. Somehow young people make the transition to adulthood. Even if the clothes and hairstyle have not changed we know when we see a 50-year-old Hell's Angel at a motorway service station today, with his wife riding with him and a packed lunch in his pannier, that they are about as likely to beat us up with a bike chain as is the elderly couple in their caravanette parked alongside.

Stanley Kubrick based the film on the American edition of the novel, which ends with the bleak assumption that the cycle of violence and exclusion from society will carry on indefinitely. But the original British edition of the novel had a further chapter which showed how one of the droogs from Alex's gang has married and rejoined mainstream society and persuades Alex to do the same. The American publisher removed this ending because it was too optimistic. Anthony Burgess deliberately planned this final chapter about commitment and coming to adulthood as number twenty-one. The film is so bleak because it has no twenty-first, no transition to adulthood.

Shaping this route to adulthood is one of the most important tasks of any society. We all of us have to navigate this life course and the extra freedoms we enjoy in the West today make it extra complicated. We cannot automatically expect to have got there by the age of twenty-one – though when Anthony Burgess published his original novel in 1962 that might not have been so fanciful. (Since then the research on delinquent young men has shown that the novelist's insight was right. The most important single factor in getting delinquents to change their behaviour is their forming a stable relationship with a woman.) The fundamental transitions of the life course – from living in one's parents' home to forming a new household with a partner – have got longer, messier, and more expensive. And they can boomerang back to parents too. And then we blame them – the kidults who have not grown up – when we have made the route to growing up to independence much harder.[1]

A group of American experts on social policy, from all across the political spectrum, tried to reach a consensus on how young people in the US could avoid long-term welfare dependency. Their conclusion was that you needed to follow three rules – do not drop out of school, do not have a baby until you have a long-term partner, and get a job, any job, even very low paid, because at least it is a start.[2] If you followed these three maxims then you were on your way to being an independent adult and most unlikely to end up trapped on welfare. This is easy to say but can be a lot harder to do.

Choosing a career and getting a job, deciding where to live and getting a place of your own, forming a solid relationship and having a baby. These are the big decisions of life – what, where, and who. They don't always feel like decisions but more like events and accidents. Even getting the order right can be a challenge. And the very idea of a right order can seem unrealistic – the middle-aged trying to impose suburban domesticity on rebellious youth.[3] But young people do actually have quite mainstream aspirations. For example, '80 per cent of young adults still want to be owner-occupiers and the age they said they would like to do this is 31. They said buying a property was dependent on feeling settled in both their working and personal life.'[4] Similarly 80 per cent of young adults expect to marry and have children.[5] And as we saw in the previous chapter even young people who are not in education, employment, or training (NEETs) have mainstream aspirations for a job and a career. We see on our TVs grainy video footage of drunken young men and, nowadays, women fighting in our high streets but deep down most of them want a decent job, a place of their own, to be in a stable relationship, and have children. One charity working with young NEETs said a young man had confessed that his great ambition was to receive a utility bill addressed to him personally. That would mean he was an adult.[6] The trouble is that moving through these stages in the transition to adulthood can look to a 20-year-old as daunting as scaling Mount Everest.

Different countries manage these transitions differently – a difference which goes right back to the fundamentals of family structure we started with in Chapter 1. In parts of Europe the welfare state does more and for longer. In Germany parents can receive child benefit in respect of their children if they are in education up to the age of 27. Scandinavian states offer more generous benefits for independent young adults. In Southern Europe it is the family which is expected do more for longer. In Italy, for example, the legal responsibility of parents for their children carries on to 26.[7] Our historic model is for young people to leave home quite soon and go out into the market. One traditional route was an apprenticeship, which in the past could well have involved staying with the master's family whilst you learned his trade. Some of the most successful apprenticeships are still residential but they are now rare and massively over-subscribed.[8] For many young people the modern equivalent of that historic English transition to adulthood via an apprenticeship is to go away to university. This is a contrast with many other Western countries, where you are more likely to stay with your parents and go to the local university.

There is substantial evidence that these transitions are becoming far more difficult in Britain than elsewhere in Europe. We have unusually high rates of teenage parenthood. We were already moving to higher rates of youth unemployment before the recession, which has hit younger people particularly hard. And getting started on the housing ladder is getting more and more difficult. We will focus on the challenge of getting a place of one's own. It is a key stage in the route to adulthood. It can also be, alongside the pension, the biggest asset an individual ever owns. So it affects both routes to adulthood and the distribution of assets across the generations.

We think we know what happened in the great housing boom: young people could not get started on the housing ladder because houses were so expensive. And that in turn delayed family forma-tion and lowered the birth rate. It seems obvious. There was indeed some increase in the average age of a first-time buyer. And people with modest incomes were not able to get started on the housing ladder at all. In 1985 34 per cent of under-25s were already home-owners: this had dropped to 19 per cent by 2005. Among 25- to 29-year-olds, owner-occupation rates were down from 62 per cent to 46 per cent twenty years later.[9] This is a sizeable reduction even if not quite the catastrophic fall in home ownership among young people you might expect given the house price increases. But when you really look at the evidence for house-buying through the last boom you have to force yourself to see what you did not expect. All through the house price boom many young people kept pushing on, eager to get started on the housing ladder and have children. Even the estimates for the average age of the first-time buyer are not quite what they seem. The average, measured as a mean, is distorted upwards by middle-aged victims of family break-up – if you split up with your partner, move into a rented property, and then buy a new place you are counted as a first-time buyer because the measure includes anyone buying from the rented sector. The mean age for a first-time buyer was up to 32 by 2007, but that figure suffers from this middle-aged spread. A better guide is the median age of a first-time buyer, which has remained just under 30.[10]

The real surprise is how many young people were still getting started despite prices shooting up by far more than their incomes. We have here a case study in the psychology of a speculative boom. In a boom like the one we had up to 2007, just about everyone believes that prices will carry on rising. That means that rising prices don't keep you out; they suck you in. You do anything you possibly can to join the feeding frenzy. This is why youthful property ownership reached its all-time high in 1988, the peak of the previous house price boom. For 20- to 24-year-olds owner-occupation rose from 35 per cent in 1984 to 41 per cent in 1988, as house prices rose. And, albeit from a much lower base, it actually rose from 20 to 24 per cent in the single year from 2005 to 2006. For 25- to 29-year-olds it rose from 60 per cent in 1985 to a historic high of 64 per cent in 1988 and again from 46 to 48 per cent from 2005 to 2006.[11] Young people were driven to buy by the belief they had to get into the market as quickly as possible. They did everything they could to get on the crucial first rung of the housing ladder.

This speculative surge was accompanied by a significant change in the composition of first-time buyers over the past twenty years. The number of single male first-time buyers remained broadly constant – roughly 115,000 single men were buying houses in the early 1980s as against 118,000 in 2004. However, the number of single female first-time buyers was up from 60,000 in the early 1980s to 95,000 in 2005. The big fall is in the number of couples buying for the first time, down from 350,000 to 210,000 in 2005.[12] So first-time buyers are more likely to be single and less likely to be couples. This looks very similar to the widening of access to university we saw in the previous chapter – middle-class families at last give a fair deal to their daughters and help them to get started in the housing market too. Then a modern middle-class marriage increasingly takes the form of two young people each of whom already has a stake in the property market combining their assets. But meanwhile poorer couples with less access to parental support and with less prospect of combining two small flats into one family house get squeezed out. The only way for them to get started was to borrow to the hilt.

High house prices in the boom sucked in young buyers on 100 per cent or 125 per cent mortgages. They borrowed ever higher multiples of salary to get a property. Mortgages for first-time buyers peaked at 3.4 as a multiple of income in August 2007 just when the crash began with the collapse of Northern Rock. The median advance was 90 per cent of the value of a property then. By spring 2009 the salary multiple for first-time buyers was down to about 3 and the median advance down to 75 per cent of the value of a property.[13]

Young buyers could hold down the initial costs by only repaying the interest, leaving the problem of repaying the capital to the future – a big change from only twenty years ago.[14] In the words of the Bank of England, 'Interest-only mortgages were non-existent in the run-up to the housing down-turn in the early 1990s, they accounted for up to 22 per cent in 2006 of new loans and 24 per cent in 2007.'[15] Improved life-expectancy with a longer working life plays a part here as well. It means that mortgages can be financed for longer, increasing the total amount that can be borrowed. All this puts up the total cost – you may well spend £500,000 over the life of a £250,000 mortgage. An illustration, provided by the Council of Mortgage Lenders (CML), shows the higher mortgage burden taken on by young borrowers in the boom. A borrower taking out a £120,000 twenty-five-year traditional repayment mortgage at 5.5 per cent would make total repayments of £221,000 over the life of the loan. Now assume a young couple start with the same actual borrowing costs and the same interest rate. But, in order to borrow more, they go for the same payments as before but covering a larger interest-only mortgage of £161,000. Then after ten years, they shift to a conventional twenty-five-year repayment mortgage. That adds up to total repayments of £385,000 over the thirty-five-year life of the loan, an increase in their total lifetime payments of almost 75 per cent. That means that the higher incomes from longer working lives of younger people are transferred to the older generation, who are able to charge higher house prices financed by the higher mortgages which younger people take on.

Having got started on the housing ladder, young people are then beneficiaries of rising house prices and can in turn gain at the expense of the generation behind, provided of course that the trend carries on. This model is not so much prudential planning for the future; it was more like fagging at some ancient public school – you may not like it when you are on the receiving end but then you become a beneficiary of the bizarre ritual and do not see why you should be the generation to discontinue it.

Once you have got over these hurdles you are ready to start a family. You have combined two incomes and perhaps two small flats to get a house. Your circumstances are then ripe to have kids. The nest is there and you have shown your commitment to each other in the modern way – sharing a mortgage contract even if not a marriage contract. Your house is rising in value so you feel more wealthy. The mini baby boom of the first decade of the century, hard to explain if, like me, you thought high house prices were a contraceptive, starts to make sense. The same speculative boom which caused young people to rush into the property market also then created the conditions for them to have children.

Young people who had got into the housing market during the boom appeared to be sitting on healthy capital gains, but as the most recent entrants they were most vulnerable to the collapse in house prices. And even in the boom times they faced higher long-term costs than they might have realized. The figures show the scale of the burden they took on. In 1995, for those households headed by someone aged 25–34 who had a house, it was worth approximately £65,000 with a mortgage of around £50,000, leaving a net asset of around £15,000. Ten years later the next group of 25- to 34-year-old homeowners were sitting on an asset that was worth around £170,000. Of this on average about £100,000 was a mortgage, leaving them a net asset then worth about £70,000.[16] So far so good. But they were much more heavily exposed to the house price crash than previous generations. Assume house prices then fell 30 per cent from £170,000 to, say, about £120,000. That reduces their net asset to £20,000, still slightly more than what that age group had ten years ago. But instead of a mortgage of £50,000 they have got a mortgage double that. And it is not being eroded by high inflation. So their debt burden is going to be heavy for quite a time. One thing that goes is any saving for the future.

They may find that lower interest rates bring a genuine easing of the monthly cash flow pressures. Their discretionary income may actually rise for a time. But that is not the whole story when boom turns to bust. They may also find themselves in negative equity. Young recent buyers are by far the biggest victims of negative equity. At the end of 2008 there were about 900,000 households caught in negative equity and of these around 600,000 or two thirds were aged under 35.[17] Indeed, the number of under-25s in negative equity is almost equal to all over-45s at about 110,000 each. The debt of these young people is not losing its value – and when inflation is negative the total burden of their debt actually rises. They do not have a decent pension so all their wealth is tied up in that property and it is wiped out. They are asset-less.

For the young people who did not get on to the ladder, mortgages now are hard to find and little housing is being built. The house price slump has not helped them as one might have expected. For a start the supply of housing has been falling.[18] House prices have fallen not because of a surge of supply of housing but because of mortgage constraints. The new constraint is the difficulty of accessing credit. The only way in is to have a hefty deposit. There has been an increase in the deposits needed to get a mortgage to a record of 25 per cent when in the boom they used to manage with 10 per cent on average.[19] With an average house price of £225,000 that means a deposit of over £50,000. The average price of properties at the bottom end of the market is £100,000 and even that means a deposit of £25,000 or a year's earnings. The average deposit is £56,000, which is double the average wage. And the trade-off is clear – the smaller the deposit the higher the interest rate so if you can only afford a smaller deposit you will pay a high interest rate. For these young buyers it is as if interest rate cuts never happened.

The only way out from this trap is to turn to the bank of mum and dad. Young buyers turned to their parents more in the boom and then even more in the bust. Financial dependence on parents has gone up in the crash: 38 per cent of first-time buyers received parental help for a property in 2007 as against 10 per cent in 1995. By 2009 the CML estimated that 80 per cent of first-time buyers under 30 were getting help from their parents, double the rate only two years earlier.[20] This is a powerful example of a generous inter-generational transfer though at the cost of lower social mobility.

———

The hidden social problem in Britain today is the sheer difficulty of getting decent affordable accommodation anywhere in the South-East or in many of our great cities as well. The cost of housing is still high. Many young people now live in desperately cramped conditions. And one of the flashpoints around immigration is its pressure on housing. In their study of social attitudes in the East End, Geoff Dench and Kate Gavron identified housing as one of the key sensitivities:

There was yet another matter about which the white East End working class found itself baffled and resentful. We have already seen that many lost their traditional jobs, to be reduced again to the welfare dependency they believed they had shaken off for ever and that their children often failed to make the critical jump into the knowledge economy and the meritocratic society. On top of this they found their traditional paths to housing blocked by new obstacles, which seemed to them systematically to favour the new-comers over themselves.[21]

BNP campaigns often focus on housing pressures. There are links between immigration and housing but, as we shall see, not quite what we might expect.

Immigration affects different people in very different ways. It is not unambiguously and equally good for everyone. What is most relevant to our argument is that, once again, it seems to work better for the older baby boomers than it does for the younger generation coming on behind. If you are one of the British-born young workers facing more intense labour competition it does not feel very beneficial for you. That smaller cohort of 20- to 30-year-olds who entered the British labour market in the last few years would have enjoyed a tighter labour market with higher pay, but instead they have experienced intense competition from a large influx of workers from abroad. This has particularly hit those who are less well-educated or less well-trained. Immigration has held down their wage relative to everyone else so immigration has probably been a factor making Britain a more unequal society. Baby boomers had tight immigration controls when they were entering the jobs market but then relaxed them when they wanted more workers coming along behind. One of the leading experts on the economics of migration summarized the evidence in the title of one of his articles, 'Affluent Americans Gain; Poor Americans Lose'.[22] It increases returns to capital and holds wages down so it rewards property-owners. It is younger people who have lost out. One of the big flows of immigration has been of domestic workers and this has made it easier for women with children to re-enter the jobs market. So immigration may have reinforced the social trends that we saw in a previous chapter, helping better-educated women but disadvantaging younger men.

There is, however, a puzzle which has not yet been explained by conventional economics. Why does it seem easier to move to the hotspots of London from, say, Cracow than from the rest of England, say, Liverpool? How come so many immigrants go to London yet that is where housing pressures are already so intense? It seems odd that immigrants should come to London when it has got the most expensive housing in Britain, indeed anywhere in Western Europe. This is not just the elite properties of Central London. Average house prices in London are much higher than in the rest of England and most of the rest of Europe. But London is also the place to which immigrants flocked. Greater London had 45 per cent of all foreign workers.[23] Forty per cent of all immigrants who come to Britain come to London.[24] It is now reaching the stage where 30 per cent of London's population was born abroad.[25] London has the most expensive housing and the most immigrants. Are these two apparently conflicting phenomena by any chance related? They are. Indeed, the links between them are crucial to understanding immigration and housing pressures in Britain. Quite simply, high house prices were one factor sucking in immigrants.

Imagine two people doing the same job in London. One has travelled from Poland and the other has come from Liverpool. Imagine that they are each earning, say, £250 per week, which is slightly more than they would get working a forty-hour week on the minimum wage. Their basic living costs such as food, transport, and clothes add up to, say, £100 a week. The biggest item by far in their spending is housing. This is what makes the difference. Imagine there is a two-bedroom flat with a total rent of £200 a week. A Liverpudlian occupies one room for which he pays a rent of £100 a week. This means that after his rent and his living costs he has got £50 left over. But the second bedroom is occupied by the Pole and he installs a bunk bed so that he can share it with a friend. That means his share of the rent is down to £50 a week. He has got £100 of disposable income left over. That is double the disposable income of the Liverpudlian.

The young man from Liverpool does not see why he should live in more cramped conditions than his family back in Liverpool occupy. The Pole may have been in a cramped Soviet period flat. He may be more willing to make sacrifices so that he can gain from the opportunities he has got coming to London. That extra £50 that he gains from under-housing himself compared with the Liverpudlian is crucial in driving the economics of immigration. He can use it to undercut the native competition. Even if he worked at a rate of £1 an hour less than the domestic competitor, he has still got more discretionary spending power as well. His willingness to be under-housed gives him a labour market advantage and it is greater if house prices are higher. (Of course, in different economic times it can be the other way round – the drama of *Auf Wiedersehen, Pet* came from the conditions of seven British builders who have to go to West Germany in the 1980s to find work and find themselves together in a cramped hut.)

There is something else he can do with the money and this is the biggest single reason why he is willing to be under-housed. He can send the money back home to his family. The Liverpudlian may wish to send some money back home as well. Fifty pounds in Liverpool buys a bit more than £50 in London but not massively more. They are part of the same national pricing structure for many consumer goods. But £50 sent back home to Poland may be worth a lot more, especially in the periods when the pound was strong relative to other currencies. It might keep elderly parents. It might help finance the purchase of a flat. We have to compare the combined earning power of money spent in London and Liverpool with the combined earning power of money spent in London and Poland. It is clearly worth more if it is divided between London and Poland, and because it is worth far more back in Poland the returns to the sacrifice of under-housing yourself in London are much greater. So it is not that our Liverpudlian is somehow a bad person compared to our Pole. It is that he or she cannot capture similar benefits for their family by under-housing themselves in London.

As housing costs rise and consume a higher and higher proportion of people's pay, so the rewards for people who are willing to under-house themselves grow ever greater. If the rent goes up to £300 a week for the whole flat then the Liverpudlian's costs rise to £150 a week and he has got no discretionary spending power left whatsoever. For the Pole his costs rise to £75 a week (half of the £150 rent for his room) and he has still got £75 of discretionary spending power left. And if rents go any higher then the Liverpudlian may just give up and thinks he might as well stay in Liverpool. But there is still some scope for our Pole to return money to Poland. The crucial proposition therefore underlying the economics of immigration in Britain is as follows. The larger the proportion of earnings consumed by housing costs, the greater the benefit of under-housing and the greater the price advantage of immigrant labour. It was not despite the high cost of housing that immigrants came to the house price hotspots in Britain to make a living – it was because of them.

If you have been served at a bar by a man from Slovakia, had your house cleaned by a woman from Brazil, had your house repainted by a Polish decorator, or your children taught by an Australian, they are probably going back to living arrangements which are far more cramped than anything that a typical British barman or cleaner or builder would accept. It is crucial to their economic advantage. There is some evidence for this hypothesis from the figures for average household size. In 2006 the mean household size across the UK was 2.4 and the median was 2. But in households with a head from the EU Accession countries it was a mean of 3.0 and median of 3.[26]

This is turn helps explain some other features of patterns of immigration. The rewards for under-housing rise the higher the difference between costs at home and abroad. When one hears of hostels or homes housing immigrant workers several people to a room, you can be sure that those immigrants are not from expensive Scandinavian countries or Germany or France. Typically, as with the tragedy of the Chinese cockle-pickers in Morecambe Bay, it is people from significantly poorer countries who are most likely to be under-housed because the rewards in terms of extra spending power back home are the greatest.

People are not willing to accept under-housing for ever. It may be bearable if you are single and in your twenties or early thirties. You can manage it as well if you are with a partner who is also working full-time. But it is much harder having a baby in circumstances like that. And it is why one of the biggest uncertainties in the debate on the recent surge in immigration was whether or not immigrants will stay. If the aim is to send remittances back home and then to go back and raise a family there, then this surge in immigration may reverse itself. That is what appears to have been happening during the recession.

House prices do not just drive immigration; they drive emigration as well. When you are young, house prices affect your disposable income. When you get older it is not the income effect that matters but it is the value of the asset. High house prices in Britain mean that you can buy much better-quality accommodation abroad either as a second home or as a retirement home. So whereas it sucks in young people who are willing to be under-housed, it has an opposite effect for older people who are, in economic terms, over-housed. They can convert some of the spare equity in their house into higher income and trade down into a smaller property. Though in theory you can do that within Britain, the gaps in house prices by size of house are not sufficient to yield a significant improvement in living standards over a fifteen- or twenty-year retirement. But if you are willing to move abroad to a place with lower house prices then suddenly the calculation becomes much more attractive. So high house prices in Britain drove emigration as well. It is older people releasing their houses that creates the opportunities for people with families to move out to family accommodation. Often it is most affordable and most attractive in the suburbs or the areas beyond London.

Putting these effects together begins to reveal the pattern of population movement in Britain. Young immigrants are sucked into London using the competitive advantage they get from high house prices (44 per cent of all Londoners were aged 20–44 compared with only 35 per cent across UK as a whole).[27] Couples with families move out from London to the areas fringing the M25 or beyond. And older people sell their houses to them as they downsize or move abroad. These are the population flows in contemporary Britain. Jack Rosenthal did a delightful comedy film twenty-five years ago called *The Chain*, tracing a set of property transactions on a single day across London. But nowadays the real chain stretches across Europe and beyond. It is a young Pole or Australian moving to London and willing to share cramped accommodation with a group of friends. It is a middle-aged couple moving out from London to a place where they may think the schools are better and houses are a bit cheaper. And it is an old person selling their house in order to downsize or move out to the Costa Brava or parts of France. In 2006 we had record levels of immigration (590,000) and of emigration (400,000).[28] And at the heart of this was a kind of convection effect with people being sucked in at the bottom of the labour market and prosperous retirees emigrating at the top. It is re-shaping the character of London. It is probably the most powerful single set of social and demographic changes which went on in Britain over the past decade. One factor was the low birth rate of the 1970s creating a shortage of new young workers twenty or thirty years later. But equally important were the high house prices of the past decade.

Big cities such as London or New York are key in accepting migrants and integrating them. It can create enormous social pressures, especially in battles over housing. But it can equally create incredibly dynamic and creative areas with concentrations of young people. They move in because of the high house prices and their willingness to be under-housed. Because they are under-housed they do not stay in their accommodation. Instead they are out in pubs, etc. That in turn drives the dynamism of the street culture and the nightlife. At its extreme there is hot-bedding, with allocation of beds divided up in twelve-hour gaps. That both feeds and makes the twenty-four-hour city possible, with people willing to work at night and sleep in the daytime.

At its most successful the sheer experience of living in one of the world's great cities can itself be integrating. Young people come together, new relationships are formed, and even if people are not sure that they are English they are sure that they are Londoners. We can observe similar effects but on a smaller scale in other great cities like Birmingham, Manchester, and Leeds. And if all of these immigrants are working and their partners are working too, then there is very likely to be a boost to GDP per capita. But it does not always work like this. The people who lose above all are the younger generation facing exceptional difficulties getting started on the housing ladder and intense competition in the labour market. Indeed, we have seen how they are linked as the high house prices suck in competitors for their jobs.

———

This account would suggest that young people were losing out in the jobs market even before the recession struck. And if we look at the evidence we can see that this was indeed happening. During the years from 1997 to 2007, which we now see was a debt-driven boom, youth unemployment was actually rising. And young people were then left particularly vulnerable when recession struck. One in five of unemployed people were aged under 25. Unemployment amongst 18- to 24-year-olds was down to 21.7 per cent of overall unemployment in 1999. Since then it has risen steadily to 31.9 per cent by November 2008.[29]

This unemployment could have potentially long-term effects:

Unemployment while young, especially of long duration, causes permanent scars rather than temporary blemishes. For the young a spell of unemployment does not end with that spell; it raises the probability of being unemployed in later years and has a wage penalty. These effects are much larger than for older people.[30]

Even at the age of 40 an episode of youth unemployment is still reducing your earnings by 9–11 per cent, and if it was prolonged by 13–21 per cent.[31]

Meanwhile employers have held on to their older workers. In fact, even during the depths of the recession employment among people over 50 kept on rising. In the period from spring 2007, when total unemployment starting rising sharply, to summer 2009 the number of older people in employment actually rose, whilst employment for young people aged under 25 fell to a record low. By the summer of 2009 there were 7.95m over-fifties in employment, comprising 27.5 per cent of all those aged over 16 in employment, the highest figures since records began. Meanwhile the number of 16- to 24-year-olds in employment fell to 3.87m by the summer of 2009, 13.4 per cent of all those in employment, both record lows.[32] This adds up to a big shift in the composition of the labour force. This is very different from some previous recessions when employers shed older workers.

It is not because young people are pricing themselves out of work. As our earlier analysis suggested, the trends are the opposite: 'The relative earnings of young people have fallen steadily since 1997 when the youth share of unemployment started to rise.' (The earnings of 18- to 21-year-olds have fallen from 49 per cent of 40- to 49-year-olds in 1997 to 46 per cent in 2008.)[33] One reason is of course that more young people are spending more time in education. But this does not explain the rise in unemployment. A better explanation may be the pensions crisis: in the past employers could make an older worker redundant and they would be a charge on the pensions scheme. That looked an attractive way of meeting redundancy costs when you have a surplus in your pension scheme. But it looks very different when there is a deficit. This effect is even stronger because this is the first recession companies have gone through with the cost of pensions directly on their balance sheets.

A further reason for the exclusion of young people from employment may be that the skills and human capital of older workers may be greater. This may be worrying evidence of weaknesses in our vocational training system. One American analysis has put the argument brutally. For the post-War period growth in the USA was driven by successive generations of new cohorts entering the labour force better educated and trained than the one before, but it is proposed that process may now be coming to an end.[34] In Britain the graduate premium has held up but that hides a wide diversity of returns and it may not be so true for individual courses. And there are some NVQs (National Vocational Qualifications) which have little value. Professor Blanchflower rightly concludes that reform of training is necessary.

These young people face competition and adversity in the labour market on a completely different scale from that which confronted the boomers entering the jobs market even in the 1970s. But in many cases they are sustained by their families. And it is these links with older generations to which we now turn.

Chapter 12

3G

Human progress surged forward about 50,000 years ago: for the first time we had a diversity of tools; we started fishing, cooking, drawing; we advanced out of Africa and across the globe. Although *Homo sapiens* had been around for 200,000 years or so this, the Upper Palaeolithic Revolution, is nothing less than the start of human culture.

What happened? The fossils left in the caves and encampments of our early ancestors are a crucial clue. They suggest that human development really took off when the ratio of old to young was transformed. The campsites of the Neanderthals and early *Homo sapiens* yield up many more jawbones of under-15-year-olds than over-30-year-olds. But about 50,000 years ago that ratio shifts dramatically so that there are twice as many jawbones for over-30s as for under-15s. A modest improvement in life expectancy meant a big increase in the chances of three generations living together – from dying at 30 when your child is 15 with no grandchildren to surviving to 35 when your child is 20 and grandchild is 5. This is a massive change in society and is key to culture and civilization.[1]

The parents might be busy hunting and gathering but the children could learn from the grandparents. They were transmitting a body of knowledge embodied in a culture across three generations. The ability to pass on what you have learned, as a tradition, is what makes human progress possible. And that is what grandparents did. Grandparents are the custodians of the intergenerational contract today as well. They can play an enormous role in lives of grandchildren, in both time and money. They are partners in three of the four contracts between the generations which we described in Chapter 5. Accounts of old age usually begin with worrying figures for dependency ratios. We can reverse that and instead recognize the contribution that the third generation make to society though their networks of exchanges, captured beautifully by Michael Young and Peter Wilmott in their classic study of *Family and Kinship in East London*:

And so it goes on – the daughter's labours are in a hundred little ways shared with the older woman whose days of child-bearing (but not of child-rearing) are over. When the time comes for the mother to need assistance, the daughter reciprocates... by returning the care she has herself received.[2]

These exchanges flourished in the strong working-class neighbourhood they studied, even though they did not live in the same house.

The classical tradition of sociology, from Durkheim to Parsons, assumed that family transfers beyond the nuclear household would just wither away. The empirical evidence shows the opposite. Whether it is measured by time or by money these ties between the generations still mean a lot. In fact many grandparents have become the new housewives.

One survey asked parents of young children about who had helped with childcare in the past week. A quarter had been helped by a grandparent as against 10 per cent a friend or neighbour and 8 per cent a day nursery.[3] Grandparents had helped 45 per cent of employed mothers with childcare as against 37 per cent who had used formal providers.[4] According to a separate survey of grandparents, of those with grandchildren under 13 between one quarter and one third report a fairly regular childcare role, about one quarter have no role at all and just under a half fall between these two positions.[5] Estimates of the value of the childcare provided by grandparents range from £3.9bn to £50bn.[6] That may be one reason why now we say, 'Darling, let's have babies while our parents are young enough to look after them.' And those ethnic minorities with different family traditions do also have intergenerational living – one in four Indian families live with paternal grandparents.[7]

Grandparents are also of great significance in shaping cultural values. The early boomers are now rather unusual grandparents. As they were such young parents in the 1960s they are now unusually young grandparents. The proportion of grandparents in the population is higher: more than half of the British population are now grandparents by the age of 54.[8] The average number of grandchildren they have is lower, which may be a reason for more engagement in their grandchildren – 58 per cent of grandparents describe themselves as friend/confidant to their grandchildren.[9]

As women live longer than men and as wives tend to be younger than husbands, the grandparent the grandchild is likeliest to get to know is the maternal grandmother. So maternal grandmothers are 35 per cent of living grandparents of 10- to 19-year-olds and over 50 per cent of the living grandparents of grown-up grandchildren.[10] This may be significant in giving them a role as custodians of the intergenerational contract – both contributing most to it and then benefiting from it. They can be a source of advice for teenagers when communication with their parents is weak. Maternal grandmothers are the older person who is by far the most likely to be cited by teenagers as a source of 'good advice' – 35 per cent of 11- to 16-year-olds say they can share things with their mum's mum which they cannot talk to parents about.[11]

There is also evidence from surveys of substantial financial transfers between living generations: 16 per cent of grandparents in their sixties and one third of grandparents in their seventies provide financial support to grandchildren.[12] An unusual piece of evidence from the former East Germany shows the strength of these transfers. East German pensioners enjoyed the greatest gains in income immediately after unification. Their total pensions were still lower than in West Germany but the gap was smaller than for younger people in work. What did they do with this extra income? They transferred a lot to their middle-aged children: 31 per cent made transfers in one year, compared with 23 per cent in West Germany. Children aged 40–55 were the main recipients. The researchers who uncovered this effect conclude that 'part of the public transfers from the employed population to the elderly in the form of pensions are handed back to their family descendants.'[13]

The more hard-bitten analyst might suggest this type of behaviour by the older generation means they are following the advice of the American bumper sticker: 'Be nice to your kids – they will choose your nursing home.' My argument is that this message is very shrewd.

––––––

You may be wondering how grandparents managed to contribute their share of these intergenerational exchanges in the past, when everyone died so much younger. We are told that average life expectancy was only 30 in the Middle Ages or 40 in the nineteenth century, for example.[14] This suggests that there were not many old people around then. And with our patterns of late marriage and childbearing that means there would not have been many grandparents. If this were true it would raise serious questions about our whole account of the historic English family – why hang around not marrying and delaying having kids until your mid- or late twenties if you are going to die by the time you were 40? Can we explain this puzzle?

The explanation is that conventional figures for life expectancy are deeply misleading and can easily lead us to misunderstand the relations between the generations. Contrary to the impression given by these familiar measures of life expectancy, older people have always been fundamental to communities, even primitive societies and certainly in Britain throughout our recorded history. Already by the seventeenth century 9 per cent of England's population was aged over 60.[15] That was probably the pattern for at least 500 years, with the exception of the demographic surge in the turbulent years of the nineteenth century when the proportion of older people may for a time have fallen to 7 per cent.

We need to disentangle the different ways in which a society can grow older. It can happen in at least three different ways, each with very different economic and social implications. Take six people. One of them dies as a child aged 5. One dies of TB aged 20. The third dies in an industrial accident aged 50. The remaining three work until they are 65 and die at the age of 75. That gives those six people an average life expectancy of 50 years. It is what Britain, and many other countries, used to be like. But the average life expectancy of 50 did not mean that there were very few old people. Average life expectancy was pulled down by the dismal attrition of death during childhood or early adulthood. Indeed, our illustrative figures would have been even more dramatic if we had counted deaths in very early infancy and used them to reduce the average even further. But once you were an adult you had a reasonable chance of getting through into your sixties, so ensuring a good mix of generations. Given our pattern of late marriage and few children, England in particular would never have felt like a particularly young country. (One might even speculate that this high proportion of old people combined with a low birth rate may be a factor in our historic political stability.)

Medicine then improves so that fewer children die and we reduce the incidence of TB. Factories become safer as well. Now imagine that all six of the people in our example work until they are aged 65 and all die at the age of 75. Average life expectancy therefore rises from 50 to 75, but it is not the case that everyone used to die aged 50 and now does so aged 75. Instead of different people dying at different ages there is a much greater chance of getting through into old age and a much narrower bunching of the ages when people die. This is what the demographers call the rectangularization of life expectancy, because instead of a drooping curve of survivors to old age we all die at about the same age. This is the first way of improving life expectancy. Average life expectancy in our example has gone from 50 to 75. But it is very misleading to imagine a group of people who used to die at 50 now die at 75. It is not like that and does not produce lots of extra years of senility and decay. Most of the extra years added to life are years of working adulthood, giving if anything a boost to the economy. That form of improvement in life expectancy has now been almost exhausted – if everyone made it to 65, life expectancy would only rise by a further one month. Because growing life expectancy in the twentieth century took the form of eliminating many of the causes of early death the experts kept on predicting that the increase in life expectancy would slow down. What has surprised them is that improvements in life expectancy are now taking a second and very different form.

Now, instead of everybody dying at 75, most make it through to 80 instead, and then on to 85. It is this type of improvement in life expectancy, pushing out the boundary, that does indeed take the form of people who were already old, judging by the standards of

their time, living to be even older. This is the much more exceptional achievement of raising life expectancy at the age of 65. This
is the figure that is now rising, as the table below shows.

Table 17. Average male life expectancy at the age of 65 in the UK[16]

1950	1960	1970	1980	1990	2000	2005	2008
12.0	12.2	12.8	14.0	15.8	18.2	19.1	21.0

We might have thought we were genetically programmed to die
at 75 but that now looks unlikely. To understand why there is no
such genetic programme we have to go to the ingenious application of the insights of Malthus and Darwin by gerontologists such
as Professor Tom Kirkwood. Malthus described a world in which
nature has a tendency to what he regarded as overpopulation.
Darwin discerned that whilst this might appear wasteful, it was
actually a precondition for enabling evolution to operate because
it meant there was an intensely competitive environment out of
which the fittest could be selected and with many more tiny
genetic experiments to choose from. In this environment you
don't die of old age – you die of cold or starvation or from preda-
tors. This means in turn there is no selection for a longevity gene
which, like a switch, would turn you off at a certain age. So there
is not a natural age of death fixing our lifespan. That is why we can
indeed imagine a world where we live far longer than today.

We fear these extra years will be years of morbidity and ill
health. There is conflicting evidence from different countries,
perhaps because they have different measures of quality of life,
and different family structures too. On balance the news is good.
It looks as if for most people these are extra years of good health.

By and large we die fitter; medical science is making progress in tackling the diseases of morbidity as well as mortality, as the table below shows – especially if you are a woman.

Table 18. Changes in healthy life expectancy (LE) at the age of 65 for males (M) and females (F)[17]

	M total LE	M healthy LE	F total LE	F healthy LE
1983	13.3	10.1	17.3	12.1
2003	16.5	12.5	19.4	14.4
Increase	3.2	2.4	2.1	2.3

The conventional wisdom is that people aged over 75 need a lot of health care. So if people live five years longer, the pessimists say, they are going to need five more years of expensive health care. But this is to misunderstand what is going on. Intensive health care is not delivered to people because they are aged 75; it is delivered to people because they are in the last year of their lives. One estimate is that for people over 65, 60 per cent of medical costs are incurred in the last twelve months of life. As people live to be 80 instead of 75, they still need expensive health care but the health care will be needed in the last year, which is five years later than before. So on this model rising life expectancy, even in the form of extra years of old age, delivers a short-term saving in health care costs as it delays the moment when people start needing expensive medical assistance.[18]

This second form of ageing can, other things being equal, change the ratio of over-60s to under-60s but that is simply a numerical relationship. It is wrong to get into the mindset of regarding this as a 'dependency ratio'. There is no rule of God or man that says that people aged over 60 have to be dependent. In fact, the research with which we began this chapter took such a ratio and interpreted it the opposite way round, with an increase in the number of older people seen as crucial to human development. Older people do not just make a massive contribution to society, but can also continue making a direct measured economic contribution.

So far we have looked at two very different long-term trends, both of which can be regarded as a society ageing. What really adds the drama is the third form of population ageing. This is what is about to hit us. It can happen alongside the other trends that we described, and can offset them, or enormously magnify them. This is when the population ages because a big cohort, called sometimes the pig in the python, gets to the later stages of the life cycle. If it is followed by a younger cohort which is smaller, then society will age even without the other two effects we have already looked at. In fact the average age of a country can rise without any change in any individual's life expectancy. It is this form of population ageing which is starting to hit us as the baby boomers reach pension age. As the cohort ahead of them is quite small we have just had a couple of decades with very little increase in the number of pensioners. In 2007 the women from the first peak of the baby boom reached pension age and in 2012 the men will. In that five years the total number of pensioners rises by 0.8 million, more than in the previous ten years.[19]

––––––––––

A pension is the intergenerational contract in its most explicit form. We might just think it is our own pension and our own savings but that does not quite catch what is going on. The bread which you might eat as a pensioner in twenty years' time does not yet exist. You cannot bake it now and store it for the future. Instead we need a way of registering our claim to bread, and other resources, when they are produced by the younger generation in the future.

A traditional way to do this is via the family, with working members of the family sharing their wages with elderly parents. In China there is still an expectation that a son will maintain his parents – a daughter's obligations are to her in-laws. This pension arrangement is why the one child policy has led, via abortion and infanticide, to a massive surplus of men over women. If China had property rights and funded pensions, families' future incomes would not be so dependent on having a son. An English parent is amazed by the sheer hard work and commitment to education of the Chinese family at their local school, but should remember that the origins of this behaviour lie in a culture where your child, especially your son, is your pension.

The English family has not traditionally worked like the Chinese – our unusually small families with more limited obligations between the generations may be one reason why financial products such as insurance and annuities flourished here. 'By about 1600 it was possible to purchase a lifetime annuity in the marketplace for oneself and one's wife.'[20] We needed such financial instruments because we did not spread claims on future resources through extended families. Instead we make a claim on these resources through a pension fund which might, for example, own shares in businesses and so take the value of some of the output as profit and dividends. This output is of course generated by the younger generation. Some of the output goes to shareholders such as pension funds so they can pay out to their elderly members. One advantage of such a fund is that it is better able than national governments to take a stake in the production of workers in other countries with very different demographics from ours.

Another way future pensioners can also make a claim on resources is via the state. The government does not need to run an equity fund and collect the dividends as revenues because it can use its power to tax the output of the next generation of workers and pass some of it on to the older generation. Either way, whether the money is being claimed via pension funds or taxes, the bread which is being baked by the working generation is ending up in the mouths of older people. And successive generations of workers accept it because they know their turn to be a recipient will come. These promises can last a long time – in fact pension promises are some of the most long-lasting we can make. The American Civil War veterans' pension fund made its last payment in 2001, 140 years after it was first set up in 1862. (The payment was to a widow who had married a very old veteran in the 1920s when he was very old and she was very young. Such marriages were quite widespread, and we might speculate on what was in it for both parties.)

There are different pension crises, depending on where you are looking from. The one which has dominated the headlines for the past few years is that companies have made promises of pensions to their employees which have turned to be out far more expensive than they thought. One reason is the improvements in the life expectancy of people after they got to 65 which we described above. These pensions are so valuable that they have been a big contribution to the wealth of the older generation. The classic response of a company to these costs and uncertainties has been to close its final salary pension scheme and move instead to a defined contribution scheme. If you are the finance director of a company, closing your generous pension scheme and setting up a new much less generous one for your younger employees looks like a solution. But it is not the end of the story. The difference between these two types of pension has profound effects on the distribution of resources between men and women and young and old.

In a final salary scheme the employee and the employer pay in during your working life and when you retire you get a pension related to your final salary. This is financed out of the big shared pot which is the company pension scheme. You carry on getting this pension, possibly uprated by inflation, for the rest of your life. Your widow, or indeed widower, has a continuing entitlement to half your pension as long as he or she survives after you. This is in effect the company acting as a mini welfare state. Its pension scheme is taking the risk of how long you and your partner will live. It is also promising to protect you from the uncertainties of life expectancy and inflation. It could only afford to do this because it thought it would carry on as a big business and successive generations of younger workers would be paying contributions that kept the whole thing going – these company schemes were closer to a pay-as-you-go pension than they were willing to admit.

It now looks an extraordinary set of responsibilities for a company to take on and only the public sector and a few very big corporations are willing to do so any longer. Even this generous arrangement has its losers as well as its gainers, at least in relative terms. Early leavers, for example, may not do very well. Another group who do relatively badly are those who may not expect to live for very long having paid in a lot – such as smokers.

A defined contribution scheme is very different. You have a personal pot of pension saving. You build it up during your working life with usually some contribution from your employer as well. After you retire you convert it into an annuity, paying you a guaranteed income for the rest of your life. Annuities can be set according to what is estimated to be your own personal life expectancy using the mass of information now available to the insurance companies that sell them. If they think you will live a long time then you will get a lower annual income for your lump sum than if you are not thought likely to last long.

There are pros and cons to both forms of pension, but a shift from one to the other involves gainers and losers. One of the biggest effects is by gender. Women live longer than men. If there are two employees with the same pension contribution record and the same salary when they retire, they get the same defined benefit pension. But the woman is likely to live longer so she will get this money for longer and hence is likely to receive more overall. If you shift to a defined contribution scheme the calculations change. Now with a given pot of money the annual annuity for the woman is going to be lower than for the man to allow for her longer life expectancy. It works the same way for smokers and non-smokers. A smoker is, so to speak, an extreme case of being a man and a non-smoker is an extreme case of being a woman. The short-lived smoker should get a much better annuity – in fact the single best piece of financial advice you will ever get is to resist the temptation to underestimate your smoking and drinking when you fill in your annuity form.

The effects do not stop there. There is no obligation for inflation protection in your annuity, so you can take more of your income upfront and risk a lower real income as you get really old. Moreover we saw that a final salary pension is required by law to protect your spouse after you die with an entitlement to half your pension. But there is no such requirement if you have a personal pension. Instead you have a choice. When you take out an annuity you can either buy an income just for yourself during the rest of your life or you can buy one for your possible future widow too. The choices men make – and it usually is men – are some of the best real-world evidence we have got about the ability of the family to act as a mini welfare state. It makes uncomfortable reading – 80 per cent of men in these circumstances opt for an annuity which just covers them and not their widow too. Instead of a big ocean liner we are each in our own craft – and in such a small craft there might not even be room for one's own spouse. For some this is invigorating, free of messy and hidden redistribution. For others it means potential losses.

The personal pension is likely to be small compared with what you could have built up in a traditional company scheme. That means losses for the younger generation, who are not going to build up a pension with anything like the value they would have had in the old company scheme. The gap between the pension of older employees and younger employees gets even wider. It is the young new recruits who are the poor bloody infantry being sacrificed as the generals fight the pensions crisis.

The biggest single effect of all these changes, however, is between the generations. But where exactly does the divide fall? It is partly between the public and private sectors, and public sector workers tend to be older than in the private sector – one reason being that they stay because of the generosity of the pension. Early boomers, who built up their pension in the good years, should be OK. But many late boomers still in their late forties or fifties are finding their pension scheme being closed to new accrual.

This tells us that the real pension crisis has not yet happened though it is rolling towards us with horrible inevitability. The real pension crisis comes over the next decades when people expect to retire and find that their new-style defined contribution is worth a pittance. This is when the real battle over resources begins and the boomers are a big powerful cohort. What will they do if especially the late boomers find they are losing out on their pensions?

One reaction to all this is to say, 'We don't need to worry, there is a great big pile of money in our house and we can use this to finance our retirement.' This transformation of the house from simply a place to live into a personal goldmine that solves every financial problem was one of the key events of the past decade. We have now had a bucket of cold water thrown over our fantasy estimates of how much our house is going to be worth. But this is still one of the most vivid ways a family wrestles with the fundamental issue of the distribution of wealth across the generations – is that wealth in the house ours to spend or for the kids to inherit?

Spending it on ourselves is what the financial services industry calls decumulation. It rests on the life cycle model of personal spending (economists focus on the life cycle and sociologists focus on cohorts). It says we smooth our income across the life cycle so first we build up our savings when we are most prosperous and then we run them down. We are supposed to spend our last day sipping our last Martini paid for with the last pound in our bank account as the mortgage on the house hits 100 per cent. It is the economic theory behind the behaviour of the 60-somethings going bungee jumping in New Zealand paid for by the money the kids thought was going to be their inheritance. This model has a very simple explanation of inheritance – it is a mistake. The mistake is made because sadly we do not know quite when we will die so we end up with assets left over in case we live longer than we do. Inheritance is like the tiresome foreign banknotes left over at end of a holiday which we give to BA for charity. At the other extreme is the bequest motive – we build up savings to pass on to our children and grandchildren.

What the boomers want to do with their money as they get older is one of the biggest financial issues of the future. Many will find that their pension does not pay as much as they hoped so they will be tempted to raid the house for as much money as they can get out of it. But they might accept a lower income in old age in order to pass something on to their children and grandchildren. A lot will depend on how well their children are doing. If the younger generation are all in well-paid jobs then their parents will keep the money for themselves.

There is some evidence of what might happen from Chris Hammet of King's College, who analyses the estates people leave. He has found they contain fewer houses than was expected. In the early 1970s 140,000 properties a year were being left. Over the next thirty years we had a lot of rhetoric about wealth cascading down across the generations. Yet it is still only 160,000 houses being left in estates now.[21] The trouble is, we don't quite know why this is happening. One reason is a fall in the death rate from 600,000 to 500,000 per year. Another reason is moving abroad. But another reason is that 30,000–50,000 properties every year are now being sold to pay for care. This is evidence of lower inheritance because of claims on income by old people themselves. One argument for cutting Inheritance Tax is that it increases the incentives for older people to save rather than consume their wealth. (Australia provides interesting evidence of how much inheritance tax matters to old people and their children. When inheritance tax was cut from a fixed date in Australia there was a fall in death rates as sick old people held on until the new tax regime came into force – tax affects behaviour so much it can even delay death.)

If older people find themselves managing on low incomes they could of course just vote themselves higher benefits. These would be paid for by higher taxes on the younger working population. It is a vivid example of one generation compulsorily taking money from another. Maybe our attitudes to issues like this just depend on where we are in the life cycle. There is already evidence of a big gap in attitudes to public spending on pensions: 30 per cent of 18- to 34-year-olds vote for raising taxes so the value of the state pension does not fall and 38 per cent vote for keeping things as they are for now, which means the value of the state pension falls over time. For 50- to 69-year-olds the figures are a much heftier 47 per cent voting for tax increases and 22 per cent for leaving them as they are.[22] Now we see why that distinction between cohort effects and life cycle effects matters so much. Will the younger generation, currently so reluctant to pay taxes to preserve the value of the pension, change their views as they get closer to pension age? If, as one might expect, their views change as they go through the life cycle, there will be further increases in the pressures on public spending.

Be it the effects of globalization on wages, the shift to lower inflation, or the impact of improved life expectancy, the baby boomers seem to have had all the luck. Or is there more to it than that? We know how the political analysts and public choice theorists would explain what is going on. Being a big generation gives you a lot of political power. Public choice theory tells us that how people vote will be affected by their interests and their political power. One study[23] compared twenty advanced Western countries to see if there was a pattern. It was very clear. For every extra year on the age of the median voter, spending on pensions rose by 0.5 per cent of GDP.

The baby boomers are a very big cohort and as a result they bring a lot of voting power with them: 71 per cent of 54- to 64-year-olds vote, and 75 per cent of over-65s, as against a national turn-out of 61 per cent. Between them these two groups cast 40 per cent of votes in the 2005 election. A 55+ party could sweep Parliament. Younger voters by contrast just do not have the same electoral power. We are in for big changes in the age of our voters over the next decade and more. The projected age of the median voter in Britain, adjusted for propensity to vote, was already 50 at the 2005 Election. It rises to 52 in 2015 and 56 in 2025, then gradually rises to 60 by 2055.[24] By far the biggest offsetting factor is not birth rate but immigration, as it shifts the age of the voter much faster. If you assume that the high immigration of the past few years continues, then voting age rises slowly but remains below 50 until 2035. It is 2020 before more than half of the total voters are aged over 50. But then you could get into very explosive territory where dividing lines of age and ethnicity reinforce each other. This is what is happening in California. Conflict between younger immigrant voters and older native pensioners can lead to generational and political gridlock.

This book is not cynical about such political power, assuming that it must always be used selfishly to favour one's own generation. We are not just solitary individuals voting for our personal interests. We are members of families and inheritors of generations stretching back in time. The book is not an attack on baby boomers – it is an appeal to them about how they use this power. It is an appeal which rests on the deepest human instincts.

Conclusion

Bladerunner used to be for me the film with the most powerful vision of the future. But now I think instead of two rather unlikely films set deep in rural France: *Jean de Florette* and *Manon des Sources*. Those two films, based on the novels of Marcel Pagnol, touched deep French fears about the prospects of the next generation.

Yves Montand acts the role of Cesar Soubeyran, a prosperous farmer. He and his unappealing nephew Ugolin want to take over the neighbouring farm with fields fed by a spring. They try to buy it but the old farmer refuses. When he dies it is taken over by a newcomer, Jean, acted by Gérard Depardieu. He struggles heroically to make the farm a success but Soubeyran and Ugolin have secretly blocked up the spring on the farm. His increasingly desperate search for water ultimately results in his death.

Jean's daughter, Manon, discovers what Soubeyran and Ugolin have done and seeks revenge for her father's death. By the end of the film Ugolin has hanged himself and Soubeyran has the shock of discovering that Jean, the man he worked so assiduously to destroy, was actually his own son. Soubeyran had been determined to continue the male bloodline through his nephew. But eventually, as a result of his own actions, the family name is extinguished with the deaths of both his nephew and his son. He dies tortured by this knowledge.

The films raise deep questions about fairness across the generations. Even though Soubeyran wanted to help his nephew and pass on his wealth to the next generation, he conspired in blocking up the spring of future prosperity and destroyed the lives of both his heirs. It is a melodramatic version of the strangely mixed emotions of so many middle-aged parents today who have achieved reasonable prosperity themselves but are increasingly anxious about how their own children can ever hope to achieve anything similar. No one can, of course, know how things will turn out. And the sheer dynamism of science and technology are the best single hope we have. But we cannot simply leave to modern science the responsibility for discharging our obligations to the future. The fabric tying the generations together is woven with many more strands than that.

There are two places above all where these obligations across the generations are discharged: the family and the nation state. We saw in Chapter 1 how there are strong connections between them, with family structure influencing both the shape of civil society and the structure of our economy. Both family and nation-state are by and large hereditary. They are the remaining vertical links in a world where many more of our connections are horizontal – to people in our own age group.

Our fears about our society and the strains in our economy reflect a breakdown in the balance between the generations. It is under threat from the baby boomers, born roughly between 1945 and 1965, not because of deliberate selfishness but because of their sheer demographic and economic power. Younger generations are losing out. The relative size of different generations has a big impact. Our short account of post-War Britain in Chapter 3 showed how the surge of young people from the immediate post-War baby boom, pouring out into adulthood, helps us understand the permissive society of the 1960s. In the 1980s the arrival of a further wave of young workers from the second peak of the baby boom made the Thatcherite transformation of Britain possible, as there were new workers who were not tied to traditional jobs in traditional indus-tries. So these twin peaks of the baby boom drove the twin social and economic revolutions of the 1960s and the 1980s. There are some who fear that society is on an irreversible process of atomiza-tion. We can be more optimistic when we understand that some of these changes are caused by these transient and unusual demo-graphic changes when countries are youthful – and we were exceptionally youthful in the period from the sixties to the eighties.

It used to be thought bad news to be a big generation as you have tougher competition for limited resources. But instead the eco-nomic and cultural evidence in Chapter 4 showed that since the War the reality has been the opposite: both in Britain and throughout the West the big boomer generation has done dispro-portionately well. They own more than half of Britain's £6tn of personal wealth. They have benefited from previous house price booms and they are also the beneficiaries of generous company pension schemes (which are now closing and not available for younger workers). It is now much, much harder for the young gen-eration to get started on the housing ladder or to build up a pension – the two main forms of personal wealth.

One objection to this argument is that younger generations are going to be a lot better off than us. If this is the case then why shouldn't we borrow money from their future? But our obligation to provide for future generations is not extinguished if we believe they are going to be richer than us. The Victorians left us fine public buildings and infrastructure such as railways which we still use today, despite their believing, rightly, that we would be better off than they were. Moreover, whilst our children and grandchildren will probably be better off than us, if we, in effect, borrow from them, then their prosperity will be blighted. And that is just what we have been doing. The boomers have been pinching too big a share of the wealth we are generating now and hope to generate in the future.

The rise in asset prices in the past decade made us all feel richer but it favoured the possessors, the baby boomers. There was a shift in wealth to that generation as they are the owners of housing and pre-crisis pensions. But they converted a once-off (and, we now see, temporary) surge in asset prices into higher incomes by borrowing against them. This delivered a temporary boost in their living standards financed by a massive reduction in saving and imposed higher costs on the next generation, who have less to inherit. It will be the younger generation who pay the price.

The amounts we save and invest are the clearest single measure of how much we value the future. Britain's savings rate fell to a catastrophically low figure of 4.5 per cent net for the entire economy, which is much less than is necessary to sustain our growth rate. This was one of the lowest ever recorded in the advanced Western world. Indeed over the twenty years 1987 to 2007 our net savings rate was the lowest of any advanced Western country.[1] The personal sector is an important part of this total. One reason our banks were so vulnerable to the credit crunch is that they had fewer savings deposits than in the past: instead they were raising funds by borrowing in the wholesale interbank market. These funds were therefore only supplied to our banks for short periods and had to be continuously re-borrowed. When they were no longer available our banking system came close to collapse. We now need to reward saving. This will mean a slow and painful process of adjustment over the next decade.

Total physical investment in Britain is also low compared with other countries. We are not endowing future generations with the transport or energy infrastructure they need to be prosperous. Even when we do have physical assets they do not necessarily belong to us, as we have had to raise funds by selling our airports or electricity-generating capacity to foreign companies. Cross-border transactions are part of the modern global economy and neither could nor should be stopped by government controls. But this fire-sale of our assets is a result of fundamental imbalances, particularly a dependence on funds from abroad to finance our balance-of-payments deficit, which are now going to have to be addressed. Meanwhile successive generations are not going to be able to enjoy the benefits of an income from these assets. The output we produce in Britain will not necessarily yield revenues for British people.

The social contract is an important part of Western political thought. I believe it is really a contract between the generations. These intergenerational contracts are at the heart of the family and the welfare state. They depend on reciprocity and we saw in Chapter 5 how recent advances in game theory and in understanding the evolution of human behaviour help us understand how reciprocity sustains co-operative behaviour and gives people a sense of well-being. Mutual exchanges between the generations are particularly fruitful in strengthening civil society. Much of what we experience as social breakdown arises from the loss of trust between the generations.

This focus on generations is a strand of thought which begins with the first sociologist, Auguste Comte, and runs through to the great twentieth-century thinker Karl Mannheim, whose essay 'The Problem of Generations'[2] is about how the succession of different generations shapes modern life. His insight is that in pre-modern societies the vertical links of family and tribe are what matter. When a culture is stable, successive generations are indistinguishable. In the modern world the crucial ties are horizontal; you are linked to other members of your generation by the particular cultural experiences you share. This can weaken co-operation between the age groups, who regard each other as alien creatures. Increasingly neighbourhoods and workplaces comprise people of the same age. When there are concentrations of very young people with very few adults anti-social behaviour flourishes. We saw in Chapter 6 how this helps explain not just the instability of countries going through their demographic transition but also the troubles on our own housing estates. Indeed, we have managed on our tough estates to create environments with such large numbers of children relative to adults that demographically they are closer to the Third World – *Lord of the Flies* is all about what happens in the extreme case of when there are no adults at all.

One way to break out of these misunderstandings between the generations is to think of other generations as like one's own but at different stages of their lives. The fundamental process of moving through the life cycle gives life its rhythm – ask people about the events which have meant the most to them over the past year, the highs and the lows, and they won't talk about politics but a wedding, the death of a relative, children's birthdays, events which mark the stages of the life cycle.

We may attach a lot of importance to future generations but conventional discount rates – the classic way economists measure value in the future – do not. They do not really attach much value to anything more than about a generation ahead. The environmental movement has led to new thinking about how we should value future generations. Chapter 7 investigated this issue and suggested a curving discount rate in the shape of a hyperbola as a way of reconciling conventional economic analysis in the short term with some value to the burdens imposed on our grandchildren. Whatever we may hope for our long-term prospects, given the extraordinary dynamism of modern science and technology, there is a predictable and clear pinch point, which appears to be most acute in about 2030. Even if we do not care about future generations, most of us will be around then when these pressures are intense. It is in our self-interest to tackle them. We just have to have the imagination to think of ourselves at different stages of the life cycle.

The world is no longer simply an America, with unlimited resources just waiting for our enterprise. We have, for example, been mining water without, as the accountants would say, properly allowing for the cost of depreciation; water stress could be a growing issue. It will be 2030 when demographic pressures are intense as the boomers age in the West and the youthful population surges in places like Africa. Demographic pressures, climate change, energy security, pressures on water and food supplies: all this adds up to a time of peril for humanity. It has rightly been called the long emergency. Beyond these material issues, the challenge of conveying our culture from one generation to the next seems much harder with the collapse of confidence in a cultural canon and the rise of militant Islam.

Our story of successive generations going through the life course provided in Chapter 8 an account of a lot of what government does. By and large the system takes money from middle-aged people and redistributes it to children and older people, not just through benefits but also in education and health care. This is rather like the redistribution that has traditionally been undertaken by the family and which to an extent still is. But as the family has shrunk so the welfare state has found itself doing more. And the welfare state tends to focus principally on the older generation, to which we do of course have inescapable obligations, whereas historically the flow of resources in families from both parents and grandparents has been to the younger generation.

For many young people negotiating the route from childhood to independence – getting started on the housing ladder, settling down in a stable partnership, or having children – is very hard indeed. Twenty-somethings become trapped in a kind of semi-adulthood. For them modern life is not fast but actually very slow. The transitions into stable employment and a stable relationship take longer than at any time since the War. This is easily misinterpreted by older generations as a rejection of these aspirations. Generally, it is not. The aspirations remain, but they are harder to achieve. It is this movement through the stages of the life course which we followed in the final four chapters. Instead of post-modern invented narratives, this is deeply rooted in the patterns of human experience.

The baby boomers and their successors have proved to be better parents than citizens. The old generation gap – the mutual incomprehension of parents and children – is disappearing, to be replaced by something less personal but deeper and more social and economic. Parents may do their best for their own children but there is still the task of ensuring a fair deal for the younger generation as a whole. A good example is the extra time parents devote to their younger children even whilst at the same time the quality of childhood is declining. The explanation of this paradox of extra parental time and poorer-quality childhood is that although parents are devoting more time to their own children, they have lost trust in other adults. They are anxious about the safety of public space and so are reluctant to let their children play freely. As a result our children are either inside in an unsupervised screen-based culture or they are outside and active but supervised. Free-range childhood has disappeared in a generation.

The growing significance of parents compared with other adults helps us to explain low social mobility in our country. The opportunities to break free from family influence are shockingly weak. The route from school to work is especially tricky for young people

UNIVERSITY OF WINCHESTER
LIBRARY

who do not have strong family backing. Getting a house of one's own is also far harder for the younger generation, unless of course they have access to the bank of mum and dad. The higher cost of housing for young people is in fact as heavy a burden as if in the past decade the government had more than doubled the national debt and left the younger generation to pay it off with higher taxes. But the fall in house prices, because it is associated with a credit crunch, is not making it easier for younger people to get on to the housing ladder. And we showed that the house price rise, to add insult to injury, has also put young people at a disadvantage in the labour market compared with migrant workers.

We have focused on the obligations we have to younger generations. But inter-generational justice is a richer idea than that: it covers all stages of the life cycle and includes obligations to older people as well as the young and the middle-aged. In 2010 the first male baby boomers become pensioners, and we then have a bigger increase in the number of pensioners over the following ten years than in the previous twenty-five. The pensions crisis means that people who retire in ten or twenty years with a personal pension will receive much less per year than someone with a traditional final salary pension. They may have to 'eat their house', which means there will be less for the next generation to inherit. Alternatively they will vote for parties promising them higher state benefits, financed by the younger generation.

The central argument in the book is that we are not attaching sufficient value to the claims of future generations. This is partly because a big disruptive generation of baby boomers has weakened many of the ties between the generations. But it is also an intellectual failure: we have not got a clear way of thinking about the rights of future generations. We are allowing one very big generation to break the inter-generational contract because we do not fully understand it. This is where politics comes in.

Politics can sometimes seem like just a cacophony of conflicting opinions. Although politicians may appeal to ideology, most people are not particularly ideological, so it leaves them cold. Montaigne expressed the scepticism which many voters feel about such deductive politics: 'It seems to me that there is a great deal of self-love and arrogance in judging so highly of your opinions that you are obliged to disturb the public peace to establish them.'[3]

That is why I have been trying to go back to fundamental experiences – the pattern of our lives as we move through the different ages of the life cycle, the changing balance of the generations, and the ties between them. This is an attempt to root politics in things which are natural and human. The family is key as it is the human universal but also helps us to understand the distinctive traditions and practices of our own society.

At its best government helps maintain the balance between the generations and helps shift resources between the different stages of the life cycle in a way that complements what families do. However, it can instead allow itself to be captured by particular generational interests that exploit this power. But this is not inevitable. Public policy can make a difference. And that means politics – good politics. What are the underlying principles that should shape what a politician does? You might say that there aren't any shared principles because political argument is about the principles we disagree on, but that isn't the whole story. We should share a belief in the basic principles of a modern liberal democracy. Can we go beyond that? What is it that enables us to distinguish between a good politician, a statesman if you like, and a bad one who is just playing the game? Look at some of the obvious historical comparisons. Why is Pitt the Younger a greater figure than Walpole? Why is Attlee a greater figure than Wilson?

Why is Thatcher a greater figure than Macmillan? Why is Churchill above all the rest? The explanation is surely that the great leaders did far more to shape the future of our country even if it meant short-term sacrifices. Good politics is about a contract between the generations in which the interests of the present generation should not automatically come first.

One opinion survey showed that more than half of voters wanted political parties to follow policies which would do good in the long term, rather than for the next year or two. This was the highest level of approval for any party political characteristic, and much higher than the 13 per cent of people who would support a party for its ideological principles.[4] This means helping to sustain the family, where these obligations are discharged one by one. It also means ensuring that no one generation uses the state for its own interests. If being a good politician is to mean anything other than being technically accomplished, it has to mean valuing the future and maintaining the contract between the generations. This lies behind our instinctive judgement about the difference between a statesman and a mere politician. As Disraeli is supposed to have said, 'A politician thinks of the next election. A statesman thinks of the next generation.'[5]

Visionaries may hope that government will wither away. Edmund Burke replied to them in his *Reflections on the Revolution in France*, one of the classic Conservative texts. He did not, as one might expect, justify government as a guarantor of order and security. Instead he appealed to government as custodian of the contract between the generations. It is a beautiful statement of the central theme of this book:

Society is indeed a contract. Subordinate contracts for objects of mere occasional interest may be dissolved at pleasure – but the state ought not to be considered as nothing better than a partnership agreement in a trade of pepper and coffee, calico or tobacco, or some other such low concern, to be taken up for a little temporary interest, and to be dissolved by the fancy of the parties. It is to be looked on with other reverence; because it is not a partnership in things subservient only to the gross animal existence of a temporary and perishable nature. It is a partnership in all science; a partnership in all art; a partnership in every virtue, and in all perfection. As the ends of such a partnership cannot be obtained in many generations, it becomes a partnership not only between those who are living, but between those who are living, those who are dead, and those who are to be born.[6]

So here we are. We have appealed to a contract between the generations. We have explained how it rests on reciprocity and how this is the origin of our moral sense. We have shown how the boomers have ended up with a large share of the national wealth and tried to set out some of the economics behind this. We have tried to address the argument that future generations will be richer, arguing that this does not extinguish the obligation. And as there is a pinch-point coming we cannot be so confident about their prosperity over the next few decades. We have offered a concession and proposed that even if we just think about ourselves in the next few decades there is a problem we have to face. We have then expanded that argument by suggesting we think of other generations as being like us but at different stages of the life cycle. We have been flattered as good parents and then challenged to be better citizens. We have appealed to our sense of self-preservation by asking what future generations will do for us when we are old and depend on them if we do not provide for them now. We have hoped for good politics – the statesmanship that comes from valuing the future. Is any further appeal left?

There remains the appeal of narrative, of tradition in its best and most sophisticated sense. We have already seen that the best way to learn responsibility and master oneself is to have a project for the future which gives purpose to our behaviour in the present and makes sense of what was done in the past. That is what drives us to reduce public debt or preserve the environment or improve educational standards. This ties together the arguments in the book. If we value the future then we can co-operate for the simple reason that we can value reciprocal benefits we hope to receive in the future. That makes reciprocity and co-operation possible. Vice versa, it is through our first experiences of such reciprocity that we can learn the value of future benefits. If someone, probably a parent, reciprocates, we begin to learn how our behaviour can bring future consequences, be they good or bad. It is hard to envisage the accumulation of social capital unless we value the future. The more we value the future so the wider the circle of co-operative reciprocal arrangements that become possible for us.

The problems of obesity or anti-social behaviour or credit card debt are not separate; they are all part of the same challenge of making self-control now worthwhile. It can be done if we see what we do today as part of a story linking past, present, and future. That is what we can do in a family and in a nation and perhaps even globally. It is what T. S. Eliot describes in his great essay, 'Tradition and the Individual Talent'. He is writing about the process of artistic creation but it applies also to our sense of who we are and what it means to inherit a tradition and pass it on:

the historical sense compels a man to write not merely with his own generation in his bones... no artist of any art, has his complete meaning alone. His significance, his appreciation is the appreciation of his relation to the dead poets and artists... He must be aware that the mind of Europe – the mind of his own country... is a mind which changes, and that this change is a development which abandons nothing en route... he is not likely to know what is to be done unless he lives in what is not merely the present, but the present moment of the past, unless he is conscious, not of what is dead, but of what is already living.[7]

Those statements are not just true for artists; they are true for all of us. The modern condition is supposed to be the search for meaning in a world where unreflective obligations to institutions or ways of doing things are eroded. The link between generations past, present and future is a source of meaning which is as natural as could be. It is both cultural and economic, personal and ethical. We must understand and honour those ties which bind the generations.

Notes

Introduction

1. Alexis de Tocqueville, 'Of Individualism in Democratic Countries' (chap. II), *Democracy in America*, vol. II, book II, Vintage Classics, 1990, p. 99.
2. Herodotus, *The Histories*, vol. I: 29–34, Oxford University Press, 1998. Another more rigorous translation is 'Until he is dead he is not happy, only lucky.'
3. The Long Now is a powerful expression coined by Brian Eno and is the name of a foundation set up by him and others. They use the idea far more ambitiously than in this volume to shift the way we think about the future so we value time-spans of thousands of years. For them the year of publication of this book is 02010.

1. Who We Are

1. Alan Macfarlane, *The Culture of Capitalism*, Blackwell, 1987, p. 151.
2. The key table is 'A scheme of the Income and Expense of the several families of England calculated for the year 1688', in *Gregory King, Two Tracts* (ed. G. E. Barnett), Johns Hopkins Press, 1936, p. 31.
3. Alan Macfarlane, *The Origins of English Individualism*, Blackwell, 1978. The quotation is from p. 163 and the figures from pp. 95 and 96.
4. F. W. Maitland, *Constitutional History of England*, quoted in Macfarlane, *Culture of Capitalism*, p. 188.
5. L. Lancaster, 'Kinship in Anglo-Saxon Society', Part II, *British Journal of Sociology*, 9, 1958, p. 375.
6. 'Family ties and the insurance they provide can only work if extended families live close to each other and therefore geographical mobility is lower.'

A. Alesina and P. Giuliano, *The Power of the Family*, Centre for Economic Performance Discussion Paper, April 2007.

7. 'Sermon of the Wolf to the English', in D. Whitelock, *English Historical Documents 500–1042*, Routledge, 1979, p. 931.

8. 'The Thegns' Guild of Cambridge', in ibid., p. 604.

9. 'The Ordinance of the Bishops and Reeves of the London District', in ibid, p. 426.

10. Macaulay, quoted in Gertrude Himmelfarb, *Poverty and Compassion: The Moral Imagination of the Late Victorians*, Vintage, 1992, p. 186.

11. The dissolution of the monasteries in 1536–40 removed long-established provision for the poor and needy. A legal framework for parish-based relief in its stead was developed over the next sixty years. The first Poor Law Act was passed in 1552. The first legislation for a compulsory local tax to pay for it was passed in 1576. This Elizabethan legislation was then consolidated in the 1601 Poor Law, which remained largely unchanged for two centuries.

12. Montesquieu quoted in Paul Langford, *Englishness Identified*, Oxford University Press, 2001, p. 5.

13. Benjamin Franklin, letter from London, 1773, quoted in *Bolingbroke's Political Writings* (ed. Bernard Cottiot), Macmillan, 1997.

14. Montesquieu, *Spirit of the Laws*, quoted in Alan Macfarlane, *The Origins of English Individualism*, p. 170.

15. *New Scientist*, 17 November 2008.

16. Emmanuel Todd, *The Explanation of Ideology: Family Structures and Social Systems*, Blackwell, 1983.

17. W. Rubinstein, *Capitalism, Culture, and Decline in Britain 1750–1990*, Routledge, 1993.

18. A. Chandler, *Scale and Scope: The Dynamics of Industrial Capitalism*, Belknap Press, 1994, and D. Landes, *The Unbound Prometheus: Technological Change and Industrial Development in Western Europe from 1750 to the Present*, Cambridge University Press, 1969.

19. Friedrich Engels, *The Origins of the Family, Private Property and the State*, quoted in Macfarlane, *Origins of English Individualism*, pp. 121–2.

20. French inheritance law changed on 1 January 2007. Your children can now sign over their inheritance to their children and miss themselves out, and likewise can sign over their inheritance to the children of their parents' union when they are from a different union, i.e. their half-siblings.

21. N. Bloom and J. van Reenen, *Measuring and Explaining Management Practices across Firms and Countries*, CEP Discussion Paper 716, March 2006,

p. 35.

22. T. Nicholas, 'Clogs to Clogs in Three Generations? Explaining Entrepreneurial Performance in Britain since 1850', *Journal of Economic History*, vol. 59, 1999, p. 709.

23. Emmanuel Todd, *After the Empire. The Breakdown of American Order*, Columbia University Press, 2003, p. 50.

24. Dr Johnson quoted in Lawrence Stone, *The Family, Sex and Marriage in England 1500–1800*, Pelican, 1979, p. 173. When Laurence Shirley, the 4th Earl Ferrers, was tried and hanged for the murder of a servant in 1760, his brother Washington succeeded him as the 5th Earl and inherited all of his estates. Holland was probably the only other European country of the period where an aristocrat could be tried for murdering a commoner and where the lines of family inheritance would be completely unaffected. I apologize to my dear brother Peter for this point.

25. Gertrude Himmelfarb, *The Roads to Modernity. The British, French and American Enlightenments*, Vintage, 2005.

26. Office for National Statistics, Focus on Ethnicity and Identity.

27. Andrew Roberts, *History of the English-Speaking Peoples Since 1900*, HarperCollins, 2008.

28. Tocqueville, *The Ancien Regime*, quoted in Francis Fukuyama, *Trust: The Social Virtues and the Creation of Prosperity*, Hamish Hamilton, 1995, p. 55.

29. Tocqueville, quoted in Seymour Drescher, *Tocqueville and England*, Harvard University Press 1964, p. 63.

30. Tocqueville, *The Ancien Regime*, quoted in Alan Macfarlane, *The Riddle of the Modern World*, Palgrave, 2000, p. 212.

31. Nancy Cott, *Public Vows: A History of Marriage and the Nation*, Harvard University Press, 2000. Chapter 1, 'An Archaeology of American Monogamy', explains the links between the American Revolutionaries' political model and their account of the family – a consensual union resting on a social contract.

32. Tocqueville quoted in Drescher, *Tocqueville and England*, p. 6.

33. Gilles Duranton, Andrés Rodríguez-Pose, and Richard Sandall, *Family Types and the Persistence of Regional Disparities in Europe*, Working Papers 2008–07, Instituto Madrileño de Estudios Avanzados (IMDEA) Ciencias Sociales, 2008.

34. Eurobarometer Survey 2001, Q35: Have you moved house in the past ten years? The countries with more than 50 per cent moving are Finland 59 per cent, Denmark 57 per cent, Sweden 56 per cent, the Netherlands, 53 per cent, and the UK 52 per cent.

35. Duranton et al., *Family Types*.
36. Richard Jackson and Neil Howe, *The Graying of the Great Powers: Demography and Geopolitics in the 21st Century*, Centre for Strategic and International Studies, 2008, p. 211.
37. The expressions come from Benedict Anderson, *Imagined Communities*, Verso, 1983; Linda Colley, *Britons: Forging the Nation: 1707–1837*, Yale University Press, 1992; Eric Hobsbawn and Terence Ranger (eds.), *The Invention of Tradition*, Cambridge University Press, 1983.
38. Hippolyte Taine, *Notes on England*, Henry Holt and Co., 1885, p. 4.

2. Breaking Up

1. 50 per cent of elderly individuals live with adult children in Japan, 42 per cent in Italy, and 40 per cent in Spain. By contrast less than 15 per cent of elderly individuals live with their children in France, Germany, the UK, and the US. See *The 2003 Aging Vulnerability Index* published by the Center for Strategic and International Studies, Washington DC. This does broadly match the divide between very low birth rates and rather higher ones.
2. Office for National Statistics, Social Trends 2007, p. 14.
3. Kathleen Kiernan, 'Lone Motherhood, Employment and Outcomes for Children', *International Journal of Law, Policy and the Family*, 1996, 10(3), pp. 233–49; shows that the educational attainments and economic outcomes for the children of lone parents are worse if the parent is not working than if he or she does. This effect is particularly marked for daughters.
4. The European System of Social Indicators, ZUMA, Mannheim, actually puts British household size on a comparable basis at 2.3, even lower than the official estimate in Social Trends.
5. Britain's Gini coefficient (a measure of how dispersed figures are in which 0 means complete equality and 1 is complete inequality) for inequality is unusually high at .36 and Sweden's Gini coefficient of inequality is much lower at .25. 'The most recent year (between 2006–07 and 2007–08) has seen a further small increase in the Gini coefficient, to reach 0.36 – the highest level since our comparable time series began in 1961': M. Brewer, A. Muriel, D. Phillips, and L. Sibieta, *Poverty and Inequality in Britain: 2009*, Commentary No. 109, Institute for Fiscal Studies, May 2009.
6. Richard Dickens and David T. Ellwood, 'Child Poverty in Britain and the United States', *The Economic Journal*, vol. 113, June 2003, pp. 219–39.

7. Arthur Brooks, *Gross National Happiness and How America Can Get More of It*, Basic Books, 2008, shows that by and large the people who try to keep these traditions going are happier than the more liberal-minded. But there is nothing to gloat about. In such a confused and fragmented world extremists tend to be happier too.

8. Every spring and autumn the EU conducts a Eurobarometer survey and records answers to the question on overall life satisfaction (Table 1.1A). Denmark has for over a decade been coming top of these surveys. In the spring 2009 survey Denmark was once again top with 98 per cent of people saying they are very or fairly satisfied with their lives, the UK was a very creditable 90 per cent, the EU average was 75 per cent and Italy was down at 60 per cent.

9. Eunice Yu and Jianguo Liu, 'Environmental Impacts of Divorce', *Proceedings of the National Academy of Science*, vol. 104, no. 51, 18 December 2007, pp. 20629–34.

10. Linda Waite and Maggie Gallagher, 'The Wages of Wedlock' (chap. 7), in *The Case for Marriage: Why Married People are Happier, Healthier, and Better-Off Financially*, Broadway Books, 2000, pp. 97–109.

11. J. Hudson, 'Inequality and the Knowledge Economy: Running to Stand Still', *Social Policy and Society*, vol. 5(2), pp. 207–22.

12. Ray Hall, Philip E. Ogden, and Catherine Hill, 'Living Alone: Evidence from England and Wales and France for the Last Two Decades' (chap. 11), in Susan McRae (ed.), *Changing Britain: Families and Households in the 1990s*, Oxford University Press, 1999, p. 274.

13. Anthony Giddens, *Modernity and Self- Identity: Self and Society in the Late Modern Age*, Polity Press, 1991, p. 6. See also chap. 3, 'The Trajectory of Self and the Brief Discussion of Family Obligations', p. 98.

14. Robert Putnam, *Bowling Alone: The Collapse and Revival of American Community*, Simon and Schuster, 2000, p. 224.

15. A good example of the optimist argument is Charles Leadbeater, *Up the Down Escalator*, Viking, 2002. For the pessimist case see Melanie Phillips, *The Sex Change State*, Social Market Foundation, 1997.

3. The Baby Boom

1. Office for National Statistics: Live births in Great Britain. A historic low point of 667,000 was reached in 1933.

2. Enid Charles, *The Twilight of Childhood*, 1933, Watts & Co., 1936 (subsequent editions retitled *The Menace of Under-Population*).

3. Advice from the Government Actuary in 1936. See John Macnicol, *The Politics of Retirement in Britain, 1878–1948*, Cambridge University Press, 1998, p. 264.

4. T. S. Eliot, 'The Idea of a Christian Society', in *Selected Prose of T. S. Eliot*, Faber and Faber, 1975, p. 285.

5. J. M. Keynes, 'Some Economic Consequences of a Declining Population', The Galton Lecture, *Eugenics Review*, vol. XXIX, no.1, 1937.

6. Royal Commission on Population: His Majesty's Stationery Office, Cmd.7695, June 1949; National Advisory Committee on the Employment of Older Men and Women, First Report, The Watkinson Report, Cmd.8693, October 1953; Report of the Committee on the Economic and Financial Problems of the Provision for Old Age, The Phillips Committee, Cmd.9333 December 1954.

7. Ina Zweiniger-Bargielowska, *Austerity in Britain: Rationing, Controls, and Consumption, 1939–1955*, Oxford University Press, 2000, shows just how low calorie intake was. The calorie intake of the middle classes fell from approximately 3,725 kcals per day in 1932–5 to a low point of 2,307 in 1947. For the working classes the figure also fell but from 2,859 in 1932–5 to 2,308 in 1947. It is also striking that calorie intake became so equal across social classes.

8. John Hobcraft, 'Fertility in England and Wales: A Fifty-Year Perspective', *Population Studies*, vol. 50, issue 3, November 1996, p. 490.

9. The average age of first intercourse fell from twenty-one years old for women born 1931–5 to twenty for women born 1936–40 and nineteen for women born 1941–5. See Kaye Wellings, Julia Field, Anne Johnson and Jane Wadsworth, *Sexual Behaviour in Britain*, Penguin Books, 1994, p. 37.

10. Philip Larkin, 'Annus Mirabilis', in *High Windows*, Faber and Faber, 1979.

11. Office for National Statistics, percentage of total first marriages with a birth within 8 months of marriage.

12. Joanna Burke, 'Housewifery in Working Class England 1860–1914', *Past & Present*, no. 143, May 1991, p. 168. The comparison between all women and then wives is imperfect but there are limits on the data and the underlying point still holds.

13. Pennsylvania State University researcher Dr Stacy Rogers interviewed 2,033

married people in 1980, 1983, 1988, 1992, and 1997 to better understand the role of income in relationships. When partners don't earn the same amount of money, the one earning less feels dependent, and the one earning more feels obligated to the other. People in both situations are less likely to divorce. This was one of the findings of the Marital Instability Over the Life Course Study: A Six-Wave Panel Study, 1980, 1983, 1988, 1992–1994, 1997, 2000. Recent British evidence found that the 1999 changes in the structure of tax credits which meant women could receive more Working Families Tax Credit if they did not have a very low-earning or non-earning partner had a 'substantial impact' on the divorce rate among the poorest households in Britain, prompting a 160 per cent rise in separations. M. Francesconi, H. Rainer, W. van der Klaauw, 'The Effects of In-Work Benefit Reform in Britain on Couples: Theory and Evidence', *The Economic Journal*, vol. 119, issue 535, 2009, pp. 66–100.

14. R. Lampard, 'An Examination of the Relationship between Marital Dissolution and Unemployment', in Duncan Gallie, Catherine Marsh, and Carolyn Vogler (eds.), *Social Change and the Experience of Unemployment*, Oxford University Press, 1994, pp. 264–98. For a later discussion see Morten Blekesaune, *Unemployment and Partnership Dissolution*, ISER working paper 2008-21.

15. Robert Rowthorn and David Webster, *Male Worklessness and the Rise of Lone Parenthood in Britain*, Oxford Centre for Population Research, Working Paper No. 30, 2007.

16. 'Men in their early fifties with an occupational pension and in the top quartile of the income distribution are 50 per cent more likely to be displaced than a man with the same age and hourly wages but no occupational pension', Nigel Campbell, *The Decline of Employment among Older People in Britain*, LSE, CASE paper, January 1999.

17. Avner Offer, 'Affluence and the Pursuit of Status', *The Challenge of Affluence: Self-Control and Well-Being in the United States and Britain since 1950* (chap. 11), Oxford University Press, 2006, p. 255.

18. Attributed to Gloria Steinem: 'a woman without a man is like a fish without a bicycle'.

19. Office for National Statistics, Marriage Statistics.

20. Kathleen Paul, *Whitewashing Britain: Race and Citizenship in the Postwar Era*, Cornell University Press, 1997, p. 86.

21. Royal Commission on Population, 1949, paragraph 329, p. 124.

22. The Colonial Secretary informed the Cabinet in June 1948 that 'the men concerned are all British subjects. The Government of Jamaica has no legal

power to prevent their departure from Jamaica and the Government of the United Kingdom has no legal power to prevent their landing.' Memorandum by Colonial Secretary to the Cabinet quoted in Randall Hansen, *Citizenship and Immigration in Postwar Britain*, Oxford University Press, 2000, p. 57. Companies, notably the publicly owned London Transport, also set up direct recruitment schemes from the West Indies in the 1950s.

23. I am grateful to Chris Cook for these calculations.

Table 19: Total of UK-born 20- to 30-year-olds, based on births twenty to thirty years previously

Date	Number in Millions
1945	8.7
1950	8.2
1955	7.3
1960	6.9
1965	7.3
1970	8.2
1975	8.2
1980	8.0
1985	8.9
1990	9.3
1995	8.4
2000	7.2
2005	6.9
2010	7.3

24. Jumana Salaheen and Chris Shadforth, 'The Economic Characteristics of Immigrants and Their Impact on Supply', *The Bank of England Quarterly Bulletin*, 2006, Q4, Table 8, p. 379.

25. The total fertility rate is defined as the average number of children a group of women would have if they experienced the fertility rate of women of each age in that specific year through their child-bearing lifespan. So you add up the rate of childbirth for a woman of 20, 21, 22, etc. in a given year and get the total fertility rate for women in that year. It is a widely used

measure but it can magnify swings. Imagine that a lot of women aged 30 in 2010 decide to delay having children until they are 35 in 2015. That lowers the total fertility rate in 2010 and raises it in 2015, even if the total number of children they have ultimately remains constant.

26. Office for National Statistics, Birth Statistics.

27. Nicola Tromans, Julie Jefferies and Eva Natamba, 'Have Women Born Outside the UK Driven the Rise in UK Births Since 2001?', *Population Trends*, vol. 136, Summer 2009, pp. 28–42.

28. I first drew attention to this new trend in an article in *The Times*, 22 May 2004.

29. M. Brewer, A. Ratcliffe, and S. Smith, 'Does Welfare Reform Affect Fertility?', CMPO 07/177, August 2007.

30. I set out the basis for this estimate in the *Sunday Times*, 22 May 2005.

31. *Ageing Report: Economic and Budgetary Projections for the EU-27 Member States 2008–2060*, Joint Report prepared by the European Commission and the Economic Policy Committee, 2009. By 2060 Germany's population is forecast to have fallen to 70.8m, France's has grown to 71.8m and the UK's is forecast to be 76.7 million

32. The classic way of measuring these effects is dependency ratios which measure the balance between the size of different generations. The very term dependency ratio for what are just figures for different age groups contains important assumptions about who is a dependant and who is not. Many a working family who can only run their lives because of support from the grandparents may feel that the dependency runs the other way. Nevertheless it is an important piece of evidence of the demographic challenges ahead.

33. Karl Mannheim, 'The Problem of Generations' (1928), in *From Karl Mannheim*, Transaction, 1993. The same volume also contains his essay 'Conservatism: a Contribution to the Sociology of Knowledge', which is one of the classic twentieth-century essays on Conservatism.

34. William Strauss and Neil Howe, *Generations: The History of America's Future 1584 to 2069*, William Morrow, 1991.

35. David Frum, *How We Got Here: The 70's: The Decade That Brought You Modern Life – For Better or Worse*, Basic Books, 2000, is an excellent statement of the argument that many of the changes we associate with the sixties really happened in the seventies.

36. Douglas Coupland, *Generation X: Tales for an Accelerated Culture*, St Martin's Press, 1991.

4. Spending the Kids' Inheritance

1. Richard Easterlin, *Birth and Fortune: The Impact of Numbers on Personal Welfare*, Basic Books, 1980.
2. The *Daily Mirror* of 29 August 2006 gave the results of a poll of members of the public. *Q* magazine, January 2006, gave the top 100 albums as selected by music enthusiasts.
3. By this method you can also work out which album is the most overrated album and the most underrated album in the *Mirror*'s top 100. Madonna's *Ray of Light* is the best performer, doing the best in spite of small cohort support, followed by Oasis, *What's the Story, Morning Glory?*, and Radiohead's *OK Computer*. Meanwhile the albums which have been carried highest by the demographic tide behind them are *Love Over Gold* by Dire Straits and *Welcome to the Pleasuredome* by Frankie Goes to Hollywood.
4. I am grateful to Chris Cook for these calculations. He explains that, using Spearman's rank correlation, there is almost no relationship between the two lists of thirty-eight albums. But, if you rank the albums in the *Mirror* list by number of 15- to 24-year-olds, it is then possible to work out a rank for the albums reflecting the degree to which albums over- or underperformed against this demographic handicapping. Albums which do well despite being released when there are few teenagers get high rankings. Albums which do poorly despite being released when there were many teenagers plunge. Once you make this adjustment, the Spearman's Rank correlation coefficient shoots up. This is consistent with the idea that the discrepancy between the rankings of thirty-eight albums is demographic.
5. Pew Research Centre, *Forty Years after Woodstock a Gentler Generation Gap*, August 2009. The extraordinary generational reach of the Beatles is striking. They were the second most popular musical performers for 16- to 29-year-olds, third for 30- to 49-year-olds, top for 50- to 64-year-olds and fourth for over-65s. The Rolling Stones were third, fourth, fourth and thirteenth respectively.
6. Richard Boreham and James Lloyd, *Asset Accumulation across the Life Course*, National Centre for Economic and Social Research and International Longevity Centre, September 2007, table 5.1. I use '65' to describe their group aged 60–69 and '75' to describe his group aged 70–79, and similarly for 50- and 25-year-olds. I am very grateful to the National Centre for Social Research for updating their figures in August 2009 to include new British Household Panel Survey data for incomes in 2005.
7. Boreham and Lloyd, *Asset Accumulation*, table 2.1. Mean net weekly house-

hold income before housing costs by age.

8. ibid., table 2.1.

9. ibid., table 5.1.

10. ibid., Appendix, table A.1.

11. ibid., table 2.1.

12. ibid., table 2.4, 'Contributions to Private Pension, by Age of Household Reference Person'.

13. ibid. table 2.2, 'Mean Monthly Household Savings, by Age of Household Reference Person'.

14. *New Statesman*, 1 December 2008.

15. $(25 \times 0.2) + (50 \times 0.7) + (75 \times 0.1) = 47.5$.

16. John Ermisch, 'Intergenerational Transfers in Industrialized Countries: Effects of Age Distribution and Economic Institutions', *Journal of Population Economics*, Spring 1989, pp. 269–84. Ehsan Khoman and Martin Weale, *Are We Living Beyond Our Means? A Comparison of France, Italy, Spain and the United Kingdom*, National Institute of Economic and Social Research, April 2008.

17. L. Keister and N. Deeb Sossa, 'Are Baby Boomers Richer Than Their Parents?', *Journal of Marriage and the Family*, 63, 2001.

18. John Bynner, Peter Elias, Abigail McKnight, Huiqi Pan, and Gaelle Pierre, *Young People's Changing Routes to Independence*, Rowntree, 2002, uses the 1958 and 1970 cohorts and the New Earnings Survey to compare earnings. Peter Elias, *Pathways, Earnings and Well-being* (chap. 4), is particularly relevant, especially p. 38.

19. ASHE and New Earnings Survey data. I am grateful to William Walter for his assistance with this research.

20. Chartered Institute of Personnel Development research for the author.

21. Department of Children, Schools and Families, NEETs Statistics, Quarterly Brief, 2009.

22. Office for National Statistics, tables for household accounts, non-financial and financial accounts.

23. UK Economic Accounts, table A64. The figures are net of liabilities like overdrafts which are not housing-related.

24. *Pensions: Challenges and Choices*, First Report of the Pensions Commission, The Stationery Office, 2004, fig. 5.4, p. 179.

25. Office for National Statistics, *The Blue Book*, 2005, table 6.1.9.

26. Alan Holmans, *Prospects for UK Housing Wealth and Inheritance*, and *Technical Report*, July 2008, published by the Council of Mortgage Lenders. Tables C9 and C14 of the *Technical Report* have been updated to spring 2009

and multiplied up to move from England to the UK. I am most grateful to Alan Holmans of the Cambridge Centre for Housing and Planning Research. I am grateful to John Adams and Chris Curry of the Pensions Policy Institute for the alternative estimates, derived from the English Longitudinal Study of Age, multiplied up to give UK estimates..

27. Andrew Benito, Jamie Thompson, Matt Waldron, and Rob Wood, 'House Prices and Consumer Spending', *Bank of England Quarterly Bulletin*, Summer 2006, p. 144.

28. Andrew Benito, Matt Waldron, Garry Young, and Fabrizio Zampoli, 'The Role of Household Debt and Balance Sheets in the Monetary Transmission Mechanism', *Bank of England Quarterly Bulletin*, Spring 2007, p. 72. Figures from chart 3, kindly provided by the Bank of England. This table shows people within age groups at the specified year. Unfortunately this data does not go back before 1995.

29. It is not easy to value accumulated pension rights. It is simpler to measure the assets of company pension schemes and the personal pensions held by insurance companies. These are what add up to £1.8tn.

30. My rough and cautious estimate is not based on as much hard evidence as I would wish. It would be a valuable contribution to the debate if the real experts produced a more authoritative version of this table.

31. Office of the Deputy Prime Minister, *Affordability and the Supply of Housing*, 2005–6, Q71.

32. HM Treasury, Pre-Budget Report, December 2004, Cm 6408, p. 96.

33. Adam Smith, 'Of the Division of Stock', *The Wealth of Nations*, bk 2, chap. 1, Oxford University Press 1976, p. 281.

33. OECD Series ADBA.

34. Martin Weale, *House Price Worries*, National Institute of Economic and Social Research, vol. 200, April 2007.

35. Kate Barker, Review of Housing Supply, March 2004, p. 124.

5. The Social Contract

1. Jonathan Sacks, *The Politics of Hope*, Vintage, 2000; David Selbourne, *The Principle of Duty*, Sinclair-Stephenson, 1994; Alasdair Macintyre, *After Virtue*, 3rd edn, University of Notre Dame Press, 2007 (1st edn, 1981); Michael Sandel, *Liberalism and the Limits of Justice*, Cambridge University Press, 1982; Elinor Ostrom, *Governing the Commons: The Evolution of Institutions*

for Collective Action, Cambridge University Press, 1990. My own earlier attempts at wrestling with this were David Willetts, *Modern Conservatism*, Penguin, 1992, and David Willetts, *Civic Conservatism*, Social Market Foundation, 1995.

2. Rousseau was given refuge in Britain in 1766, helped by Hume. But he then bitterly accused David Hume of plotting against him. There was no such plot. But Hume was perhaps too intensely concerned to protect his reputation as *Le Bon David*. The dispute has gained iconic significance with entire books devoted to it as it reveals the difference between Romantic rebellion and Classical reason, a comparison made all the more vivid by their shared atheism.

3. Its significance has been brought out brilliantly by Brian Skyrms in *The Stag Hunt and the Evolution of Social Structure*, Cambridge University Press, 2004.

4. Jean-Jacques Rousseau, *A Discourse of Equality*, quoted in Skyrms, *The Stag Hunt*, p. 1.

5. David Hume, *A Treatise of Human Nature* (ed. L. A. Selby-Bigge), bk iii, section v, 'Of the Obligation of Promises', Oxford Univeristy Press, 1975, pp. 520–21.

6. I have particularly drawn on Ken Binmore's excellent *Natural Justice*, Oxford University Press, 2005; and also Paul Seabright, *The Company of Strangers: A Natural History of Economic Life*, Princeton University Press, 2004; Stephen Pinker, *The Blank Slate: The Modern Denial of Human Nature*, Penguin Putnam, 2002; Matt Ridley, *The Origins of Virtue*, Viking, 1996. Hayek has an interesting example of this type of argument in *The Fatal Conceit: The Errors of Socialism*, Routledge, 1988. The structure of this chapter draws especially on Martin Nowak, 'Five Rules for the Evolution of Co-operation', *Science*, 2006, 314, p. 1560.

7. In fact much of the latest theory is really a fleshing-out of Book Three of his *Treatise of Human Nature* – it is extraordinary what he accomplished without knowledge of evolution or genes or game theory to help.

8. Elainie Madsen, Richard Tunney, George Fieldman, Henry Plotkin, Robin Dunbar, Jean-Marie Richardson and David McFarland, 'Kinship and Altruism: A Cross-Cultural Experimental Study', *British Journal of Psychology*, vol. 98, 2007, pp. 339–59. It is also described in Binmore, *Natural Justice*, pp. 103–4.

9. John Dupré has warned powerfully about this fallacy in *Darwin's Legacy: What Evolution Means Today*, Oxford University Press, 2003. Many serious philosophers are most uncomfortable with what they dismiss as the natu-

ralistic '*Just So* stories' of the evolutionary biologists, maintaining that we cannot move from descriptions of how evolution may have worked to moral judgements about how we should behave. In response the evolutionary biologists dismiss what Daniel Dennett has called the 'sky hooks' on which moral philosophers suspend our religious or moral principles with no explanation of what the sky hooks themselves are attached to. A sky hook is the modern equivalent of the *deus ex machina*, which neatly resolved all the tricky loose ends in a plot by flying in a classical god in a theatrical machine. The alternative preferred by Daniel Dennett is a crane which lifts us up but remains firmly based on the ground itself. That is what these naturalistic accounts of our obligations to others are trying to offer. I myself favour those who believe nowadays we have to offer a naturalistic account: it is the best type of argument to use in the public realm, whatever our personal religious beliefs may be.

10. This is the natural law tradition of Aristotle and Thomas Aquinas, enriched by modern disciplines such as evolutionary biology and game theory. Richard Dawkins, in *The Selfish Gene*, does himself go way beyond what would conventionally be seen as selfishness in his account of our behaviour.

11. Tony Ashworth, *Trench Warfare 1914–1918: The Live and Let Live System*, Pan Books, 2000, p. 146.

12. Robert Axelrod, *The Evolution of Co-operation*, Basic Books, 1984.

13. Seabright, *Company of Strangers*, p. 56.

14. Margaret Thatcher's full quote is less brutal than the version which has gone down in the folklore. Even *Woman's Own*, where it first appeared, gave a shortened version, so you have to go back to the original COI transcript to find what she actually said. Here it is: '... who is society? There is no such thing! There are individual men and women and there are families and no government can do anything except through people and people look to themselves first. It is our duty to look after ourselves and then also to help look after our neighbour and life is a reciprocal business and people have got the entitlements too much in mind without the obligations, because there is no such thing as an entitlement unless someone has first met an obligation' (Thatcher archive COI transcript 23 September 1987).

15. David Hume, *Treatise of Human Nature*, p. 521

16. The Milgram experiment involved an authority figure getting people to apply severe electric shocks to subjects, not knowing that they were actors who were simulating pain. Professor Philip Zimbardo studied in the Stanford prison experiment the psychological effects of becoming a prisoner or

prison guard. Volunteers randomly assigned to the role of prisoner or guard soon absorbed the role and lived it out all too energetically.

17. Michael Oakeshott, *Rationalism in Politics*, Methuen, 1962, p. 105.

18. The barter economy analogy is from Nowak, 'Five Rules'.

19. Adam Smith, 'The Theory of Moral Sentiments', quoted in Avner Offer, 'Between the Gift and the Market: The Economy of Regard', *Economic History Review*, L, 3, 1997, p. 452.

20. L. Bickman, A. Teger, T. Gabriele et al., 'Dormitory Density and Helping Behavior', *Environment and Behavior*, 5(4), 1973, pp. 465–90. This greater co-operation in smaller halls of residence does not, however, show up as a difference in satisfaction with living in different places – students living in the big crowded dorms did not report that they were less happy with their community even though there was clearly less co-operative behaviour.

21. A Parliamentary answer to the author on 19 February 2007 (Ref 119112) showed 3.33 per cent of the school population excluded in schools with under 1,000 pupils and 6.85 per cent in the few schools with more than 1,500 pupils.

22. Leda Cosmides and John Tooby, 'Cognitive Adaptation for Social Exchange', in Jerome Barbour, Leda Cosmides, and John Tooby (eds.), *The Adapted Mind: Evolutionary Biology and the Generation of Culture*, Oxford University Press, 1992.

23. E. Hermann et al., 'Humans Have Evolved Specialized Skills in Social Cognition: The Cultural Intelligence Hypothesis', *Science*, 317, 7 September 2007, pp. 1360–65.

24. I am grateful to Gervas Huxley and Marloes Nicholls for this example.

25. Jane Austen, *Pride and Prejudice*, chap. 48 in particular.

26. Seabright, 'Murder, Reciprocity and Trust', *Company of Strangers* (chap. 3), pp. 48–53.

27. S. Bowlse, 'Group Competition, Reproductive Levelling and the Evolution of Human Altruism', *Science*, 314, 8 December 2006, pp. 1569–72.

28. Charles Darwin, *The Descent of Man*, John Murray, 1879, p. 161.

29. Richard Dawkins would argue that group selection is simply the selection of what is rational self-interested behaviour by individual vampire bats.

30. Binmore, *Natural Justice*, p. 9.

31. If vampire bats are rather unappealing, you may prefer an experiment conducted by a Victorian naturalist, Sir John Lubbock. He managed to get ants intoxicated on water laced with alcohol and then observed whether these insensible ants were assisted by sober ants. 'The sober ants were somewhat puzzled at finding their intoxicated fellow creatures in such a disgraceful

condition' but they carried fellow members of the same colony back to their nest but not drunken ants from other colonies who were dropped into water. Sir John Lubbock, *Ants, Bees, and Wasps: A Record of Observation of the Social Hymenoptera*, 1882, p. 111.

32. Helen Haste, *Mapping Britain's Moral Values*, Nestlé, 2000.

33. Avner Greif, 'Reputation and Coalitions in Medieval Trade: Evidence on the Maghribi Traders', *Journal of Economic History*, vol. 49, no. 4, 1989, pp. 857–82. In the words of Avner Greif's classic paper: 'The Maghribi traders overcame the contractual problems associated with agency relationships by organizing such relationships through a non anonymous organizational framework, the coalition. Within the coalition an internal information transmission system served to balance asymmetric information and a reputation mechanism was used to ensure proper conduct. This reputation mechanism explains the observed "trust" relations among the traders. The "trust" did not reflect a social control mechanism or the internalization of norms of behaviour... rather the Maghribi traders established a relationship between past conduct and future economic reward... Since this fact was known beforehand to all traders, agents could acquire a reputation as honest agents.'

34. Binmore, *Natural Justice*, p. 11.

35. Frans de Waal, *Primates and Philosophers: How Morality Evolved*, Princeton University Press, 2006, p. 29.

36. Paul Zak, 'Values and Value', in Paul Zak (ed.), *Moral Markets*, Princeton University Press, 2008, p. 267.

37. Jefferson quoted in George Will, *Statecraft as Soulcraft: What Government Does*, Simon and Schuster, 1983, p. 53.

38. Robert Frank, *Passions Within Reason: The Strategic Role of the Emotions*, W. W. Norton, 1988.

39. Binmore, *Natural Justice*, p. 83.

40. Daria Koch et al., 'Diminishing Reciprocal Fairness by Disrupting the Right Prefrontal Cortex', *Science*, 314, 2006, p. 829.

41. De Waal, *Primates and Philosophers*, pp. 45–9.

42. Benjamin Nelson, *The Idea of Usury: From Tribal Brotherhood to Universal Otherhood*, Princeton University Press, 1949, appears to be the origin of the phrase.

43. Nicholas Anthony, *Prospect*, September 2006, p. 68.

44. Haste, *Mapping Britain's Moral Values*.

45. James Q. Wilson, *The Moral Sense*, Free Press, 1993. Wilson finds a 'general pattern of warm familial relationships' in several separate pieces of

research, p39. He cites Samuel P. Oliner and Pearl M. Oliner, *The Altruistic Personality: The Rescuers of Jews in Nazi Europe*, New York Free Press, 1988.

46. Nancy Folbre, *Family Time: The Social Organization of Care*, Routledge, 2004, and C. B. Mulligan, *Parental Priorities*, University of Chicago Press, 1997, cited by Sarah McLanahan, 'Diverging Destinies: How Children are Faring under the Second Demographic Transition', *Demography*, 41(4), 2004, pp. 607–27.

47. Exodus, 20:12.

48. Axel Gosseries makes a useful distinction between descendant and ascendant contracts in 'Three Models of Intergenerational Reciprocity', in Axel Gosseries and Lukas Meyer (eds.), *Intergenerational Justice* (chap. 4), Oxford University Press, 2009.

49. A good recent summary of the philosophical debate is Gosseries and Meyer (eds.), *Intergenerational Justice*. J. C. Tremmel (ed.), *Handbook of Intergenerational Justice*, Elgar, 2006, is another useful collection of essays.

50. I am grateful to Matthew Willetts for this point – itself a good example of intergenerational exchange. It does of course assume that we do not discount the interests of future generations.

51. Emily Grundy and John Henretta, 'Between Elderly Parents and Adult Children: A New Look at the Intergenerational Care Provided by the Sandwich Generation', *Ageing and Society*, vol. 26, 2006, pp. 707–22, quotation from p. 717. She focuses on women aged 55–69 who had at least one adult child and one living parent or parent-in-law. And also E. Grundy, 'Reciprocity in Relationships: Socio-economic and Health Influences on Intergenerational Exchanges between Third Age Parents and Their Adult Children in Great Britain', *British Journal of Sociology*, vol. 56, 2005, pp. 233–55. She concludes: 'If you help a child, with time or money, you are more likely to help a parent and this is after allowing for class, income etc and marriage.' The data does also show stronger help among the married.

52. Kimberly A. Wade-Benzoni, 'A Golden Rule Over Time: Reciprocity in Intergenerational Allocation Decisions', *Academy of Management Journal*, vol. 45, no.5, 2002, pp. 1011–28.

53. John Rawls, *A Theory of Justice*, Oxford University Press, 1972.

54. ibid., sections 22, 44, and 45. David Gauthier, *Morals by Agreement*, is a conspicuous exception. I am grateful to Georgina Testa for drawing out its significance for me. The quote is from section 44, p. 284.

55. ibid., section 44, p. 285.

56. ibid., p. 128.

6. Ages and Stages

1. Geoff Dench, 'Exploring Parents' Views', in A. Park, J. Curtice, K. Thomson, M. Phillips, and E. Clery (eds.), *British Social Attitudes, the 25th Report* (chap. 5), Sage, 2009, p. 114.

2. Alison Park, 'The Generation Game', in Roger Jowell, John Curtice, Alison Park, Katerina Thomson, Lindsey Jarvis, Catherine Bromley, and Nina Stratford (eds.), *British Social Attitudes, the 17th Report 2000/01* (chap. 1), National Centre of Social Research, 2001, p. 103.

3. Helen Haste, *Mapping Britain's Moral Values*, Nestlé, 2000.

4. Michael Wilmot and William Nelson, *Complicated Lives*, Wiley, 2003, pp. 86–7.

5. Howard Schuman and Jacqueline Scott, 'Generations and Collective Memories', *American Sociological Review*, vol. 54, June 1989, pp. 359–81.

6. Professor Stephen Zeldes of Columbia University cited in *Professional Pensions*, 4 December 2008, p. 6.

7. David Bell and David Blanchflower, *What Should be Done About Rising Unemployment in the UK?*, University of Stirling, 2009, p. 16.

8. The life cycle model of consumption was developed by Franco Modigliani, for which he won the Nobel Economics prize in 1985. It suggests we aim for a broadly stable level of consumption across our lives so we borrow when we are young, save when we are middle-aged and run down our savings when we are old. It lies behind the behaviour we describe in Chapter 4 and we will return to it when we discuss the role of government in Chapter 8.

9. I am grateful to Una McCormack for this point on the life course.

10. Dench, 'Exploring Parents' Views', p. 116.

11. Jacqueline Scott, 'Changing Households in England – Do Families Still Matter?', *Sociological Review*, vol. 45, no. 4, November 1993, p. 601.

12. T. S. Eliot, *Collected Poems*, Faber and Faber, 1974.

13. Paul Seabright, *The Company of Strangers*, Princeton University Press, 2004, p. 138.

14. Alison Park, The Generation Game, in British Social Attitudes Survey, 2000

15. Jacqueline Scott, Duane F. Alwin, and Michael Braun, 'Generational Changes in Gender-Role Attitudes: Britain in a Cross-National Perspective', *Sociology*, vol. 30, no. 3, 1996, p. 485.

16. Robert Putnam, 'Tuning in, Tuning out: The Strange Disappearance of Social Capital in America', *Political Science and Politics*, 1995, 28(4), pp. 664–83.

17. Michael Johnston and Roger Jowell, 'Social Capital and the Social Fabric', in

Roger Jowell, John Curtice, Alison Park, and Katarina Thomson (eds.), *British Social Attitudes, the 16th Report: Who Shares New Labour Values* (chap. 9), Ashgate, 1999. I am grateful to Rein Jensons for his assistance with this research.

18. ibid., p. 188.

19. Robert Putnam, 'Social Capital: Measurement and Consequences', in *The Contribution of Human and Social Capital to Sustained Economic Growth and Well-Being*, International Symposium report, OECD and HRDC, 2000.

20. E. L. Glaeser, D. Laibson, J. A. Scheinkman and C. L. Soutter, *What is Social Capital? The Determinants of Trust and Trustworthiness*, NBER paper 7216, July 1999, Table 1.

21. Robert Wuthnow, *Loose Connections*, Harvard University Press, 1998, and Les Lenkowsky, 'Review of *Bowling Alone*', *Commentary*, October 2000.

22. Glaeser, Laibson, Scheinkman, and Soutter, *What is Social Capital?*, pp. 21 and 22. Also you return much less if you were an only child than if you have siblings, showing again the importance of the family as the place where reciprocity is first learned.

23. The responses to the question whether most people can be trusted are as follows: 61 per cent of people aged under 40 and 52 per cent of over-40s in 1959 say yes; then 40 per cent of under-40s and 47 per cent of over-40s say yes in 1990. The source is *Civic Culture in World Values Survey*, cited in Peter Hall, 'Social Capital in Britain', *British Journal of Political Science*, vol. 29, 1999, pp. 417–61, at p. 432.

24. Paolo Grenier and Karen Wright, 'Social Capital in Britain: Exploring the Hall Paradox', *Policy Studies*, vol. 27(1), 2006, pp. 27–53.

25. Hall, 'Social Capital in Britain', pp. 417–61, p. 433. Page 429 has a generational chart which appears to show we also have a long civic generation followed by a decline. But Hall says this is a life cycle effect and has a chart showing more engagement with age, certainly up to 50.

26. Ben Page of Ipsos MORI.

27. Miller McPherson, Matthew E. Brashears, and Lynn Smith-Lovin, 'Social Isolation in America: Changes in Core Discussion Networks Over Two Decades', *American Sociological Review*, vol. 71, 2006, pp. 353–75.

28. A survey for *Bliss* magazine, 2004. In a survey of over 2,000 students aged 13–15 only 4 per cent agreed with the statement that 'marriage is old fashioned and no longer relevant'. C. Hill, *Sex under Sixteen?*, Family Education Trust, 2000.

29. Office for National Statistics figures on marriages in England and Wales.

30. Rosie Boycott, *Daily Mail*, 19 March 2004.

31. United Nations 2008 population data Table A.12, *Median Age of the Population by Country* and research by Richard Fairbanks and Paul Hewitt for the Centre for Strategic and International Studies. See also Richard Jackson and Neil Howe, 'Battle of the Youthful Bulge', *National Interest*, July/August 2008.

32. The controversial German demographer Gunnar Heinsohn has set out this theory in *Sons and World Power: Terror in the Rise and Fall of Nations*, published as *Söhne und Weltmacht: Terror im Aufsteig und Fall der Nationen*, Bern, Orell Füssli, 2003. For evidence of the interest of the US military see Patrick Hughes, Director, Defense Intelligence Agency, Evidence to the Senate Select Committee on Intelligence 5.2.97. 'A global threat and challenge to the United States is the youth bulge phenomenon which historically has been a key factor in instability.' An earlier more cautious historical account is Jack Goldstone, *Revolution and Rebellion in the Early Modern World*, University of California Press, 1991. For a sceptical warning not to forget the role of institutions and policies see Garran Therborn, 'NATO's Favourite Demographer', *New Left Review*, 56, March–April 2009.

33. Linda Richter, 'Studying Adolescence', *Science*, vol. 312, 30 June 2006, p. 1902.

34. UN World Population Prospects: The 2008 revision, United Nations, 2009.

35. David Page, *Developing Communities*, Joseph Rowntree Foundation, 1994, p. 19, and David Page, *Building for Communities*, Joseph Rowntree Foundation, 1993. See also Graham Martin and Judi Watkinson, *Rebalancing Communities: Introducing Mixed Incomes into Existing Rented Housing Estates*, Joseph Rowntree Foundation, 2003.

36. Research by Phil Rees and Danny Dorling cited in the *Economist*, 22 May 2004.

37. CIPD Employee Relations Report 2004, pp. 6–7.

38. McPherson, Brashears, and Smith-Lovin, *Social Isolation in America*, pp. 353–75.

39. Francis McGlone, Alison Parker, and Ceridwen Roberts, 'Kinship and Friendship: Attitudes and Behaviour in Britain 1986–1995', in Susan McRae (ed.), *Changing Britain: Families & Households in the 1990s* (chap. 5), Oxford University Press, 1999, p. 149.

40. L. J. Kotlikoff and A. Spivak, 'The Family as an Incomplete Annuities Market', *Journal of Political Economy*, vol. 89, no. 21, 1981.

41. Nicholas Eberstadt, 'World Population Implosion?', *The Public Interest*, Fall 1997, p. 21.

42. M. Rokeach and S. J. Ball-Rokeach, 'Stability and Change in American Value Priorities, 1961–1981', *American Psychologist*, vol. 44, pp. 775–84. Daniel Kah-

neman and Alan B. Kruger, 'Developments in the Measurement of Subjective Well-Being', *Journal of Economic Perspectives*, 20, 2006, pp. 3–24.

43. Kay Hymowitz, *Marriage and Caste in America: Separate and Unequal Families in a Post-Marital Age*, Ivan Dee, 2006.

44. I am grateful to Harry Benson of the Bristol Community Family Trust for this analysis.

45. K. Kiernan, 'Childbearing Outside Marriage in Western Europe', *Population Trends*, vol. 98, Office for National Statistics.

7. Why Bother About the Future?

1. Then as now it is the full title that matters and his was *An Essay on population as it affects the future Improvement of society, with remarks on the speculation of Mr Godwin, Mr Condorcet and other writers*. First published in 1798, published in Penguin Books 1982.

2. A geometrical progression is one where the starting number is multiplied by a fixed number – if it is by 2 then your sequence would go 2, 4, 8, 16, etc. An arithmetical sequence adds a fixed number time after time. So sticking with our example using 2, it would go 2, 4, 6, 8, etc. Malthus thought 'Population, when unchecked, increases in a geometrical ratio. Subsistence increases only in an arithmetical ratio' (p. 71).

3. *The Economics of Climate Change*, The Stern Review, HMSO, 2006, and Cambridge University Press, 2007.

4. *The Collected Speeches of Margaret Thatcher* (ed. Robin Harris), HarperCollins, 1997, p. 341.

5. Charles Dickens, 'Telescopic Philanthropy', *Bleak House* (chap. 4).

6. A good discussion of hyperbolic discounting is George-Marios Angleton, David Laibson, Andrea Repetto, Jeremy Tobacman, and Stephen Weinberg, 'The Hyperbolic Consumption Model: Calibration, Simulation, and Empirical Evaluation', in George Loewenstein, Daniel Read, and Roy Baumeister (eds.), *Time and Decision: Economic and Psychological Perspectives on Intertemporal Choice*, Russell Sage Foundation, 2003.

7. As our economy grows so future generations will be much richer. But how much extra happiness does Nick Stern think this will bring us? When our descendants are all millionaires in today's terms, how much will another 1 per cent more income be worth to our richer descendants as against another 1 per cent of our income today? Nick Stern's model suggests that the value

of both should be the same. By selecting what economists call a value for the elasticity of the marginal utility of consumption (usually called the 'eta' in the literature) of 1, Stern has assumed that an extra 1 per cent of GDP now is equal in psychological value to an extra 1 per cent of GDP in the future.

Stern has a social discount rate close to zero so £1,000 now will be worth £1,000 in the future. We can also assume that we will get the same amount of utility from an extra 1 per cent of GDP today as we will from an extra 1 per cent of GDP in the future. It is when we combine these two assumptions that the real difficulties begin. The low discount rate means we are willing to incur costs today for benefits in the future – sacrificing £1,000 of output now for £1,100 in ten years' time looks a very good deal. But to get the same amount of happiness in that richer world we are going to need even more money than that because it may be a lower proportion of GDP. The assumption about marginal utility says that wherever you are on the income scale, now or in the future, the psychological damage of losing 1 per cent of your income is the same. A society which lived by these two assumptions would have very high savings for the future to avoid feeling worse off then. Professor Partha Dasgupta suggests, for example, that we would be saving 97.5 per cent of our national income (*National Institute Economic Review*, vol. 199, 2007, pp. 4–7) because we would be willing to sacrifice a lot of money today to provide for the future. We would never say that we do not need to worry about people in the future because they will be richer – that is the eta assumption – but we would say that benefits in the future are worth as much as benefits today – that is the discount rate assumption.

Lord Stern has replied with a concession. He accepts that actually as we get richer an extra given sum of money is worth less and less to us. So instead of an eta of one we could increase it to, say, two, meaning that the marginal utility of income halves. But he then adds, rather mischievously, that his critics have made a case not just for redistributing income from rich future to poor now, but also have to accept it means redistributing from people who are rich now to people who are poor now. It is one of the oddities of the political line-up in this debate that some of the experts who are keenest on the argument that we should not be redistributing away from us to the rich future are not so keen on applying this to incomes today.

That we save so little reveals that we are not valuing the future in the way which Nick Stern's model suggests. This is the key critique from leading economists such as Professors Nordhaus, Weitzman, and Dasgupta. They argue that behind Stern's technical analysis there is a moral appeal which does not accurately reflect our current behaviour.

8. A lively contribution to the controversy is Nigel Lawson, *An Appeal to Reason: A Cool Look at Global Warming*, Duckworth Overlook, 2008. He makes some very telling remarks about the economics of all this, though one suspects he is rather too dismissive of the scientific evidence on global warming.

9. The *South Park* episode is from April 2004.

10. This analysis draws heavily on a paper by John Beddington, Chief Scientific Adviser to HM Government, 'Food, Energy, Water and the Climate: A Perfect Storm of Global Events?', conference on Sustainable Development, London, March 2009.

11. UN World Population Prospects, 2008 Revision, March 2009.

12. *A Note on Rising Food Prices*, World Bank Policy Research Paper, No. 4682.

13. Y. Shen, T. Oki, N. Utsumi, S. Kanae, and N. Hanasaki, 'Projection of World Water Resources under SRES Scenarios. Part 1: Water Withdrawal', *Hydrological Sciences*, 53(1), pp. 11–33.

14. In 2008 business investment in the UK was running at 10.9 per cent of GDP and Gross Fixed Capital Formation was 17.5 per cent of GDP – both below the average for OECD countries; ONS.

15. David Laibson, 'Golden Eggs and Hyperbolic Discounting', *Quarterly Journal of Economics*, May 1997 pp. 443–77.

16. The remark is sometimes attributed to an American Congressman but the earliest record of it is Sir Boyle Roche, during Grattan's Parliament in Dublin in the 1790s.

17. The case of Phineas Gage has fascinated people ever since and has been widely written about. It influenced the early development of neurology as it revealed different parts of the brain had different functions.

18. Avner Offer, *The Challenge of Affluence: Self-Control and Well-Being in the United States and Britain since 1950*, Oxford University Press, 2006.

19. Derek Wanless, *Our Future Health Secured: A Review of NHS Funding and Performance*, September 2007.

20. World Health Organization 2001/2 survey on health behaviour in school-aged children. Out of twenty-four European countries providing data England's rate for girls was the highest and for boys the second-highest.

21. Adam Smith, *A Theory of Moral Sentiments*, bk IV, chap. 2, para. 6, Oxford University Press, 1976, p. 189. David Hume also thought this capacity was important: 'There is no quality in human nature, which causes more fatal errors in our conduct, than that which leads us to prefer whatever is present to the distant and remote...' (*Treatise of Human Nature*, bk III, part ii, section vii, 'Of the Origin of Government' (ed. L. A. Selby-Bigge), Oxford University

Press, 1975, p. 538). Note the title of the chapter where this point is made – Hume is considering how we get ourselves into circumstances where this sort of prudence is rewarded and gives a role for government not unlike Sunnstein and Thaler have recently proposed in 'Nudge'.

22. Offer, 'Body Weight and Self-Control', *The Challenge of Affluence* (chap. 7).

23. Lowenstein, Read, and Baumeister (eds.), *Time and Decision*, p. 204.

24. Walter Mischel, 'Father-Absence and Delay of Gratification', *The Journal of Abnormal and Social Psychology*, vol. 63(1), July 1961, pp. 116–24.

25. The paper is a University of Oregon Working Paper by K. Krause and W. Harbaugh published in 1999. Alternatively, I guess children could do the experiments on adults.

26. C. Peter Herman and Janet Polivy, 'Dieting as an Exercise in Behavioural Economics', in Loewenstein, Read, and Baumeister, *Time and Decision*. The quote is from p. 478.

27. Derek Parfit, *Reasons and Persons*, Oxford University Press, 1992.

28. Shane Frederick, 'Time Preference and Personal Identity', in Loewenstein, Read, and Baumeister, *Time and Decision* (chap. 2), pp. 89–113.

29. Fifty-three is the age of your author as he writes that so apparently it does not get better than this cognitively. 'In cross-sectional data of prime borrowers in ten credit markets, middle-aged adults borrow at lower interest rates and pay fewer fees relative to younger and older adults. Fee and interest payments are minimized around age 53… Age-related changes in experience and cognitive function provide the leading explanation for the patterns that we observe.' Sumit Agarwal, John Driscoll, Xavier Gabaix, and David Laibson, 'The Age of Reason: Financial Decisions over the Lifecycle', 21 October 2008, Social Science Research Network, http://ssrn.com/abstract=973790.

30. Maybe the involvement of these two different parts of brain helps to explain hyperbolic discounting – we value $10 tonight over $11 tomorrow yet $111 in a year and a day over $110 in a year. See Samuel McClure et al., 'Separate Neural Systems Value Immediate and Delayed Monetary Rewards', *Science*, 306, 2004, p. 503.

31. The examples in this and the following paragraph come from Kimberly A. Wade-Benzoni, 'Legacies, Immortality, and the Future: The Psychology of Intergenerational Altruism', *Ethics in Groups: Research on Managing Groups and Teams*, vol. 8, pp. 247–70.

8. What Governments Do

1. Hillard Kaplan and Michael Gurven, 'The Natural History of Human Food Sharing and Co-operation: A Review and a New Multi-Individual Approach to the Negotiation of Norms', in Herbert Gintis, Samuel Bowles, Robert Boyd, and Ernest Fehr (eds.), *Moral Sentiments and Material Interests: The Foundations of Cooperation in Economic Life*, Massachusetts Institute of Technology, 2005.
2. There is an excellent review of these arguments in Ronald Lee, 'Intergenerational Transfers and the Economic Life-Cycle: A Cross-Cultural Perspective' in Andrew Mason and Georges Tapinos (eds.), *Sharing the Wealth: Demographic Change and Economic Transfers between Generations*, Oxford University Press, 2000.
3. This way of thinking was set out very well by Jane Falkingham and John Hills in *The Dynamic of Welfare, the Welfare State and the Life Cycle*, Prentice Hall/Harvester Wheatsheaf, 1995.
4. The figures for spending by age groups are for the financial year 2003–4, the last year for which the government has done this analysis, published in the House of Commons Health Select Committee Report, *Public Expenditure on Health and Social Services*, 2006.
5. HMRC income tax receipts data 2007/8 and DWP benefit expenditure tables 2007/8
6.

Table 20: Who pays income tax? (£bn)

	Men	Women
Under 25	3	2
25–34	16	8
35–44	33	11
45–54	30	10
55–64	19	6
65–74	6	2
75 and over	2	1
	109	40

Source: HMRC Survey of Personal Incomes 2006–7

7. Calculations by the House of Commons Library based on DWP claimant count and average weekly amount claimed.

8. John Hills, 'Future Pressures: Intergenerational Links, Wealth, Demography and Sustainability', in John Hills, Tom Sefton, and Kitty Stewart (eds.), *Towards a More Equal Society? Poverty, Inequality and Policy since 1997* (chap. 15), Policy Press, 2009, p. 327.

9. Nick Barr, *The Welfare State as Piggy Bank*, Oxford University Press, 2001. Strictly speaking, the piggy bank function involves both mutual insurance against misfortune and personal accounts which directly link what you pay in when you are working and what you get out when you are, for example, a pensioner.

10. John Hills, 'Distribution and Redistribution', *Inequality and the State* (chap. 8), Oxford University Press, 2004, p. 197.

11. Lloyd George, assisted by Winston Churchill, introduced the contributory principle for health care in 1911 having introduced non-contributory means-tested pensions in 1909. We then spent the next half-century reversing this arrangement and moving to a contributory pension system and a non-contributory NHS. The pre-War arrangement still leads some people to believe that their national insurance contributions pay for the NHS, which in turn may be one reason for the relative popularity of national insurance over income tax. Some other advanced Western countries such as Germany and the USA have kept the contributory principle for health care.

12. The researchers did not find 'A positive impact of income heterogeneity on the size of these programmes'. F. Breyer and B. Craig, 'Voting on Social Security: Evidence from OECD Countries', *European Journal of Political Economy*, 13, 1997, pp. 705–24.

13. Paul Samuelson, 'An Exact Consumption-Loan Model of Interest with or without the Social Contrivance of Money', *Journal of Political Economy*, LXVI, December 1958, pp. 467–82. The quotation is from p. 471.

14. Avner Offer in a recent paper, 'The Economy of Obligation: Contract Ambiguity and the Welfare State' (July 2009, unpublished), argues that maintaining these pay-as-you-go contracts is a key function of government.

15. Rational expectations theory says that families adjust their behaviour to government issues of debt, recognizing that it means higher taxes in the future and that deficit-financed spending has not made them any better off really. This theory is therefore arguing that ultimately it is families who decide the balance of costs between the generations and they will adapt their behaviour to offset what governments do. It is an interesting idea but given the scale of the government flows we are considering here it looks implausible.

16. Hills, 'Distribution and Redistribution', p. 199. A lot has happened since these estimates were produced but they are the most recent we have.

17. HM Treasury, *Long-Term Public Finance Report: An Analysis of Fiscal Sustainability*, March 2008, table 4.1, p. 36. I am grateful to Edmund Cannon of Bristol University for his analysis of these projections.

18. I am grateful to Edmund Cannon of Bristol University for the analysis on which this point rests.

19. Chris Curry, Pensions Policy Institute, presentation at International Longevity Centre Seminar on Public Spending and the Effect of Changes in Life Expectancy, June 2009.

20. The Treasury's official forecasts include an extra line for non-age-related spending, which it shows falling by 2.3 per cent of GDP between 2007 and 2047, from 20.4 per cent to 18.1 per cent. The Treasury has refused to answer questions from the author asking for a breakdown of this line. It appears to be a modest increase in several public spending programmes, which could be where some of the long-term costs of the projected population surge would be shown. But this increase is then more than offset by a big fall in the non-age-related benefits. These effects are all hidden in the one line which the Treasury will not disaggregate.

21. John Hills, 'Future Pressures', p. 329.

22. Reported in a speech by Mervyn King, Governor of the Bank of England, 21 October 2008.

23. Thomas Jefferson, letter to James Madison, 6 September 1789, in Adrienne Koch and William Peden (eds.), *The Life and Selected Writings of Thomas Jefferson*, Random House, 1944, pp. 488–93. The issues in the letter have been widely discussed. See W. Andrew Achenbaum, 'Public Pensions as Intergenerational Transfers in the United States', in Paul Johnson, Christopher Conrad, and David Thomson (eds.), *Workers versus Pensioners: Intergenerational Justice in an Ageing World* (chap. 7), Centre For Economic Policy Research and Manchester University Press, 1989. It is also discussed in Victor Muniz-Fraticelli, 'The Problem of a Perpetual Constitution', in Axel Gosseries and Lukas Meyer (eds.), *Intergenerational Justice* (chap. 14), Oxford University Press, 2009.

9. Time for Childhood

1. Report Card 7, 'Child Poverty in Perspective: An Overview of Child Well-Being in Rich Countries', UNICEF 2007. Sue Palmer, *Toxic Childhood: How the*

Modern World is Damaging Our Children and What We Can Do About It, Orion Books, 2006, sets out the arguments very well.

2. Staffan Linder, *The Harried Leisure Class*, Columbia University Press, 1970, was a path-breaking account of these ideas.

3. A further example of this is the extraordinarily packed CVs young people now present. Assuming they are not works of fiction, they are spending their time far more intensely and purposefully than the boomers a generation ago. Robert Putnam suggests one reason for the apparent increase in voluntary activity by young people is that they are improving their CVs having learned that employers value it.

4. Admittedly, one piece of empirical research, on New York taxi drivers, did suggest they had a target income and all went home when it rained. See George Loewenstein, Daniel Read, and Roy Baumeister (eds.), *Time and Decision: Economic and Psychological Perspectives on Intertemporal Choice*, Russell Sage Foundation, 2003, p. 468.

5. Future Foundation, *The Changing Face of Parenting: Professional Parenting, Information and Healthcare*, Experian report for Calpol, August 2006.

6. Eric Knudsen, 'Sensitive Periods in the Development of the Brain and Behaviour', *Journal of Cognitive Neuroscience*, vol. 16, no. 8, 2004.

7. Sarah-Jayne Blakemore and Suparna Choudhury, 'Development of the Adolescent Brain: Implications for Executive Function and Social Cognition', *Journal of Child Psychology and Psychiatry*, 47:3/4, 2006, pp. 296–312.

8. Two powerful critiques of early-years determinism are Jerome Kagan, *Three Seductive Ideas*, Harvard University Press, 1998, and John Bruer, *The Myth of the First Three Years*, Free Press, 2002.

9. ICM, 1999, cited in Frank Furedi, *Paranoid Parenting*, Allen Lane, 2001, chap. 5.

10. I am grateful to Professor Jonathan Gershuny at Oxford University, our leading expert on time use, for providing raw data from the most recent Multinational Time Use Studies (MTUS) surveys on which this chapter draws. The data has been analysed by Chris Cook, to whom I am also most grateful.

11. Sylvia Ann Hewlett, *When the Bough Breaks: The Cost of Neglecting Our Children*, Basic Books, 1991.

12. W. Keith Bryant and Cathleen D. Zick, 'Are We Investing Less in the Next Generation? Historical Trends in Time Spent Caring for Children', *Journal of Family and Economic Issues*, vol. 17 (3/4), Winter 1996, pp. 365–92.

13. Using the same international MTUS dataset as the UK figures.

14. Kirsten Asmussen, Judy Corlyon, Hanan Hauari, and Vincent La Placa, *Supporting Parents of Teenagers*, Research Report No. 830, Policy Research Bureau, March 2007.

15. Calculations by Chris Cook from the MTUS dataset.

16. Mark Bryan and Almudena Sanz, *Does Housework Lower Wages and Why? Evidence for Britain*, ISER Working Paper 2008–3.

17. James Flynn, *What is Intelligence?*, Cambridge University Press, 2007.

18. Claire James and Sally Gimson, *Families and Neighbourhoods*, Family and Parenting Institute, 2007.

19. The World Values Survey 2005–2007. This is a different survey, and a later one, from that cited in Chapter 6.

20. Perry Francis and Harwinda Tiwana, 'Unpaid Household Production in the United Kingdom 1995–2000', *Economic Trends*, January 2004, p. 58, shows a 25 per cent fall in gross unpaid household production of voluntary activity.

21. Survey conducted by UCL Jill Dando Institute of Crime for ADT, May 2006.

22. Clare Sharp, Judith Aldridge, and Juanjo Medina, 'Delinquent Youth Groups and Offending Behaviour: Findings from the 2004 Offending, Crime and Justice Survey', Home Office Online Report 14/06.

23. Julia Margo and Mike Dixon with Nick Pearce and Howard Reed, *Freedom's Children: Raising Youth in a Changing World*, Institute for Public Policy Research, 2006, p. 13.

24. Tim Gill, *No Fear: Growing Up in a Risk Averse Society*, Calouste Gulbenkian Foundation, 2007, pp. 157 and 158, cited in Sue Palmer, *21st Century Boys: How Modern Life is Driving Them off the Rails and How We Can Get Them Back on Track*, Orion Books, 2009.

25. Palmer, *21st Century Boys*.

26. Richard Layard and Judy Dunn, *A Good Childhood: Searching for Values in a Competitive Age*, Penguin, 2009, p. 38.

27. Margo and Dixon, *Freedom's Children*, p. 14.

28. 97 per cent of children from deprived backgrounds and 48 per cent of children from affluent backgrounds have a TV in their bedroom. 93 per cent of children from deprived backgrounds have a DVD or video player in their room compared to 41 per cent of affluent children. Deprived children are classified as children living in part of the 15 per cent most deprived areas in the UK; affluent as in the 15 per cent most affluent areas in the UK. Source: Agnes Nairn and Jo Ormond with Paul Bottomley, *Watching, Wanting and Wellbeing: Exploring the Links*, Family Parenting Institute, 2007, p. 14

29. Sonia Livingstone and Magdalena Bober, *UK Children Go Online: Final Report of Key Project Findings*, LSE, 2007, p. 3.

30. 1985–1989.

31. Economic and Social Science Research Council, 'Children are Falling Behind in Maths and Science', *The Edge*, issue 21, March 2009, which draws on M.

Shayer, *Have the Norms for Volume and Heaviness for Year 7 changed since the mid-70s?* Report to the ESRC RES-000-22-1379.

32. Steve Johnson, *Everything Bad is Good for You: How Today's Popular Culture is Actually Making Us Smarter*, Riverhead, 2005.

33. The World Health Organization, *Inequalities in Young People's Health: Health Behaviour in School-Aged Children: International Report from the 2005/6 Survey*, 2008, shows the UK is top of the league for the number of 13-year-olds who have been drunk at least twice a week. The number of 15-year-old girls who have had sex is also much higher than the OECD average.

34. Sarah-Jayne Blakemore's research shows how malleable teenagers' brains are. Sarah-Jayne Blakemore and Suparna Choudhury, 'Development of the Adolescent Brain: Implications for Executive Function and Social Cognition', *Journal of Child Psychology and Psychiatry*, 47:3/4, 2006, pp. 296–312, and Sarah-Jayne Blakemore, *Brain Development during Adolescence and Beyond*, The Institute for Cultural Research, Monograph Series No. 51, 2006.

35. James Flynn, 'Requiem for Nutrition as the Cause of IQ gains: Raven's Gains in Britain 1938–2008', *Economics and Human Biology*, 2009.

36. James Flynn, quoted in the *Sunday Telegraph*, 8 February 2009.

10. Schools and Social Mobility

1. John Hassler and José Vincente Rodríguez-Mora, *IQ, Social Mobility and Growth*, CEPR Discussion Paper Series No. 1827, March 1998.

2. Arnaud Chevalier, *Just Like Daddy: The Occupational Choice of UK Graduates*, University College, Dublin, and Centre for Economic Performance, LSE, 2002.

3. Jo Blanden, Alyssa Goodman, Paul Gregg, and Stephen Machin, *Changes in Intergenerational Mobility in Britain*, Centre for Economic Performance, Discussion Paper, December 2001, p. 4.

4. Ipsos MORI and the Sutton Trust, *Social Mobility*, 2008.

5. Marcus Richards, Rebecca Hardy, Diana Kuh, and Michael Wadsworth, 'Birth Weight and Cognitive Function in the British 1946 Birth Cohort', *British Medical Journal*, 322, 2001, pp. 199–203.

6. Michael Young, *The Rise of the Meritocracy*, Thames and Hudson, 1958. New edition with a new introduction by the author, Transaction Publishers, 1994.

7. F. A. Hayek, 'Equality, Value and Merit', *Constitution of Liberty*, Routledge and Kegan Paul, 1960, chap. 6.

8. Steve Machin, Paul Gregg, and Jo Blanden, *Intergenerational Mobility in Europe and North America*, Sutton Trust, 2005.
9. Given the inverse snobberies of Britain even people with white-collar middle-class jobs sometimes like to describe themselves as working class. The British Social Attitudes Survey 2007 reported 37 per cent of people describing themselves as middle class and 57 per cent as working class.
10. Panel on Fair Access to the Professions, *Unleashing Aspiration: The Final report of the Panel on Fair Access to the Professions*, July 2009, p. 20; *Phase 1 Report: An Analysis of the Trends and Issues Relating to Fair Access to the Professions*, April 2009, p. 21; and *Fair Access: Good Practice, Phase 2 Report*, May 2009, p. 20. The original figures come from a paper by Lindsay Macmillan, *Social Mobility and the Professions*, Centre for Market and Public Organisation, University of Bristol. Here is a summary of her key table based on the average monthly net family income at the age of 16 of people who are subsequently in various professions aged 33/34. It shows how much higher these family incomes were than the national average for 16-year-olds in 1958 and then in 1970. Some of the changes are very striking indeed – such as for accountants and journalists.

Table 21: Difference in family income above national average for people who join professions (per cent)

	1958	1970
Doctor	43	63
Lawye	40	64
Lecturers and professors	21	11
Teachers	18	17
Bankers	13	32
Artists, musicians, writers	13	8
Stockbrokers and traders	11	14
Engineers	9	17
Scientists	8	16
Journalists and broadcasters	6	42
Nurses	4	10
Accountants and actuaries	0	40

11. John Goldthorpe, 'Class Inequality and Meritocracy: A Critique of Saunders and an Alternative Analysis', *The British Journal of Sociology*, vol. 50(1), pp. 1–27.

12. Fernando Galindo-Rueda and Anna Vignoles, 'The Declining Relative Importance of Ability in Predicting Educational Attainment', *Journal of Human Resources*, vol. 40(2), 2005, pp. 335–53.

13. Jo Blanden, Paul Gregg, and Lindsey Macmillan, 'Accounting for Intergenerational Income Persistence: Non Cognitive Skills, Ability and Education', *Economic Journal*, vol. 117 (519), 2007, pp. 43–60.

14. Yvonne Roberts, *Grit: The Skills for Success and How They are Grown*, Young Foundation, 2009.

15. Angela Duckworth and Martin Seligman, 'Self-Discipline Outdoes IQ in Predicting Academic Performance of Adolescents', *Psychological Science*, vol. 16, no. 12, 2005, pp. 939–44.

16. Leon Feinstein, 'Inequality in the Early Cognitive Development of Children in the Early 1970 Cohort', *Economica*, vol. 70, 2003, pp. 73–97.

17. The research shows 'A pupil from a poor family is 17 percentage points less likely to go to a good school.' S. Burgess and A. Briggs, *School Assignment, School Choice and Social Mobility*, CMPO 06/157.

18. Sutton Trust, *Rates of Eligibility for Free School Meals at the Top State Schools*, October 2005, p. 4.

19. Research by Tom Loveless of Brookings in the USA.

20. Department for Children, Schools and Families, *School Admissions Code*, The Stationery Office, 2009.

21. Sutton Trust, *No More School Run: Proposal for a National Yellow Bus Scheme in the UK*, June 2005, p. 16.

22. See David Willetts, 'Better Schools and More Social Mobility', speech to the CBI Conference on Public Service Reform, 16 May 2007.

23. 'Opportunities to become a professional via a no-graduate route are becoming rarer... Only 27 of *The Times* Top 100 Employers accept alternative entry routes.' The Panel on Fair Access to the Professions, *Phase 1 Report: An Analysis of the Trends and Issues Relating to Fair Access to the Professions*, April 2009, p. 45.

24. Government Statistical Service, *Education Statistics for the United Kingdom*, 1979 and 1992.

25. Department for Innovation, Universities and Skills, *Participation Rates in Higher Education: Academic Years 1999/2000–2007/2008 (Provisional)*, DIUS SFR 02/2009, 31 March 2009.

26. Steve Machin and Anna Vignoles, 'Educational Inequality: The Widening

Socio-Economic Gap', *Fiscal Studies*, vol. 25, no. 2, 2004, pp. 107–28.

27. Blanden, Gregg, and Macmillan, 'Accounting for Intergenerational Income Persistence'.

28. Jo Blanden, Alyssa Goodman, Paul Gregg, and Stephen Machin, *Changes in Intergenerational Mobility in Britain*, Centre for Economic Performance, Discussion Paper, December 2001, p. 15.

29. Office for National Statistics, *Focus on Families*, Palgrave Macmillan, 2007.

30. Blanden, Goodman, Gregg, and Machin, *Changes in Intergenerational Mobility in Britain*, p. 11.

31. This was the model in the former Soviet Bloc countries of Eastern Europe and is to some extent in Germany. Personal choice matters less and there is greater use of aptitude and other testing to steer young people towards types of career.

32. 'At the workshops with young people, all of the participants expressed some form of aspiration, many of which were highly specific.' Based on thirty-six workshops across the UK with young NEETs. Geoff Hayward, Stephanie Wilde, and Richard Williams, *Engaging Youth Enquiry: Consultation Report*, Rathbone/Nuffield Review, 15 October 2008.

33. Deborah Wilson, Simon Burgess, and Adam Briggs, *The Dynamics of School Attainment of England's Ethnic Minorities*, CMPO Working Paper 05/130, October 2005.

34. World Health Organization, *Inequalities in Young People's Health: Health Behaviour in School-Aged Children. International Report from the 2005/06 Survey*, eds. Candace Currie, Saoirse Nic Gabhainn, Emmanuelle Godeau, Chris Roberts, Rebecca Smith, Dorothy Currie, Will Picket, Matthias Richter, Antony Morgan, and Vivian Barnekow, University of Edinburgh: Child and Adolescent Health Research Unit, 2008. England has the highest number of 11-year-olds with three or more close friends and the highest number of 15-year-old girls with three or more close friends at 91 per cent. But we are in the bottom half of the league table for all ages for the number of children who find it easy to talk to their mother – 72 per cent of 15-year-old girls compared with an average of 77 per cent. Only 50 per cent of 15-year-old girls find it easy to talk to their father, again below the average. I am grateful to Ryan Shorthouse for this point.

35. Department for Education and Skills, Eleanor Ireland, Sarah Golden, and Marian Morris, *Evaluation of Integrated Aimhigher: Tracking Surveys of Young People*, DfES and National Foundation for Educational Research, Research Report 811, 2006, p. 44.

36. ibid., p. 62.

37. Nick Buck, *Does Area Matter? Neighbourhood and Individual Influences on Social Capital*, Institute for Social and Economic Research, University of Essex, 2005.
38. Jonah Lehrer, *Proust was a Neuroscientist*, Houghton Mifflin Harcourt, 2007.
39. Sarah-Jayne Blakemore, *Brain Development during Adolescence and Beyond*, Institute for Cultural Research Monograph Series No. 51, 2006.
40. Stanley Baldwin, *On England* (1926), Penguin, 1937, p. 13.

11. Houses and Jobs: Generation Crunch

1. There is now a rich literature on the subject of transitions to adulthood stimulated in the USA by Jeffrey Arnett's work on 'Emerging Adulthood'. A good guide to the British debate is John Bynner's article 'Rethinking the Youth Phase of the Life Course: The Case for Emerging Adulthood?', *Journal of Youth Studies*, vol. 8, no. 4, December 2005, pp. 367–84, which includes references to evidence on the stabilizing effects of long-term relationships, especially with non-delinquents. Professor Gill Jones, *Young Adults and the Extension of Economic Dependence*, The National Family and Parenting Institute, Policy Discussion Paper, is another useful guide. One radical argument is that the source of the problem is the modern idea of adolescence, which should be abolished, as argued by the leading American psychologist, Robert Epstein, *The Case against Adolescence: Rediscovering the Adult in Every Teen*.
2. *The New Consensus on Family and Welfare*, American Enterprise Institute, 1987.
3. Some critics might object to the idea of a 'right' order. A good example is Professor Gill Jones writing for the National Family and Parenting Institute: 'It is not feasible to talk in terms of successful or unsuccessful transitions to adulthood, since "success" and "failure" are likely to be constructed differently by young people, their parents and policy makers' (Policy Discussion Paper, *Young Adults and the Extension of Economic Dependence*.) The risk with this relativism is that it can enable older generations to shed their responsibility for unhappy and delayed transitions to adulthood.
4. *Understanding First-Time Buyers*, Council of Mortgage Lenders, May 2005. I am grateful to Bob Pannell and the Council of Mortgage Lenders, who have been of great assistance with the housing figures in this chapter.
5. *Observer*, 28 May 2006.
6. Author's conversation with Sandy Campbell of Working Rite.

7. Jones, *Young Adults and the Extension of Economic Dependence.*

8. A good example of a residential apprenticeship is Network Rail's apprenticeship scheme based at HMS *Sultan* in Gosport which involves the young people staying on a naval base alongside naval cadets. The popular calls for National Service are an appeal to that tradition of leaving home but remaining under some supervision whilst learning a useful skill.

9. Department of Communities and Local Government, Survey of English Housing, Table S118 for 2005/6. Estimates for 1985 from the DOE Labour Force Survey Housing Trailer.

10. CML analysis of mortgage advances to first-time buyers. There is a major discontinuity in the data in 2005 which makes comparison over time difficult.

11. DOE Labour Force Survey Housing Trailer for earlier figures and Department of Communities and Local Government Survey of English Housing for later figures.

12. Analysis by Chris Cook of figures on number and gender of first-time borrowers and buyers.

13. CML Table ML2 First-Time Buyers: Lending and Affordability/Bank Search Regulated Mortgage Survey.

14. Nowadays there are interest-only products with no repayment vehicle alongside. Endowment mortgages, whatever their subsequent tribulations, were interest-only mortgages but with a repayment vehicle as well.

15. Tomas Hellebrandt, Sandhya Kawar, and Matt Waldron, 'The Economics and Estimation of Negative Equity', *Bank of England Quarterly Bulletin*, Q2 2009, p. 116.

16. Richard Boreham and James Lloyd, *Asset Accumulation across the Life Course*, Nat Cen and ILC, September 2007, Appendices A.1, A.2, and A.3.

17. CML end 2008 estimates for negative equity. The five-year age group with by far the largest exposure was 25- to 29-year-olds with 260,000 households in negative equity. 30- to 34-year-olds are next with 190,000 households in negative equity.

18. A good analysis of the difficulty of access to the housing market now is in the paper by the National Housing and Planning Advice Unit (NHPAU), *Housing Requirements and the Impact of Recent Economic and Demographic Change, on Prospects for First-Time Buyers.*

19. Council of Mortgage Lenders press release of 9 July 2009.

20. Council of Mortgage Lenders, *Understanding First Time Buyers*, May 2007, and press release 9 July 2009.

21. Geoff Dench, Kate Gavron, and Michael Young, *The New East End: Kinship,*

Race and Conflict, Profile Books, 2006, p. 155.

22. George J. Borjas, *Atlantic Monthly*, vol. 278, issue 5, November 1996. See also David Coleman and Robert Rowthorn, 'The Economic Effects of Immigration into the United Kingdom', *Population and Development Review*, 30 (4), December 2004, pp. 579–624.

23. John Salt and Jane Millar, 'Foreign Labour in the United Kingdom: Current Patterns and Trends', *Labour Market Trends*, October 2006, pp. 335–52.

24. Jumana Saleheen and Chris Shadforth, 'The Economic Characteristics of Immigrants and Their Impact on Supply', *Bank of England Quarterly Bulletin*, Q4 2006, p. 382.

25. Amy Ellis, UK Resident Population by Country of Birth, *Population Trends*, no. 135, Spring 2009, Office for National Statistics, pp. 20–28.

26. Letter from Karen Dunnell, Head of the Office for National Statistics, to the author, 5 February 2007.

27. Office for National Statistics, *Focus on London Population and Migration*, 2005.

28. Office for National Statistics, 'Note on Population, Migration'.

29. David N. F. Bell and David Blanchflower, *What Should be Done About Rising Unemployment in the UK?*, University of Stirling, 2009, p. 27.

30. ibid., p. 16.

31. ibid., p. 37 .

32. Office for National Statistics Labour Market Statistics, September 2009, and House of Commons Library.

33. Bell and Blanchflower, *What Should be Done...?*, p. 33.

34. Jacob Funk Kierkegaard, *The Accelerating Decline in America's High-Skilled Workforce: Implications for Immigration Policy*, Peterson Institute for International Economics, 2007.

12. 3G

1. The conclusion of the research is: 'We therefore think significant longevity came late in human evolution and was a fundamental component tied to the population expansions and related behavioural innovations associated with modern humans.' Rachael Caspari and Sang-Hee Lee, 'Old Age Becomes Common Late in Human Evolution', *Proceedings of the National Academy of Sciences of the United States of America*, vol. 101, no. 30, 27 July 2004, pp. 10895–900.

2. Quoted in Geoff Dench and Jim Ogg, *Grandparenting in Britain: A Baseline Study*, Institute of Community Studies, 2002, p. 8. One of Michael Young's many insights was the importance of grandparents for intergenerational exchange – the pressure group Grandparents Plus has been called his last brainchild, and one of his intellectual companions, Geoff Dench, is responsible for much research on grandparents.

3. Caroline Bryson, Anne Kazimirski, and Helen Southwood, *Childcare and Early Years Provision: A Study of Parents' Use, Views and Experience*, DCSF Research Report 723, 2004. They state, 'Almost nine in ten (86 per cent) families had used some form of childcare or early years provision – be it regular or ad hoc – within the last year. Over that period, a greater proportion of families (67 per cent) had used informal care than formal care (57 per cent). Of all providers, families were most likely to have used grandparents. Half of families (49 per cent) had done so at some point in the last year... Two-thirds of families had used childcare in the last week: 41 per cent had used formal care, and 42 per cent had used informal care. As with use over the last year, out of all the childcare providers, families were most likely to have used a grandparent for childcare during the past week (26 per cent). Used by 12 per cent of families, out of school clubs (on or off school sites) were the most commonly used type of formal provision in the last week.'

4. *Rethinking Family Life: Exploring the Role of Grandparents and the Wider Family*, Grandparents Plus, 2009, p. 11.

5. Dench and Ogg, *Grandparenting in Britain*, p. 87.

6. *Rethinking Family Life*, p. 5.

7. ibid., p. 35.

8. Dench and Ogg, *Grandparenting in Britain*, p. 32.

9. Ben Page, *Families and Children Key Issues*, Ipsos MORI, Age Concern Research Services, 2006.

10. Dench and Ogg, *Grandparenting in Britain*, p. 37.

11. *Rethinking Family Life*, p. 14, and Grandparents Plus, *'My second Mum and Dad': The Involvement of Grandparents in the Lives of Teenage Grandchildren*, September 2009.

12. ibid., p 15.

13. Martin Kohli, Harald Künemund, Andreas Motel, and Marc Szydlik, 'Families Apart? Intergenerational Transfers in East and West Germany', in Sara Arber and Claudine Attias-Donfut, *The Myth of Generational Conflict: The Family and State in Ageing Societies*, Routledge, 2000, pp. 88–99.

14. In 1901, according to the Office for National Statistics, baby boys were expected to live for 45 years and girls 49 years. US life expectancy of a white

male at birth was 38 in 1850 and 42 in 1890, US Department of Health and Human Services Vital Statistics Reports.

15. Pat Thane, *Old Age in English History*, Oxford University Press, 2000. See especially her excellent opening chapter 'Did People in the Past Grow Old?.' She points out that 'the average age at death of the nine seventeenth-century Archbishops of Canterbury was 73 and the average age of appointment was 60', p. 4.

16. The First Report of the Pensions Commission, *Pensions: Challenges and Choices*, The Stationery Office, 2004, fig. 1.1 and ONS.

17. DWP measure of performance against indicator 31 – increase in healthy life expectancy at age 65.

18. The Treasury applied this argument in its 2006 report on long-term fiscal trends. It did not increase its forecast for life expectancy but it managed to cut its forecast of long-term NHS spending by 1 per cent of GDP. It did this by taking account of the 'finding that a high proportion of lifetime utilisation of health care costs is concentrated in the final year of life' (HM Treasury, *Long-Term Public Finance Report: An Analysis of Fiscal Sustainability*, December 2006, p. 34). It was taking a transitional saving on public spending from improving life expectancy. Nowhere in the document is the effect of this assumption explained.

19. In 1997 there were 10.7 million people of state pension age resident in the UK; in 2007 it was 11.4 million and in 2012 is expected to be 12.2 million, according to the Office for National Statistics communication to the author, June 2008.

20. C. G. Lewin, *Pensions and Insurance before 1800: A Social History*, Tuckwell Press, 2003, p. 134.

21. Research by Chris Hammet of King's College, London.

22. Office for National Statistics, Pension Trends, *Attitudes to Pensions: The 2006 Survey*, DWP, 2007, fig. 5.12. The figures are the author's estimates by visual inspection of charts.

23. F. Breyer and B. Craig, 'Voting on Social Security: Evidence from OECD Countries', *European Journal of Political Economy*, 13, 1997, pp. 705–24.

24. Philip Booth, 'The Young Held to Ransom – A Public Choice Analysis of the UK State Pension System', *Economic Affairs*, vol. 28, no. 1, p. 6.

Conclusion

1. ONS reply to Parliamentary Question by the author, 16.1.08, and Ray Barrell and Martin Weale, *Fiscal Policy: Fairness between Generations and National Saving*, National Institute of Economic and Social Research, September 2009. Imagine an economy which is generating output of £1tn a year from fixed capital of £6tn. For its output to grow by 3 per cent a year its capital also has to grow by about 3 per cent, which is £180bn a year in this example. That means 18 per cent of its output has to be set aside for investment. Those are the kind of figures other advanced Western countries achieve for their levels of net investment and saving. We fall far short of them.

2. Karl Mannheim, 'The Problem of Generations', in Kurt Wolff (ed.), *From Karl Mannheim*, Transaction Publishers, 1993, pp. 351–98.

3. Montaigne quoted in Kieran O'Hara, *After Blair: Conservatism beyond Thatcher*, Icon Books, 2005, p. 49.

4. A survey for the Fabian Society by YouGov in 2004.

5. Another attribution is to James Clarke.

6. Edmund Burke, *Reflections on the Revolution in France* (1790), Everyman, 1976, pp. 92–3.

7. T. S. Eliot, 'Tradition and the Individual Talent', from *The Sacred Wood: Essays on Poetry and Criticism*, Methuen, 1920.

Index

Page references in **bold** refer to tables

UNIVERSITY OF WINCHESTER
LIBRARY